PHILOSOPHY AND POLITICS IN CHINA

哲學與政治在中國

三十年代對辯証唯物論的論戰

辛酉 麥思鳴著

WERNER MEISSNER

Philosophy and Politics in China

The Controversy over Dialectical Materialism in the 1930s

TRANSLATED FROM THE GERMAN BY
RICHARD MANN

STANFORD UNIVERSITY PRESS
STANFORD, CALIFORNIA
1990

Stanford University Press
Stanford, California
English translation © 1990 Werner Meissner
Originally published in German in 1986 by
  Wilhelm Fink Verlag, Munich, as *Philosophie und Politik
  in China: Die Kontroverse über den dialektischen
  Materialismus in den dreissiger Jahren*
Originating publisher of English Edition:
  C. Hurst & Co. (Publishers) Ltd., London
First published in the U.S.A. by
  Stanford University Press, 1990
Printed in Great Britain
ISBN 0-8047-1772-9
LC 89-51664

PREFACE

In the following study I have made an attempt to throw new light on the emergence of Maoism in the 1930s, especially on the basis of the Chinese Communist ideology: dialectical materialism. My research on this subject started in the 1970s when I began my studies in sinology, thanks to a scholarship from the Volkswagen Foundation. Always interested in Western and Chinese philosophy, I read Stuart Schram's book *The Political Thought of Mao Tse-tung*, and, like all students interested in politics, studied the *Selected Works* of Mao. I decided to investigate the philosophical background to Chinese Communism in the 1930s, and found the names of Ai Ssu-ch'i, Yeh Ch'ing and others in Father Brière's history of Chinese philosophy.

After having collected the available Chinese material on dialectical materialism, I started reading them but found they lacked a genuine philosophical content, compared for example with the original works of Hegel and Marx. Partly discouraged, I put the material aside. What should I write? A philological outline, repeating phrases by the Chinese authors on Western philosophy? The boring question remained: Why had all these theorists written so many articles and books on philosophy and science, dialectics, logic and so on, and criticised each other to such an extent? What was the real core of all their efforts? Was it possible that they had not been talking about philosophy at all but about something else? It struck me that to criticise the level of their philosophical statements from a philosophical point of view would be doing them injustice, only showing my own bias and misunderstanding of their real intention.

After having reached this point, I began to decipher the whole corpus of Chinese dialectical materialism in the 1930s as a self-contained system of analogous thought. The method and its results can be found in this book. They are, of course, open to radical critiques.

The manuscript was finished in 1983, and appeared in German in 1986. Since then, several studies have been published on the genesis of Chinese Marxism before 1949, and I have incorporated their findings into the English edition. However, the basic thesis on Chinese dialectical materialism has not been changed, although I needed to modify and expand some of my arguments.

Finally, I would like to extend my thanks here to all the institutions and persons who made their contributions to this study: the Volkswagen Foundation, which created the financial conditions; the library of the Department of Political Science of the Free University of Berlin, which always supported in a most generous fashion the acquisition of Chinese material; and last but not least, Professor Jürgen Domes, former Director of the Arbeitsstelle 'Politik Chinas und Ostasiens' of that department.

Berlin, April 1989   WERNER MEISSNER

CONTENTS

vii

Contents

1. INTRODUCTION

The philosophical basis for the ideology of the Chinese Communist Party (CCP) is dialectical materialism (*pien-cheng wei-wu lun*). The general, definitive version, never superseded up till the present, is set out in the works 'On Practice' (*shih-chien lun*) and 'On Contradiction' (*mao-tun lun*), of which Mao Tse-tung is officially named as the author in China.[1] An attempt is made in the present work to open up the sources from which Chinese dialectical materialism originated. The path to these sources leads us back to Shanghai in the 1930s, where a philosophical controversy broke out in 1934 among intellectuals with a leftist orientation. It reached a climax in 1936–7 and finally died out in 1939.

The object of this controversy was the 'New Philosophy' (*hsin che-hsüeh*). This was identical to Soviet dialectical materialism, of which the literature had been translated into Chinese since the beginning of the 1930s. Those documents on the 'New Philosophy', written in the course of the controversy, form the materials from which Chinese dialectical materialism originated. I am not aware of any Chinese publication later than 1939 which goes beyond the framework of what had already been written in the preceding years. Since then the 'New Philosophy' has undergone neither an intellectual deepening nor any other changes. For this reason our inquiry covers only the years 1934–9.

Two theoreticians, above all, were involved in the genesis of the 'New Philosophy'. One of them was Ai Ssu-ch'i (1910–66), joint publisher of the Communist magazine *Tu-shu sheng-huo* (Study and Life) in Shanghai, author of one of the major works of Chinese Marxist philosophy, *Ta-chung che-hsüeh* (*Philosophy for the Masses*), and from the autumn of 1937 one of Mao's closest collaborators in Yenan over questions of ideology. The other was Yeh Ch'ing (1896–), originally a member of the CCP and in the 1930s author of numerous works on the history of Western philosophy, especially materialism, and after 1939 a member of the Nationalist Party (Kuomintang). On the other hand, the role of Mao Tse-tung as a Marxist philosopher was insignificant in the genesis of dialectical materialism in China.

The main purpose of this work is to reveal the background to the controversy over the 'New Philosophy' and to trace the process of development which culminated in dialectical materialism standing as a self-contained system. A second goal is to discover the effects of this system on the intra-party decision-making processes, on the one hand, and in relation to society as a whole on the other. A third goal is to establish how much importance should be attached to Chinese dialectical materialism in the context of the general reception of Western thought in China.

Method

As to the method used in this study, I have first tried to analyse the relevant Chinese texts like similar texts by Western authors. The results were discouraging. The authors talk about 'philosophy', 'science', 'materialism', 'idealism', 'dialectical materialism', 'logic', 'objectivity', 'knowledge' and even 'truth'; in a word, they freely use the whole vocabulary of Western philosophy, but in the end one concludes that, compared to Western descriptions, the terms are strangely flat and life-less, that the texts are full of repetitions, that the applied concepts are not defined and that the logic leaves much to be desired.

Out of deference to a foreign culture, judgement may be suspended in the hope of being pleasantly surprised by the next discussion on 'philosophy', but the second essay is hardly distinguishable from the first, or the third from the second and so on. Nevertheless, before judging these discourses, one should be clear that such a judgement applies at first only to what one has seen oneself in each particular concept. The Chinese theoreticians are hardly affected by this judge-ment, since it transpires that what one has read into their texts was never there in the first place. Therefore, before trying to interpret the Chinese texts, we had first to make a critical examination of our own approach in order to find a methodological basis capable of making the texts understandable.

A starting-point is an examination of translation problems – the problems of translating a concept of Western philosophy into Chinese, and of retranslating the Chinese concept into a Western language. There is a considerable danger that concepts can change their meaning through the process of being adopted into a totally different area of speech and culture, particularly when concerned with abstract and not concrete terms. The danger is diminished if the translator of the foreign concept has acquired an insight into its content, its connotations and its whole cultural and social context, and then seeks areas of similar meaning in his own language and culture. The greater the knowledge and comprehension of the foreign concept, the less is the chance of misunderstandings. The danger of a mistake in translation exists both where a concept in a Western language is translated into Chinese, and vice versa.

As for the first case, it can be ascertained that the adoption of concepts from Western philosophy by the Chinese dialectical materialists was not accompanied by a sufficient preoccupation with European intellectual history. For the second case – the question of retranslation by Western scholars – it can be said that this was carried out as if the Chinese Communist theoreticians had made an adequate study of Western philosophy. The danger consists in investing a retranslated concept – e.g. 'hsing-shih lo-chi' / formal logic – with a content which is in turn determined by one's own knowledge of philosophy. This danger is always present, since one is obliged to use a dictionary, which of course does not provide the full meaning of the concept.

For example, let us take a work entitled *Hsin che-hsüeh lun-chan* and translate that as 'Controversies over the New Philosophy'. Impressed by the concept 'philosophy' (*che-hsüeh*), which above all one associates with the search for truth and immediately goes on to associate with the history of Western philosophy, one will then read the text as if it referred to the work of a Western philosopher. However, one is making the false assumption that the Chinese dialectical materialist is also writing about philosophy in the Western sense of the word; thus it is impossible for one to understand the real content of the text. One attempts to compare the author's ideas and his applied concepts with those of Western philosophy, assuming that his understanding is the same as one's own, or at least similar to it.

If the Chinese concepts of 'materialism', 'idealism', 'objectivity' and suchlike have a different meaning from their verbal counterparts in Western philosophy, how and where can this be determined? If one wants to establish the meaning of these discourses, attention should be directed to two aspects: first, the structure of the text and, secondly, the factors related to their publication.

All the texts are based on a certain structure. The authors do not describe or define any concepts, but only the relations between them. Each discourse contains a representation of the relationship between concept A and concept B (e.g. 'philosophy' and 'science', or 'formal logic' and 'dialectical logic'), which is completely independent of the intellectual content the respective concept would have for a Western reader. The difference between the writings lies in the fact that the relationships between concept A and B are differently represented.

However, the structure contained in each discourse gives no clue as to why the author wrote it. One finds the reason not in the essay itself, but outside it in such external factors as the date and place of publication of the piece, the author's affiliation to a particular political group, and current political events at the time of publication.

If one were to sketch the political conflicts between and within the various political groups diagramatically, the resulting diagram would be congruent to the structure of essays published at the same time; in other words, the political conflict is reflected in the sense of having an analogous counterpart in the 'philosophical essays', and the various 'philosophical' positions are structurally identical to the respective political positions.

It is theoretically conceivable that one could find in the essays both a philosophical statement and at the same time an attempt to justify a decision on a political question from a philosophical point of view. In this case, one could still speak of the essay having a philosophic substance in which the political question is embedded. The philosophy would still then possess a certain autonomy, and the author's opinion would originate from his efforts to arrive at a judgement – made with the greatest possible objectivity – of the matter under consideration. However, this way of thinking is not to be found in any of the essays. Hence:

– The political situation does not form the background of the essay, in which the philosophical drama is played out as if in a theatre, but the political conflict is the real content of the 'philosophical' discussion.

– The political conflict determines every philosophical statement, the relationships between the respective concepts, and indeed the time of publication.

– Every development that brought about a change in the political conflict had as the result to bring about a change in the relationships between the respective 'philosophical concepts'.

– Conversely, every change in the relationship between the philosophical concepts signals forthcoming changes, or changes that have already taken place, in political conflicts.

– Because of these reciprocal functions, none of the philosophical concepts used can possess any intellectual content. Indeed, they are absolutely empty.

– If the concepts possess no intellectual content, then they are also interchangeable. If they are empty and interchangeable, they are no longer philosophical concepts.

Therefore, as we describe and analyse the texts, we will no longer use the word 'concept', but rather 'signs' and 'symbols'. By the word 'symbol' we mean a sign which has been endowed with a meaning not contained in the symbol itself. The symbol represents something which has no counterpart in substance, but which can only be expressed through symbols. The 'philosophical concepts' like 'philosophy', 'science', 'logic', 'matter' and 'spirit', can therefore only be understood as symbols, which stand for a position in a political conflict, and which have nothing to do with the actual content of the concepts as they are understood in Western philosophy. Thus the relationship between the respective symbols in the text does not represent a substantive counterpart, but only an analogous counterpart to a political conflict.

The signs and symbols themselves have nothing in common with the content of the political conflict, since it is only the relationship between them that is analogous to the political struggles. The moment the symbolic classification is imposed upon the 'philosophical concepts' they become empty formulae.

However, this apparent lack of philosophical content cannot be equated with intellectual chaos or nonsense, although a series of these texts can give such an impression; for this type of 'philosophical nonsense' is based on a structure which must be constantly decoded afresh and which, taken in isolation, is very logical. If one can continuously remind oneself that the texts are not concerned with philosophy, they come to life as soon as one is able to decipher them, having previously appeared so dead and stereotyped. The disappointment one had felt over the emptiness of the concepts is replaced by fascination with a type of communication that allows for extensive dispute over a political theme without ever calling a spade a spade.

To give just one example of what this implies, we must not make the mistake of interpreting the remarks of a Chinese Communist theoretician about Kant and his theory of knowledge as expressing the interest of this author in German idealism, and thus take his comments to be indicative of a particular position on questions regarding epistemology. Even our simple judgement 'The Chinese theoretician is of the opinion that Kant is an idealist' is already false. Rather, we must ask: when, where and how did the theoretician express himself on Kant? – who else expressed judgements on Kant? – and what is the structural difference between the statements? Only thus can the meaning of the statement be revealed. Hence, we can conclude that in all the statements it was not Kant who was being talked about; rather, those involved were

concerned with profoundly important concrete questions, usually of a
military-strategic nature.

In the past many studies on Chinese Marxism by Western scholars
concentrated mainly on the analysis of the theoretical works of Mao
Tse-tung. His standing as a Marxist philosopher was never questioned and the Western concept of philosophy had been uncritically
transferred to his texts. Indeed, many excellent studies set out to clarify
the questions as to whether the works 'On Practice' and 'On Contradiction' were written in 1937, and in several studies the political background was also mentioned. However, the next step – realising
that the political conflicts themselves formed the contents of the 'philosophy' – was not taken. If we examine only the texts of one author, it
is very difficult to discover the function of these texts for certain limited
political purposes. At best we can have a hunch. Only the inclusion
of all available texts from the same period and on the same theme,
and their analysis according to the criteria mentioned above, can
furnish proof that the 'philosophical' essays are not concerned with
philosophy, but that all 'philosophical concepts' merely symbolise political conflicts.

Since up till now many texts from the 1930s have only been drawn
upon, if at all, to clarify the original versions of the theoretical works of
Mao Tse-tung, and since at the same time Chinese characters like *che-
hsüeh* and *k'o-hsüeh* in these texts have been uncritically re-translated as
'philosophy' and 'science', the impression has been given that in China
one is simply dealing with an Asiatic variety of Marxist philosophy,
Soviet Marxist philosophy, or mainly autochthonous Chinese philosophy, and that these varieties, though not attaining the level of Western
philosophy, can none the less be designated as philosophy. Therefore, in
the debates on Chinese Marxism there were numerous attempts to
support these judgements by means of comparisons with European
Marxist philosophy and Soviet philosophy, and by proving the existence
of autochthonous elements such as the Yin-Yang doctrine and even Neo-
Confucianism in Chinese Marxism.[2]

If it should turn out that the conceptual apparatus of Chinese
dialectical materialism has no more than a symbolic function, then it is
superfluous to investigate what the Chinese Marxist theoreticians had
adopted from European philosophy in addition to the intellectual
traditions of their own country.

In a consideration of dialectical materialism in China it can be held
against this functionalist aspect that a theory used by the holders of

political power cannot serve an exclusively functional purpose, but that there must also be a positive ideological substance to guide the decision-making process, in the sense of an ideology of development.[3] Nevertheless, if the presence of such a substance in Chinese dialectical materialism cannot be proved, then the only remaining question concerns its function in politics.

The concept of 'esoteric communication', already coined for the study of Soviet sources, intrudes in this connection. This means an instrument for the transmission of controversies within a leadership élite to the sub-élites, with the object of furnishing the latter with an orientation. The ideological language used is constructed in such a way that the true purport of the transmitted information remains hidden from the mass of the population and can only be decoded by someone proficient in the terminology used and sufficiently knowledgeable concerning quarrels within the leadership élite to be able to connect particular formulations with the actual substance of the controversy. The analysis of the ideological line, in comparison with changes in direction on the political scene, can convey information about those changes.[4]

All these observations on method can be designated with the concept 'qualitative content analysis'. Furthermore, we have the method linked to the concept 'esoteric communication'. However, these methods ignore essential factors needed in order to understand the texts. For example, it is possible and even probable that the leadership élite use other channels of communication to inform their sub-élites of impending changes. This still does not answer the question of which functions this type of communication fulfils alongside that of informing the sub-élites. Finally, it is possible that those who practise this type of communication may indeed use formulae which are objectively empty but in which they believe, or did once believe. Should this unity between subjective conviction and legitimising thought be found *not* to exist, the 'empty formulae' will be suspected of an ideological fraud. But if this unity *does* exist, the question must be asked: how does one characterise a thought which believes certain concepts that are empty, while still using these concepts to legitimise one's political actions?

In the case of Chinese dialectical materialism, several factors coincide:

1. The belief in concepts like 'materialism', 'dialectic' and so on is part of a world-view with the help of which one can shape the country's future. It is this belief which not only uses 'esoteric communication' for the transmission of political conflicts to the sub-élites. Thus a

theoretician who believes dialectical materialism to be the only true philosophy of the proletariat, and in turn identifies the proletariat with the CCP, can argue vehemently in his essays against ideological 'leftist and rightist deviationists' and thus achieve two objectives simultaneously. Through his identification, as a theoretician, of dialectic, party, proletariat and science, there is revealed in his statements the 'esoteric' level, where the lines of the internal party struggle over certain conflicting goals can be understood. At the same time, these statements have a propaganda effect beyond this sphere and thus serve to legitimize a certain political action within the framework of a seemingly progressive view of life. Since it can be demonstrated that the belief rests upon a basic ignorance of the actual content of the concepts applied, the concepts 'science', 'philosophy', 'materialism' and so on have no empirical content, and thus the suspicion arises that, as far as they are concerned, one is dealing with myths.

2. 'Science', 'philosophy', 'materialism' etc. are at one and the same time both myth and symbol. Believed in as a myth, the terms can also be used in the sense described above as the means of legitimation and 'esoteric communication'. As a result, the myths 'philosophy', 'science', 'materialism', 'dialectic' etc. are believed in as 'magic weapons' (Ai Ssu-ch'i). They are like foreign gods, in which one has more confidence than in one's own.

In the course of reading the texts, I was partly reminded of the mythical and even totemistic thinking described by Cassirer, Durkheim and Lévy-Bruhl:[5] in this manner of thinking, where nothing can be found which logicians call discursive, there is an overlapping of the totemistic structure from the organisation of the tribe to the organisation of the world. This is thought of and explained as analogous to the social structure of the tribe. However, with dialectical materialism in China, the social base unit is no longer the tribe but rather the party. The statements made in the texts concerning the cosmos, society and thinking are not based on logical analysis, but correspond exactly to certain political opinions, which in turn are linked to factions in the party. And here we have one important characteristic of Chinese communist ideology: the 'philosophical' organisation of the world is performed by the authors according to intra-party struggles, and thus reflects the socio-political structure of the party. The various contradictions in the cosmos, society and in thinking are described 'scientifically' in a way that corresponds exactly to the contradictions within the party. This is the real core of the so-called 'scientific philosophy' of 'dialectical materialism' in China.

A further aspect of mythical thinking is that the names and symbols both have a special importance. A symbol is understood as strength in a mythical sense; it is never just a conventional sign for an object but, for the mythical consciousness, a real part of it. The symbol does not merely represent the whole; it is the whole. Therefore, whoever takes possession of the name gains power not only over the object but also over an opponent. Perhaps this explains the importance of ideological controversies in China, and at the same time reveals that the controversies are concerned not only with 'esoteric communication' but also with a mythical level of consciousness, where the symbol for 'dialectic', and so on, is tantamount to a substantial force which is seen as at least partly decisive in overpowering the opponent.

3. The connecting link between this seemingly curious, mythical form of thinking and the legitimation of political action is thinking in 'analogous counterparts' and symbolic classifications, as sketched above. Thus it is possible that mythical and legitimising thought can split apart after a certain length of time – at the latest, when the myth has proved itself to be unrealisable. This is the moment when pure legitimation begins. When the myth is destroyed, mythical thinking is reduced exclusively to 'esoteric communication' and legitimation. In the beginning was the myth; at the end the legitimation of power.

The decline of the myth does not proceed uniformly. It begins with those who have concocted it – who, however, for the sake of legitimising their power, are interested in the maintenance of the myth by the 'masses'. In this way the myth turns into camouflage, into 'esoteric communication'. Thus an exact knowledge of intra-party struggle at every point is necessary in order to understand such communications. The only people in possession of such knowledge are, on the one hand high-ranking party members, and, on the other, opponents outside the party in a position to gain access to secret information. In order to maintain the myth, the struggle must be expressed not only in secret party documents, to which only insiders have access, but also in the form of a literary genre that makes use of analogy, parable and simile. These are immediately understandable to insiders; nominal members are given at least a trace of insight, while the 'masses' are given the myth, which legitimises control. The opponent also gets a 'trial balloon', which he then intercepts and, according to his interests, returns in his own manner – without, of course, expressing himself concretely. Thus a 'philosophical' ping-pong game emerges – an intellectual type of game of which the Chinese theoreticians are undoubtedly masters.

When readers unfamiliar with these ways of thinking and these political conditions read such texts they will laboriously seek the historical truth, searching for the logic behind the arguments presented and believing that remnants of Western thinking are to be found, which the authors could have adopted. They will engage in methodical research to discover whether Kant, Hegel and Marx have been correctly understood, and which linguistic difficulties occasioned by the Chinese language may have obstructed the reception of their works.

The party functionary, who must be trained in the reading of such texts, is spared such mental gymnastics since he already knows after the first pages for whom the bells tolls and, in the worst case, that it is tolling for him.

The methodological notes cited here are introductory, and are designed to enable the texts to be more easily understood. Some of the more essential aspects can only be touched on here, but in the course of this study, especially in Part V, we attempt to treat them more extensively.

Outline

Hitherto we have emphasised the analogy between the structure of the texts and political conflicts. To prevent any misunderstanding, it should be re-stated that judgements given here are expressly limited to dialectical materialism in the 1930s. It is not our object to establish whether this should also hold true for other parts of the CCP's ideology or even for Chinese thought in general. Other studies on historical materialism and the Communist science of history[6] suggest that, if the method described here were applied to the corresponding sources, the results would be similar to those of our studies.

I have avoided beginning with a presentation of the history of the dialectic, especially of the materialistic dialectic and the traditional Chinese dialectic, although such a chapter is appropriate to our overall theme. We will be able to see that an exact knowledge of what has been understood as dialectic in Europe and traditional China is irrelevant for an understanding of the texts studied here. As our preceding methodological statements show, one's own ideas on Western philosophy tend to obstruct rather than free one's vision of the political core of the 'philosophical' struggles as one reads the texts.

On the other hand, it is necessary to summarise briefly the history of the dialectic in the Soviet Union up till the beginning of the 1930s, and the process of its depletion, since the final fruit of this process formed the 'intellectual material' from which the Chinese Communist theoreticians derived their knowledge of European philosophy in general, and of Marxism in particular. We will examine the development of Soviet philosophy only in relation to those themes which later led to controversy among the Chinese theoreticians.

Several works analysing the narrow dependence of Mao Tse-tung's theoretical works on Soviet sources, and his plagiarism, have already appeared (Wittfogel, Takeuchi Minoru, Schram, Lippert, Wylie, Knight, Fogel),[7] so they do not need to be discussed extensively here. Wittfogel notes the fact that approximately 40 per cent of Mao's work *Dialectical Materialism* is plagiarism, while the other parts hardly deviate at all from Soviet models.

The same goes for the works of the other Chinese theoreticians. The whole gamut of Chinese writings on dialectical materialism is based mainly on three Soviet works.[8] The first is the *Course of Instruction in Dialectical Materialism* by Sirokov and Aizenberg, published in Moscow and Leningrad in 1931, translated into Chinese by Li Ta and published in 1932 as *Pien-cheng fa wei-wun lun chiao-ch'eng*. The second work was an article from the 1935 edition of the *Great Soviet Encyclopedia*, with the title 'Dialectical Materialism', edited and partly written by Mitin and Ral'cevic. The translation by Ai Ssu-ch'i and Ch'eng I-li was made from a Japanese translation of the original and published in 1936, with the title *Hsin che-hsüeh ta-kang* (A Brief Survey of the New Philosophy). The third work, by Mitin and Razumovskij, was entitled *Dialectical and Historical Materialism*; its first part was published in Moscow in 1933, and parts of it appeared in the Chinese translation by Ai Ssu-ch'i in March 1939 in the book *Che-hsüeh hsüan-chi* (Selected Philosophical Works).

All these Soviet texts were concerned polemical writings against 'Mechanism', 'Bukharinism', 'Deborinism' and 'Trotskyism' in Soviet philosophy and politics. They were not even found worthy of mention by Loren Graham in his study *Science and Philosophy in the Soviet Union*.[9] The works of the Chinese theoreticians move solely within the framework provided by the Soviet works. They assume the same form of polemic and do not refer to the original works by Marx and Engels. Knight's observation regarding the lack of original citations from the works of the classical authors in Mao's writings[10] is also true of the works of the other Chinese Communist theoreticians. One can therefore proceed on the assumption that the history of dialectical materialism was not adopted on the basis of original sources, but rather that the Chinese theoreticians adopted a standardised form of dialectical materialism from the Soviet Union, which was a direct product of the quarrels between Stalin's faction in the Communist Party of the Soviet Union (CPSU) and its opponents mentionend above: the 'Mechanists', 'Bukharinists', 'Deborinists', and 'Trotskyists'. We deal with this problem in the first part of this book.

The reception of Soviet dialectical materialism as prefabricated, legitimising thought, and the analogous structure of the Chinese works, require that we place a chapter on the development of domestic politics in China in the 1930s in Part II (chapters 5–9), ahead of the actual analysis of the texts, because in the former the struggles in the CCP which are relevant to the 'philosophical' controversies occupy the focus of interest along with their links to the Comintern's policy towards China. A particular effort is made to elaborate the various positions held within the CCP on the question of a United Front with the Nationalist Party (Kuomintang).

The review of the struggles over the United Front is followed by the presentation and analysis of the texts on dialectical materialism in Part III (chapters 10–16). There is extensive quotation from the texts of the two most important theoreticians, Ai Ssu-ch'i and Yeh Ch'ing, in order to show the full extent of the 'analogous counterpart' mentioned above, right down to the individual characters/signs. With these newly-acquired 'tools', we begin Part IV (chapters 17–19) with an examination of the theoretical works ascribed to Mao Tse-tung, 'On Practice' and 'On Contradiction', in which there is an attempt to show their relative importance in the controversy and in intra-party struggles.

In the Conclusion all the 'philosophical concepts' or symbols examined are listed in a glossary and classified according to their political and military meanings. Finally, an appraisal is given, in ten points, of Chinese dialectical materialism.

Literature

The Chinese literature on dialectical materialism in the 1930s includes a variety of pamphlets, magazine articles and monographs. In our examination and selection of the material, we have particularly taken into account those works whose authors were the main targets in the theoretical quarrels. Because the attacks were aimed mainly at Ai Ssu-ch'i and Yeh Ch'ing, their works consequently occupy the central place. Most of these works were first published as magazine articles, only appearing later in the form of books. As far as possible, the articles and reprints are compared to determine possible changes which could prove important. In addition, there are a number of authors whose only purpose was to oppose or support one or the other side in the quarrels. Hence their articles hardly differ from those of Ai Ssu-Ch'i and Yeh Ch'ing; they are simplified plagiarism. Examination and analysis of these works are indeed necessary, but a presentation of the train of thought expressed in them would be superfluous, because they basically repeat themselves. As a consequence of the great amount of ritualised and standardised language in all the articles, and the constant harmony of the arguments, they are only mentioned when necessary. However, this does not hold true for those articles in which differing positions can be found with regard to Ai Ssu-ch'i and Yeh Ch'ing, as in the case of Ch'en Po-ta and T'an Fu-chih. Therefore, in selecting articles, the guiding principle has been that they exemplified a certain trend within dialectical materialism.

It was helpful in the gathering and selection of material that many of the articles were published in collective volumes shortly after their original appearance, a procedure already recognisable from the controversies over *k'o hsüeh yü jen-sheng kuan* (Science and World-View) in 1923 and over the social history of China from 1927.[11] The articles published in the omnibus editions represent a relatively dependable cross-section of the literature on the controversy, as an examination of the rest of the literature reveals. However, because the omnibus books include only a part of the most important literature, they were supplemented by the selected literature according to the criteria already mentioned. One certainly can not claim completeness for all the material analysed; this would only be possible when the archives in the People's Republic of China for this type of material have been opened to outsiders.

The literature in Western languages that we use is divided according to three themes: 1. the history of Soviet philosophy; 2. the history of China in the 1930s; and 3. modern Chinese intellectual history. Regarding Soviet philosophy the works of Ahlberg, Wetter, Bochenski, Joravski, De George, Negt, Graham and Jordan are prominent, although Graham's book does not deal with the period under consideration here. The works of the Russian theoreticians Deborin,

Mitin and Bukharin have unfortunately only been translated in extracts.[12]

All Western authors agree, when it comes to judging Soviet philosophy in the 1920s and '30s, that basically it serves the general need for legitimation of post-revolutionary society (Negt), as well as the legitimation of individual political actions by the CPSU (especially Ahlberg), and that the function of dialectical materialism in the Soviet Union hardly extends beyond this role. Since the controversies in the Soviet Union over philosophy are well documented and not of central importance for the understanding of Chinese dialectical materialism, an additional study of Soviet philosophy on my part was not required.

The same is true of Western literature concerning Chinese history in the 1930s, especially the second United Front between the CCP and the Kuomintang. Here one can mention the works of McLane, Kataoka, Harrison, Domes, Van Slyke, Kuo, Benton, Wylie, Ch'en, and recently Shum and Garver.[13] Most of them have striven to work on the struggles within the CCP over the correct tactics to pursue in the United Front on the basis of previously inaccessible documents. It can no longer be denied that a serious conflict developed in the CCP in the 1930s over the party's role in the United Front between the Comintern-supported 'Wang-Ming line' and the 'Mao Tse-tung line'. An echo of this struggle can be found in the individual commentary of the publishing committee of the *Selected Works* of Mao Tse-tung and in the autobiographies of Otto Braun, Chang Kuo-t'ao, and Wang Ming;[14] in the latter the authors are concerned with their personal accounts, having been involved in the events. A perusal of the *Wang Ming hsüan-chi* (Selected Works of Wang Ming)[15] delineates clearly the military-strategic differences between the factions, especially in volume 5 (thus confirming the main arguments of McLane, Kataoka, Benton and others, which appeared before Wang Ming's works were published).

In the voluminous literature on modern Chinese philosophy, the controversy over dialectical materialism has hitherto hardly been noticed. Very short comments can be found in the following works: O. Brière, *Fifty Years of Chinese Philosophy*; Brière's article 'L'effort de la philosophie marxiste en Chine', and Kwok, *Scientism in Chinese Thought*;[16] Brière's book gives an excellent survey of the individual currents in Chinese philosophy from the beginning of the twentieth century and is impressive in its abundance of lexical information. It is largely based on the work of Kuo Ch'an-po, *Chin wu-shih nien chung-kuo ssu-hsiang shih* (A History of Chinese Thought in the Last Fifty Years).[17]

However, the few notes concerning the controversy between Ai Ssu-ch'i and Yeh Ch'ing over Marxist philosophy do not go beyond a short philosophical-historical description, and neglect political references – as does Brière's article, somewhat more extensive as it is. Both works nevertheless provided the starting-point for our own study.

Kwok's excellent study also contains a small section on the controversy over dialectical materialism.[18] He had set out to examine the development of the comprehension of modern science by the Chinese intellectuals, but treats the texts of Marxist theoreticians like other texts of European philosophy – a basic misunderstanding, as argued above. He approaches the sources as if they were in an intellectual vacuum and without the slightest reference to the domestic politics of the period.

The article by Chen Cheng-ti on 'The Controversy over New Philosophy, 1935–1937', recently published in Japanese, is the only study to appear so far that deals directly with our subject, but the author does not mention the political relevance and implications of the controversy; he regards the debate on dialectical materialism as merely a repeat of the debate in the Soviet Union, and his main explanation of why the Marxists criticised Yeh to such an extent was their lack of confidence in his political reliability. However, Chen already uses some of the important sources for our purpose.[19]

Raymond Wylie's *The Emergence of Maoism*, solidly documented and hitherto the most important book on the theoretical development of Chinese Marxism before 1945, unfortunately deals only with Yeh Ch'ing's attacks on Mao in the 1940s, but not with the controversy between Yeh and Ai in the 1930s. And Fogel's book *Ai Ssu-ch'i's Contribution to the Development of Chinese Marxism*,[20] also recently published, contains only a few lines on the subject under consideration here, although it provides an excellent and profound insight into the career of Ai Ssu-ch'i.

In conclusion, I must mention three authors and their works, who are not referred to again in this study but to whom I owe much of my understanding of Chinese Communist world-views and their social functions. These are Karl Mannheim's works on the sociology of knowledge, the works of Ernst Topitsch on mythical models in epistemology and his comments on the concept of 'empty formulae', and Marcel Granet's work *La pensée chinoise*.[21]

Part I. SOVIET PHILOSOPHY UP TO 1930s

2. 'OVERBOARD WITH PHILOSOPHY!'

In the first few years after the October Revolution of 1917, there were initially a multitude of philosophical currents in Russia, which were able to develop side by side with relatively little hindrance. With the removal of most of the philosophy professors from their posts in 1921-2, materialism was finally able to assert itself as the dominant philosophical direction. Its representatives were supporters of the Revolution, and generally understood materialism as a progressive and revolutionary way of thinking, based on knowledge of modern science. Caught up in the general intellectual and social awakening of the period, they placed their hopes in science as a means of freeing Russia from its backwardness and building a new society. All representatives of materialism had one point in common: they had intensively studied the substance of the main currents of European philosophy and the modern sciences of the nineteenth century, and had treated them in their works and attempted to make them applicable to Russian society.

However, materialism was not a unified, closed system. It also embraced the theories of the 'vulgar materialists' Minin and Encmen, who established connections with Russian nihilism of the nineteenth century; the empiriomonism of Bogdanov, which seized on elements of empiriocriticism from Mach and Avenarius; the 'mechanical materialists' Stepanov and Timirjazev, who based themselves particularly on the natural sciences; and finally Bukharin, who has to be classed mainly with the 'Mechanists', as well as the 'dialectical materialists' Lenin and, following him, Deborin.[1]

The various opinions on the system of materialism did not concern the materialists for as long as the struggle to protect the Revolution and consolidate the new social order continued. But as the Bolshevik party consolidated its control in the early 1920s, the resistance of its opponents virtually ceased and materialist philosophy was institutionalised as the specified way of thinking in the Russian universities; thus the 'United Front' between the various schools of thought in materialism collapsed. The subsequent controversy was first dominated by the

16

'vulgar materialists' and then by the 'mechanical materialists' who later developed from them, *vis-à-vis* the 'dialectical materialists'.

The supporters of 'vulgar materialism' were of the opinion that all phenomena of a higher order could be traced back to those of a lower order: organic life to chemical processes, chemical to physical, and finally physical to mechanical. In their opinion, the reduction of all phenomena in nature, society and intellectual thought to mechanical-determinist principles made all philosophy superfluous. Instead, the natural sciences would assume this position, since they alone offered the prerequisites of being able to research and measure all material processes – including human thought as a purely physiological process of the brain – thus making them verifiable. This view implied that Marxism as a philosophy should also give way to a positivistic science.[2]

Thus Minin, in his work *Overboard with Philosophy* published in 1922, championed the thesis that philosophy, including Marxism, was merely a relic of bourgeois ideology. He justified his argument as follows: 'There are three ways of grasping the world: religion, philosophy and science. Marxists go astray – as one tends to say – between these three pine-trees: instead of immediately throwing the ship's commanders overboard and leaving no survivors, as the first act after the revolution and philosophy too . . . the proletariat should be left only with science, and nothing but science, and not some philosophy.'[3]

A similar attitude to philosophy was expressed in a pamphlet by the biologist Encmen. He claimed that the concept '*Weltanschauung*' (world-view) was merely an invention of the exploiter and would disappear once the dictatorship of the proletariat had been established. As a substitute for the philosophy of Marxism, Encmen created a 'Theory of a New Biology', which he propagated as a 'direct and necessary development of the real, orthodox Marxism'.[4]

Encmen's ideas seemed to have widespread currency and influence among Soviet youth, especially the party youth – so much so that Bukharin, as well as Deborin, saw in them a danger for Marxism and sharply criticised the 'Theory of a New Biology'.[5]

A far greater danger for Marxist philosophy was the 'mechanical materialism', originating from 'vulgar materialism'. While the latter soon lost its importance because of its lack of a scientific basis, 'mechanical materialism' developed into a real danger for the 'dialectical materialists'. Its supporters differed from the 'vulgar materialists' not so much in their basic ideas as in their professional qualifications. Standing behind the 'Mechanists' were the members of the famous state institute for scientific research, named after the well-known natural scientist Timirjazev.

Just like the 'vulgar materialists', the 'Mechanists' questioned the right of all philosophy to exist. Marxism was for them purely a positive science. 'For the Marxists,' wrote Stepanov, 'there is no individual area of "philosophising", separated from science; for the Marxists, materialist philosophy consists of the final and general results of modern science.'[6] Along with their rejection of philosophy, the 'Mechanists' had another conception of dialectics as well. Unlike Engels and Lenin, they did not regard it as an autonomous science and a scientific method of research. Engels, and later Lenin, had attempted to explain the origin of motion with the help of the 'law of the unity of opposites', which stated that the struggle of opposites, in which the unity of every single thing disintegrates, is the single driving force behind its own development. Every object is set in motion from within, by the struggle between its own inherent opposites. The 'Mechanists' maintained, on the contrary, that it was not the internal opposites which were the decisive factor of every movement and development, but rather that every movement was caused by external factors. Accordingly, they rejected the application of the 'law of unity of opposites' to research in the natural sciences, and considered the dialectic as something mysterious that was to be applied to reality rather than developing from within it.

The 'Mechanists' also contradicted another law of 'dialectical materialism', namely the 'law of transformation from quantity to quality'. Engels had maintained in his work *Dialektik der Natur* that the developmental process of every object takes place in qualitative leaps. All development proceeds, to begin with, in the form of a quantitative change, but when it has reached a certain stage, it is transformed into a new entity by undergoing a 'leap'. This 'leap', as the law understood it, was for example the transition from inorganic to organic matter, or the revolutionary change from a capitalist to a socialist society. In contrast, the 'Mechanists', referring to the natural sciences, argued that all matter consisted of identical particles, and thus a qualitative 'leap' was an impossibility – the alleged qualitative changes could all be explained by quantitative changes in the number and group arrangement of the particles.[7]

However, this rejection of the 'qualitative leap' by the 'Mechanists' was related not merely to research in the natural sciences, since they considered consciousness and all social phenomena as only an expression of chemical and physical processes – here they relied especially on the research of the Russian physiologist I.P. Pavlov and his theory of 'conditioned reflexes'.[8] By transferring ideas from the natural sciences to intellectual thought and society, they were obliged to support the thesis that the development of all objects, including social ones, was distinguished not by 'qualitative leaps' but rather by a progressive, linear development. They were thus opposed to the 'dialecticians', who insisted on a conception of development based on discontinuous 'revolutionary leaps'.

The socio-political connotations of 'Mechanist' ideas are clearly exemplified in the person of Nikolai Bukharin. Bukharin, who in no way thought of himself as a 'Mechanist', and had criticised the 'Mechanists' in certain respects, stood closer to them than the 'dialecticians' over the question of dialectics. His role in the struggle is of particular importance, in that he was among the leading members of the CPSU. He was also a longtime member of the Politburo, editor-in-chief of *Pravda* and, in 1926, Zinoviev's successor as General Secretary of the Comintern.[9]

Bukharin, like Lenin, accepted the 'unity of opposites', although, while Lenin sought the origin of every movement and development in the objects themselves, in their innate contradictions, Bukharin, like the 'Mechanists', saw the origin of movement as lying outside the object. Indeed, he too considered every movement as a struggle between the contradictions; however, differing from Lenin, he saw it as a struggle between an object and its environment. For Bukharin, everything formed a closed 'system', composed of various elements and in an unstable state of equilibrium. Any disturbance of this equilibrium, and the resulting motion, were caused by external factors; thus the state of equilibrium was dependent upon the environment. 'The relationship between system and environment is the decisive quantity,' Bukharin wrote, 'since the whole situation of the system, the basic forms of its movements (decrease, development, stagnation) are determined by this relationship.'[10] Bukharin's 'theory of equilibrium', which did not deny the 'qualitative leaps' in development as the 'Mechanists' did, still considered development the result of external influence, and thus offered his political opponents the opportunity of placing him close to the 'Mechanists', thereby designating his political ideas 'anti-Marxist' and 'undialectical'.

3. THE VICTORY OF THE 'DIALECTIC'

After 1925 there erupted a violent controversy between the 'Dialecticians' and the 'Mechanists' over their positions in the afore-mentioned debate. Criticism of the 'Mechanists' was led by Abram Moiseevic Deborin, the most important representative of dialectical philosophy in the period after Lenin, who sought in his works to extend the philosophy of dialectical materialism and give it a systematic basis.[11]

The publication for the first time of Engels' *Dialektik der Natur* in 1925 gave Deborin the arguments with which, by reference to Engels and Lenin, he attacked the scientific thesis of the 'Mechanists'.[12] He recognised that their thesis – whereby Marxism existed only as a positive science and not a philosophy – represented a danger for Marxism as an autonomous philosophy, and was capable of determining the social development of the Soviet Union. Thus science threatened to take control and be the judge of all socio-political decisions made by the exponents of Marxism. So Deborin several times pointed to the connection between Marxist philosophy and the existing social order, and warned that if the leading role of philosophy was superseded by science, socialism could be imperilled.

What is the meaning of the slogan 'Overboard with philosophy'? Isn't it really clear that, if such a current were to gain predominance among the Marxists, this would lead to a capitulation of Marxism *vis-à-vis* the bourgeois-philosophical teachings, to a capitulation of Marxism in regard to the ideology of the bourgeoisie? Translated into everyday usage, such a triumph of the anti-philosophers would inevitably mean the intellectual capitulation of the proletariat. Moreover, intellectual capitulation is already the beginning of political capitulation.[13]

While the 'Mechanists' saw no room for philosophy in a socialist society and associated a rational social order with science, especially the natural sciences, being given priority, Deborin was convinced that the survival of a socialist society could be guaranteed only if Marxist philosophy had primacy in the areas of science and culture. From this standpoint there arose the claim that Marxist philosophy, especially the dialectic, had to be a constitutive element of the sciences. Scientists, according to Deborin, should apply dialectical method in their research. Otherwise the danger might arise of the natural sciences as well as the social sciences committing 'ideological errors' and 'political treason'.[14]

He substantiated this clear formulation particularly in his work 'Materialist Dialectic and Natural Science',[15] where he describes the essential meaning of the dialectic in the framework of a review of history since Hegel:

Marxism, or dialectical materialism is a self-contained *Weltanschauung*, consisting of three basic components: the materialist dialectic as the general scientific methodology (including the theory of knowledge), the dialectic of nature as the methodology in the natural sciences, and the dialectic of history (historical materialism).[16]

Deborin understood the dialectic as an 'abstract science of general laws of motion', a 'general methodology'; as such, it probes the categories and laws which are already found in the total reality. Since these categories and laws have supposedly taken concrete form in reality, he arrives at the concept of the dialectic as a scientific method. Thus, following Engels, he demands that scientists should form an alliance with dialectical philosophy and assume its methods.[17] Moreover, he held that this alliance was necessary because the natural sciences, through their empirical methods, had already accumulated an 'enormous mass of positive knowledge', which called for explanation and systematisation.[18] According to Deborin, the explanation and systematisation could only be achieved through the application of the dialectic:

The dialectic philosophy already contains at its highest developmental level the analysis, the examination of details and an understanding of the particular in connection with the totality. The dialectic encompasses a synthesis of the universal and individual, intuition and intellectual thought, theory and practice, empirical natural science and the theoretical, i.e. 'philosophy'.[19]

At the same time, Deborin did not want the 'alliance' with the natural sciences understood in the sense that the dialectic should be imposed upon the latter; for him this was impossible because the dialectic supposedly lay in the objects themselves. The internal connection, which the natural sciences were finally to uncover with the help of the dialectic in their research, existed 'objectively', according to Deborin, and that which appeared in consciousness, theory and as dialectical law was merely a reflection of what already existed in the objects. Assuming the unity between 'subjective' and 'objective dialectic' he stressed that the establishment of internal linkages 'was not to be understood in the sense that we would bring in the linkage from without'.[20]

Deborin's struggle against the 'Mechanists' lasted for five years and ended with their condemnation' at the Second All-Union Conference of the Marxist-Leninist Research Institutes, which took place at the Communist Academy in Moscow in April 1929. Deborin, who produced the conference report, summarised the charges against the 'Mechanists' as follows: they refused to use dialectical method to overcome the 'crisis in the natural science', they considered the dialectical natural sciences, as understood by Engels and Lenin, as 'metaphysical natural sciences' and considered it necessary to return to 'mechanistic natural sciences'. Furthermore, the 'mechanists' maintained, on the grounds of their 'positive-empirical' approach, that social laws could be referred to physical, chemical and biological principles. Finally, they denied the special importance of quality in the developmental process, reducing it to purely quantitative changes.[21]

The condemnatory decree 'Concerning the Present Problems of Marxist-Leninist Philosophy' declared that the 'Mechanists' were guilty of an obvious deviation from the positions of Marxist-Leninist philosophy.[22] However, their condemnation was important not only for the further development of Soviet philosophy; it also had grave consequences for those who supported this 'deviation'. Shortly after the end of the conference, the 'Mechanists' were removed from all key positions in philosophy and science and replaced by Deborin's supporters, who from now on controlled the philosophy department at the state publishing house and the articles on philosophy in the *Great Soviet Encyclopedia*. Thus all 'mechanist' publications were now under their control.[23] The victory of Deborin's teachings was reflected in his personal advancement as well: he ran the Institute for Philosophy in the Communist Academy and in 1929 became a full member of the Academy of Sciences of the Soviet Union.[24] The triumph of 'dialectical philosophy' was complete.

4. THE END OF 'PHILOSOPHY'

It is not merely the personnel changes resulting from the Second All-Union Conference that arouse scepticism, but also the philosophical content of the arguments presented by both sides. Doubts had already been raised by the discussion over the question whether the dialectic was extrinsic or intrinsic to objects, thus posing the further question whether the problem had to do with the theory of knowledge at all. The 'Mechanists' attempted to evade the demand that they should apply the dialectic as a method. On the one hand, they maintained they were indeed themselves dialectical materialists, but, on the other, insisted the dialectic could be found only through research into the objects themselves and could not in any way be imposed upon them. However, this contradiction was really only the reverse side of the same coin. It is substantially the same whether one begins a study with the intention of dissecting the dialectic out of the objects, as the 'Mechanists' pretended to do, or whether, like the dialecticians, one has used the dialectic from the beginning, thus establishing it as an *a priori* principle.

This can also be said of the controversy over Bukharin's 'theory of equilibrium'. Bukharin had maintained that the change and development of a system was a function of the environment or milieu; the dialecticians concluded from this argument he had championed the thesis that the cause of motion lies not within the object, in a struggle of the inherent opposites, but rather externally. However, the important thing is what one considers as an object or system, and which individual parts are subsumed under these concepts. If, for example, one were to consider people as a system and nature as an environment, as Bukharin does, then the environment plays the determining role; it is the external factor. If one were to combine human beings and the environment into one system or consider them as a 'unity of opposites', nature is then no longer an external factor but rather an internal contradiction. The causes of motion are suddenly once again the inner opposites. The formulation 'unity of opposites' or 'system' can thus be so conceived that each author is able to express his own interests and concepts and can also impute that his opponents are deviating from the 'true laws of the dialectic', although the latter themselves rely on the same laws. If the discussions on the dialectic as a method of inquiry were not the result of a misunderstanding, which can hardly be assumed, then all they could have been were sham philosophical battles, and the arguments employed must have had some other meaning.

Deborin first alluded to this when he established a direct connection between the dialectic as a method of research and the existence of the new social order in the Soviet Union. The leading role of dialectical philosophy was by then already equated with the control of the CPSU; philosophy thus had the function of legitimising the social system and its representatives. The position of the 'Mechanists' regarding the independence of research, and their resistance to the assumption of the dialectic, supposedly to help them solve the 'crisis in the natural sciences' – all this contained within it the possibility of jeopardising the party's social policy. Since this potential contradiction even possessed an organised base in the party, 'Mechanism' had to be banned as a 'deviation from Marxist-Leninist philosophy' in order to acquire legitimation for the exclusion of a certain wing of the party. This being so, it was unimportant whether the views of the 'mechanists' or those of the 'dialecticians' approximated more closely to the truth. It is only possible to get to grips with the true meaning of the discussion if the arguments presented by each side are seen respectively as a form of legitimation for concrete political ideas and interests in the framework of the development of internal politics in the Soviet Union, and understood as an expression of conflicts over political goals and power.

While the legitimation of the new social order as a whole and the control of the CPSU were still addressed in the discussion over the role of dialectical philosophy, the debate over Bukharin's 'theory of equilibrium' was related to concrete domestic and inter-party questions: the future development of Soviet society after the period of the 'new economic policy'.

After 1928 there emerged clear differences within the party over the abandonment of the 'new economic policy' introduced by Lenin. Stalin pleaded for rapid industrialisation, the necessary capital for which should be obtained through the collectivisation of agriculture and the liquidation of the kulaks. To attain this goal, 'all measures against the kulaks, including the total confiscation of their property and their banishment beyond the borders of the afflicted areas and provinces' were to be implemented.[25] Bukharin understood the necessity of industrialisation as well, but his view was that of a peaceful transformation of the private sector to socialism. He feared the use of violence against the kulaks could endanger Soviet control and even lead to its collapse. Bukharin – as well as Rykov, the then Premier, and Tomsky, leader of the trade union

International – spoke out against an aggravation of the 'class struggle' and in favour of a policy of moderation towards the kulaks. If Stalin wanted to enforce his plans for collectivisation, he had first to break the opposition to them within the party. What could be better than to accuse his opponents in the party of being guilty of a 'mechanist' philosophical deviation, thus legitimising his own plans? The conception of the 'Mechanists' regarding the development of nature and society without 'qualitative leaps', which they tried to support with the help of their knowledge of natural science, could be interpreted in a simplified way as advocating an evolutionary path and a moderate policy towards the kulaks. The rejection of 'qualitative leaps' in nature was equated with a rejection of the 'class struggle', the attainment of socialism through violent action.

At the beginning of 1929, Stalin criticised the group around Bukharin, Rykov and Tomsky as a 'right-deviation within a party' and levelled the following detailed charges against them:

(1) that they advocated a deceleration of the development of industrialisation;
(2) that they wished to limit the establishment of a collective economy, since this supposedly had no role to play in the agricultural sector;
(3) that they advocated complete freedom of private trade;
(4) that they were against the liquidation of 'capitalist elements' in the towns and the countryside; and
(5) that they were opposed to taking measures against the kulaks, and were against taxing them excessively, which would protect them.'[26]

Stalin charged the Bukharin group with 'opportunism' and 'capitulationism' *vis-à-vis* the kulaks, that their attitude favoured the 'improvement of chances for capitalist elements', and that a renunciation of state regulation of the grain market, as the group envisaged, would endanger the Soviet system and the 'dictatorship of the proletariat'.[27]

Bukharin's 'theory of equilibrium' was in this respect an ideal connecting point, allowing his opponents to describe his advocacy of a moderate policy towards the kulaks as 'anti-Marxist', 'mechanistic' and 'undialectical'. If one were to apply this theory to the domestic political situation, it would have the following meaning: the development of society towards socialism and industrialisation can not be realised by means of violent action against the kulaks, but can be triggered only by an external factor: the struggle against the kulaks can not be the decisive factor in such a development. But for the 'dialecticians' it was the other way round. By referring to the 'unity of opposites' they implied only the struggle against the kulaks, i.e. that between the internal opposites in society, could lead to the hoped-for 'self-movement' towards socialism. They therefore accused Bukharin of propounding the idea that the condition of society was determined by 'equilibrium' and 'harmony' between the classes and not by 'class struggle'. Bukharin himself had never applied his theory to the kulak question; on the contrary, there are a number of instances in his works where he unambiguously declares himself in favour of 'class struggle' and the 'change from quantity to quality'.[28] However, by pointing to a lack of precision and partly contradictory statements in his texts, the 'dialecticians' branded him as a supporter of the 'mechanists'.

Thus it was not merely by chance that the removal of the 'mechanists' from all key positions in academic philosophy in the spring of 1929 was paralleled by the elimination of the Bukharin group from all party and state bodies. Here it becomes clear the struggle against the Bukharin group, and Stalin's support of the 'dialecticians' in their struggle against the 'Mechanists', were both based on a reciprocal alliance of utility. The Deborinists, with their dialectic, provided Stalin with the 'philosophical' arguments he used against the 'Mechanists' and Bukharin, and in turn were now able to move into key positions which their opponents had held previously.

Yet, the dialectic had still not come into its own. The victory of Deborin and his supporters lasted only a year. Already within a few months of the II All-Union conference, a third group began to criticise the Deborinists on the grounds that it considered itself the true guardian of dialectical materialism, accusing Deborin of 'Hegelianism' and 'left-deviationism'. This group comprised party ideologists who, unlike the Deborinists and 'Mechanists', were merely Stalin's 'philosophical' mouthpiece and applied philosophy exclusively as a means of legitimising political measures.

Stalin himself supplied the terminology for the condemnation of Deborin's 'philosophy'; he designated it 'Menshevist idealism', placing it close to 'Trotskyism'.[29] The condemnation was followed in January 1929 by an official decision of the CC of the CPSU[30] whereby the partial division between philosophy and party was removed. From this point on, philosophy passed into the control of the party and its dominant wing, led by Stalin.

At the head of the new group stood the party ideologues Mitin, Judin and Ral'cevic. In their arguments against Deborin's philosophy, which they attempted to prove through distorted selection and obfuscation, they claimed that in the latest quarrels which had sealed the fate of 'philosophy', only political questions were involved. Deborin was accused of the separation of philosophy from present political problems, of methodological formalism, and of philosophical impartiality. But criticising him proved difficult because his philosophy had, in essence, been accepted by the new 'dialecticians' and had become the core of Bolshevik state ideology. In order to find at least some points of criticism, Mitin and his supporters did not shy away from employing certain 'mechanist' arguments which had been used against Deborin.[31]

There is only one vital point to be found in Mitin's criticism of Deborin; it concerns the supposedly different interpretations of the 'unity of opposites'. Deborin had written of the antinomies in Kant: 'Kant places the thesis *vis-à-vis* the anti-thesis and attempts to prove that the thesis excludes the anti-thesis, and therefore that it can not be reconciled or resolved. On the other hand, the positive dialectic sees the thesis and anti-thesis as opposites, which do not exclude each other but, rather, are reconciled.'[32]

However, in Mitin's opinion the essential point of the dialectic lay not in the reconciliation of opposites, but in their struggle. In accordance with Lenin, he considered the 'unity of opposites' to be relative but the struggle between them to be absolute.[33] Still, even on this issue the difference between the positions of Deborin and Mitin seems to have been fabricated. This can only be established if one misconstrues the 'reconciliation of opposites' in the process of perception as the reconciliation of opposing interests in politics – something that Mitin had obviously achieved. Moreover, all Deborin's other works show him to have stood completely in line with the Leninist dialectic.[34] Even Deborin's criticism of 'Mechanism', which was comprehensively adopted by Mitin and his supporters, is indicative of the pugnacious character of his dialectic rather than of a desire to 'reconcile the contradictions'. It is characteristic of Mitin's style of criticism that the passages cited all came from rather old publications. Deborin's passage concerning the 'reconciliation of contradictions' dates from 1924.[35] This action says more about the intentions of the critics than about the content of their criticism.

Why did Deborin's 'philosophy' meet with the same fate as 'mechanism'? Why was the former 'confederate', who had fought so meritoriously against 'mechanism', found guilty and condemned for 'deviation' from true 'Marxist-Leninist philosophy'? There were probably two explanations. First, the value of 'philosophy' as a means of justifying a political position must have become clear to the party during the struggle against 'right-deviationism'. Hence, the control of 'philosophy' by the party had become necessary. On the other hand, Deborin had not developed his 'philosophy' under the party's protection; he himself had been a Menshevik till 1917 and then an independent, only joining the CPSU in 1928. Deborinism was therefore a relatively independent 'philosophy'.

Not until his condemnation and the replacement of his supporters by malleable party ideologists were the party able to win control of 'philosophy' and thus exclude all possibility of criticism of Stalin and his policy based on dialectical materialism. Henceforward, the unity of 'dialectical philosophy' and the party allowed for the legitimation of every political measure while denying the possibility of criticism of the party on the basis of 'dialectical philosophy'. The rise of Stalin marked the end of this development. He became the 'philosopher' of 'Marxism-Leninism', and his works were declared to be generally binding and a creative interpretation of the works of Marx, Engels and Lenin.

The history of philosophy in Russia since the October Revolution is one of its continual depletion and functionalisation for political purposes. The first phase, up till the institutionalisation of materialism in the universities in 1921–2, was distinguished by the attempt to form social reality according to philosophical content and, by establishing a new social order, to bring the two into harmony. One can thus speak of this phase as a unity of philosophical and legitimising thought. This unity was bound to collapse at the moment when the desired realisation of the philosophical content failed to materialise, or when its fulfilment proved to be exceedingly difficult. Thus the ruling party's drive for legitimation bore on society with increasing severity. The legitimising function of philosophy had to increase, while its substantive differentiation decreased.

In the second phase, which included the struggles between the 'Mechanists' and 'Deborinists', an already strongly canonised form of dialectical materialism was created with the appearance of Deborin's 'philosophy'. His references to Engels and Lenin, in relation to the 'Mechanists', now revealed dogmatic tendencies, and he sought to defend 'true philosophy' against 'deviation' from the eternal 'laws' laid down by Marx, Engels and Lenin. The aspect of Deborin's 'philosophy' which favoured the legitimation of control was by then so dominant that one could hardly speak of a 'philosophical' content. However, the development continued: in the third phase, following Deborin's condemnation, 'philosophy' served merely to legitimise a party faction's claim to total power, a process which finally reached its climax in the dictatorship of Stalin. 'Philosophy' had been definitively emptied of its intellectual content and become the handmaid of politics. It no longer contained the function of epistemology; its task was to justify, in the name of the 'dialectic', political measures such as the collectivisation campaign, the widespread liquidation of the kulaks, and the 'purges' of Stalin's political opponents in the party.

In order to assess dialectical materialism in China, it is important to note that it was largely from Mitin's works that Chinese theoreticians gained their knowledge of European philosophy in general, and of Marxism in particular. Those were the same works which had served in the condemnation of the 'Mechanists' and 'Deborinists'. Thus the birth of Chinese dialectical materialism began at the point when Marxist philosophy in the Soviet Union had ceased to exist: Chinese theoreticians adopted Soviet dialectical materialism as an ideal prescription for their political struggles without ever having grasped the intellectual dimension of Marxism in the history of European thought or having informed themselves of it through other sources.

Part II. THE STRUGGLE OVER THE SECOND UNITED FRONT

5. FROM 'ABSOLUTE OPPOSITES' TO 'ALLIANCE'

The close link between current politics and philosophy became manifest in the development of Soviet philosophy up till the early 1930s. Politics had prevailed to such an extent that philosophy had been emptied of its content, and had passed fully into the control of the party. In view of the adoption of Soviet dialectical materialism by Chinese theoreticians, we have to address the question of which political factors were decisive in the development of this world-view in China. This question can best be answered by presenting a short survey of events in the 1930s with particular reference to the emergence of the United Front.

The history of China in the 1930s was determined by the following major events: Japan's expansion into Manchuria in 1931; the 'extermination campaigns' by the national government against the Chinese Communists in the soviet areas and the ensuing 'Long March' of 1934–5; the 'Hsi-an incident' of December 1936; the all-out attack on China by Japan in 1937; and the second 'United Front' between the CCP and the Kuomintang, which came about directly after the Japanese advance and temporarily ended the civil war between the two which had gone on since 1927.[1]

The CCP's strategy after the Japanese invasion in 1931 can be divided into two phases. The first was distinguished by an 'absolute contradiction' *vis-à-vis* the Kuomintang and by vain attempts to induce large parts of Chinese society to fight against both it and Japan. The tactic used in this case was the 'United Front from below'. In several proclamations, the Chinese soviet government in Chianghsi under the chairmanship of Mao Tse-tung demanded the uniting of all social and political forces for the struggle against the Kuomintang and Japan. This move was in response to the direct threat to the soviet areas posed by the 'extermination campaigns' of the national government at the beginning of the 1930s. For as long as Japan limited itself to the occupation of Manchuria, Chiang Kai-shek considered his primary political and military goal to be the destruction of the Communist movement. In order to avoid all-out war with Japan, so as to enable him to concentrate his forces on the elimination of the Communists, Chiang Kai-shek pursued a conciliatory policy towards Japan; hence, according to the CCP, the struggle against Japan was coupled with that against the Kuomintang.

In the second phase, after the loss of the soviet area in Chianghsi and the 'Long March' to North Shensi, the party gradually reassessed its tactics in relation to the United Front, leading to the decision in 1937 to renew cooperation with the Kuomintang. The goal was now a United Front that included the Kuomintang, and from which the CCP hoped to obtain a desperately-needed respite from further 'extermination campaigns'. The change in tactics over the United Front was precipitated firstly by the rapid deterioration of the Soviet Union's international situation and secondly by the danger of a renewed 'extermination campaign' by the national government against the new CCP bases in North Shensi.

Where international relations were concerned, the Soviet leadership proceeded from the assumption that a new world war was imminent in which, at the worst, they might have to fight on two fronts – against Nazi Germany and Japan, two states that were pursuing extremely expansionist goals. To counteract these twin dangers, the VII World Congress of the Comintern decided in the summer of 1935 on new guidelines for co-operation between Communist parties and bourgeois forces, with the goal of a new 'unity of action in the struggle against fascism, offensive capital and war'.[2] Regarding the threat to the Soviet Union from Japan, China was to play a key role for the Comintern: only through a reinforcement of the hitherto weak Chinese resistance to the Japanese invasion could Japanese troops be tied down and thus kept away from the Soviet border. Hence, one of the most urgent goals of the Soviet Union's China policy had to be the ending of the Chinese civil war, a rapprochement between the CCP and the Kuomintang and the launching of a war of resistance to be waged by all parties.

The new guidelines of the VII World Congress were expressed by the CCP in the 'August 1st Manifesto' in 1935.[3] This contained an appeal for the formation of a United Front against Japan and demanded the inclusion of all anti-Japanese forces regardless of their various interests and political affiliations. The CCP suggested the establishment of a 'government for national defence', including all political parties, social groups and organisations that were prepared to participate in the war of resistance against Japan. Furthermore, they demanded the formation of a 'united anti-Japanese army' with a unified high command, to be led by the 'government of national defence'. However, this offer did not apply to the Kuomintang and Chiang Kai-shek, who were to be excluded from the formation of such a government. Nevertheless, the proposal already implied a readiness to compromise, and was the first step on the way to future co-operation with the Kuomintang.

The Comintern realised that an effective resistance to Japan and the hoped-for weakening of Japanese pressure on the Soviet Far East would not be possible without the Kuomintang, the strongest political and military entity in China. While it attempted to bring the CCP into a United Front with the Kuomintang, the Soviet government was at the same time negotiating a non-aggression pact and the granting of large-scale military assistance with the Nanking government in the event of Chiang Kai-shek deciding on war with Japan. Its major goal here was not the release of Communist units for the war – the Red Army had only just begun to regroup again after the costly 'Long March' and had only 40,000 soldiers at its disposal – but rather to let the strong and well-armed Nationalist units finally march against Japanese forces. If it wanted to achieve this goal, it had to try to persuade the CCP to make far-reaching compromises in relation to the Kuomintang so that it would agree to a United Front.

The interests of the Soviet Union's China policy partly accommodated those of the CCP, since the latter's situation in North Shensi threatened to deteriorate even further. The advance of Communist units on Shensi had ended in defeat in the spring of 1936;[4] thus, the CCP wanted to deter Chiang Kai-shek from further extermination campaigns against it. On May 5, 1936, the 'Revolutionary Military Committee of the Red Army' addressed a direct appeal to the government in Nanking to stop the civil war and begin negotiations with the CCP for a United Front in the war of resistance against Japan.[5]

In the same month Wang Ming, who as Comintern delegate of the CCP in Moscow and Member of the Presidium of the ECCI had already initiated the 'August 1st Manifesto', in his article 'The Struggle over the Anti-Japanese People's Front in China' advocated the inclusion in the United Front of the Kuomintang and Chiang Kai-shek. He explained this change in tactics by the fact that the Communists had not succeeded in incorporating the greater part of the Nationalist troops in the struggle against Japan, or in detaching those Kuomintang elements that were pressing for the war of resistance to begin.[6]

Wang Ming's article did not merely reflect his personal opinion; he was one of Stalin's close adherents and wrote as a member of the ECCI.

In September 1936 the General Secretary of the Comintern, Dimitrov, also demanded the establishment of a national United Front to include the Kuomintang.[7] On the surface it seemed as if the CCP and the Comintern were pulling together; however, as will soon be clear, they both followed widely divergent interests within the United Front.

6. WHO SHOULD LEAD THE
UNITED FRONT?

The Nationalist government in Nanking rejected the CCP's offer of negotiations on an armistice and the formation of a United Front, commenting that it still had not given up hope of a peaceful understanding with Japan, and continued its preparations for a new 'extermination campaign'; this was to be led by Chang Hsüeh-liang's army, whose units were mostly from Manchuria, besides provincial troops from Shensi under the command of Yang Hu-ch'eng; these units were stationed together in south Shensi.[8]

The CCP now attempted to hinder the start of the 'extermination campaign' in two ways: by intensive propaganda for a United Front among the officer corps and troops of the 'North-East Army' (Tung-pei Army), which came from Manchuria, and by offers of negotiation to the Nanking government in which it declared itself ready for extensive compromises.

In quick succession the CCP made two offers to the Nanking government to end the civil war. These were to be of special importance in the controversy over dialectical materialism: In a 'Letter from the Communist Party of China to the Kuomintang of China' dated August 25, 1936, the CCP declared itself ready to make compromises:

We stand for the setting up of a unified democratic republic for the whole country and the convening of the parliament elected by universal suffrage, and we support an anti-Japanese national salvation congress representative of all the people and all the anti-Japanese armed forces in the country, and a unified national defence government for the whole country. We hereby declare: as soon as a unified democratic republic is set up for the whole of China, the Red areas will become one of its component parts, the representatives of the people of the Red areas will attend the all-China parliament, and the same democratic system will be set up in the Red areas as in other parts of China.[9]

This 'letter' was published somewhat later in the magazine *Kommunistische Internationale*, from which one can conclude it had the approval of the Comintern.[10] The content of the 'letter' held out the prospect, for the first time, of the dissolution of the Communist soviet government and the inclusion of all territory under its control in an All-Chinese republic on the basis of general elections, in the event of a government of national defence being formed. This offer must clearly have led to a considerable difference of opinion within the CCP, because only a short time later, on September 17, the Politburo of the CC of the CCP adopted a 'Resolution on the New Situation in the Movement to Resist Japan and Save the Nation and on the Democratic Republic'. This renewed the offer of August 25, but with an important addition: the resolution stated that 'by strengthening the Chinese Communist Party's role of political leadership in the national United Front, by greatly consolidating the Red political power and the Red Army' the conditions could be created for the establishment of a democratic republic.[11]

This resolution was important in that for the first time it stressed the 'leading role' the CCP was to play in the United Front, with the Kuomintang being included, not excluded. At the same time, the resolution underscored the necessity of securing the party's political and organisational independence and of expanding and consolidating Red power. These 'conditions' for a 'democratic republic' had not been mentioned in the 'letter' of August 25. One can thus conclude that parts of the CC were clearly afraid that the offer to dissolve the Red areas could lead to a weakening of the party's organisational independence and the possible loss of the territory it controlled.

Both documents reveal the basis of the party's seemingly contradictory tactics *vis-à-vis* the United Front. On the one hand, the party declared itself ready to incorporate its Red areas into a 'democratic republic' and to submit itself to the results of general elections. By way of compensation, the party hoped for the elimination of the Kuomintang's one-party dictatorship, the legalisation of the CCP and for the possibility of its becoming active in organisation and propaganda at a national level. On the other hand, in the long term the maximum consolidation of Red power and the Red Army and the extension of the Red areas would inevitably lead to renewed conflict with the Kuomintang, all the more so given the party's resolution of September 17, in which it laid claim to the leadership of the United Front.

The Comintern, taking its own interests into account, was keen to avoid another confrontation between the CCP and the Kuomintang, which would weaken the anti-Japanese resistance. Thus it had to press for political 'good behaviour' from the CCP within a 'democratic republic', in which the leading military and political role of the Kuomintang could at no time be jeopardised. The passage in the September 17 resolution on leadership in the United Front and the consolidation of Red power could hardly have been welcomed by the Comintern.

These various appraisals of the CCP's role in the United Front were to appear more sharply in the following months, finally becoming the core of a struggle within the party. In the controversy over dialectical materialism, the period between August 25 and September 17 is important because it marked a decisive break in the philosophical controversies. Moreover it seems to have been linked directly to the leadership question within the United Front.

7. THE 'HSI-AN INCIDENT' AND ITS CONSEQUENCES

The CCP's propaganda among units of the 'North-East Army' and the unwillingness of the latter's to begin the campaign of extermination, led finally to the event which has gone down in history as the 'Hsi-an Incident'. The reaction to the Incident of the Comintern and the CCP revealed once again the two sides opposing interests.

Chiang Kai-shek went in December 1936 to Hsi-an, the army head-quarters, in order to direct the 'extermination campaign' personally.[12] But after issuing the order to begin the offensive on December 11, the following morning he was taken prisoner by soldiers of the 'North-East Army'. Generals Chang Hsüeh-liang and Yang Hu-ch'eng explained in a telegram to the national government that they would release Chiang Kai-shek as soon as a number of demands were met. These included the demand that the civil war should cease, and that the Nanking government should be reorganised by incorporating all political parties and groups within it.[13]

The reactions of the Comintern and the CCP to the 'Hsi-an Incident' differed: the imprisonment of Chiang Kai-shek took the Chinese Communists completely by surprise. In contrast to their offers of August 25 and September 17 concerning cooperation with him, Mao Tse-tung and other leading comrades were supposed to have demanded that Chiang, the 'traitor of the people', should be deposed and placed on trial before a 'people's court'.[14] Even more revealing was Moscow's attitude; in a personal telegram, written by Stalin, from the Comintern to the CCP on December 13, 1936, it was stated that the 'Hsi-an Incident' was a plot instigated by Japanese agents. Stalin demanded that the CCP exploit the situation resulting from Chiang's imprisonment by advocating his release, thereby helping to facilitate cooperation with him.[15]

Neither Chiang nor the government in Nanking was ready to accept the demands; instead Nanking was planning a 'punitive expedition' against the mutinous troops of Chang Hsüeh-liang and Yang Hu-ch'eng. This would have further fragmented the Kuomintang forces and postponed indefinitely the start of the war of resistance, a development that would have been in Japan's interests but not those of Soviet Far Eastern policy. Stalin now subordinated the interests of the CCP to those of the Comintern; so the CCP, yielding to instructions from Moscow, advocated the release of Chiang, thus improving the chances of ending the civil war and establishing the planned non-aggression pact between Nanking and Moscow.[16]

The imprisonment of Chiang Kai-shek was little understood by the Chinese public. In fact, the action even seemed to be rebounding against the Chinese Communists, because of suspicions that the imprisonment of Chiang was a result of Communist propaganda among the troops of the 'North-East Army'. As a result of the willingness of the government in Nanking to send troops to Hsi-an, a lack of public support and of the recommendation for his release from the Comintern and the CCP, Chiang was finally freed on December 25 and returned to Nanking.

The 'Hsi-an Incident' had two consequences: firstly, the primary goal of hindering the 'extermination campaign' had been achieved, since the 'North-East Army' would probably not be ready to comply with the renewed order to go on the offensive after Chiang's release; and secondly, Moscow had made an important step forward in its efforts to bring about co-operation between the CCP and the Kuomintang.

Two months after the 'Hsi-an Incident' the CCP, in a telegram to the 3rd Plenum of the Kuomintang, offered four guarantees as a basis for co-operation:

1. The policy of armed insurrection to overthrow the national government will be discontinued;
2. The Workers' and Peasants' Democratic Government will be renamed the Government of the Special Region of the Republic of China, and the Red Army will be redesignated as part of the National Revolutionary Army and come under the direction of the Central Government in Nanking and its Military Council respectively;
3. A thoroughly democratic system based on universal suffrage will be implemented in the areas under the Government of the Special Region;
4. The policy of confiscating the land of the landlords will be discontinued and the common programme of the anti-Japanese United Front carried out resolutely.[17]

The Kuomintang formulated four demands in response to this offer:
1. the liquidation of the Red Army;
2. the liquidation of the soviet government;
3. the termination of 'Red propaganda' and recognition of the 'Three People's Principles';
4. the cessation of the class struggle and renunciation of armed rebellion as a means of gaining the Party's ends.

The text of demands 1 and 2 is especially revealing in regard to the 'philosophical controversy', since we have here two important points, which are reflected in the debates on dialectical materialism:

1. 'The unity of the military organization and command is a prerequisite for the effective control and leadership of the armed forces. The co-existence of soldiers with incompatible ideologies is inadmissible. Therefore, the so-called Red Army and other Communist units with various misleading names must be entirely abolished.

2. The unity of administration is a prerequisite for national unification. The simultaneous existence of two administrations independent of each other is intolerable. Therefore, the so-called Soviet government and other Communist organs which question administrative unity, must be abolished.'[18]

In the philosophical controversy these two points will be discussed in terms of 'philosophy of identity' and 'formal logic'.

At the same time, Chiang Kai-shek promised freedom of expression, and an amnesty for political prisoners, as well as the regrouping of the nation's best military forces. Thus, both sides staked out their basic positions for a United Front – positions that remained far apart.

The ending of the 'extermination campaign' and the Kuomintang's offer of an amnesty meant that, with the demand for the liquidation of the Red Army and of the soviet government, no military action was suggested. What was desired was rather a capitulation as the starting-point for negotiations, which in practice could involve the Red Army being renamed and placed under the Nanking government's control. On the other hand, the CCP made two concessions which had not been included in earlier offers: it renounced the establishment of a 'democratic republic' and the reorganisation of the national government as preconditions for its participation in the United Front. However, the possible renaming and attachment of the Red Army to the national government raised the question of the extent to which such an army could still be controlled by the CCP. Finally, the renunciation of the expropriation of the landlords amounted virtually to an abandonment of the agrarian revolution and thus struck at the very foundation of the party's existing strategy. Furthermore, the leading role of the party in the United Front was no longer mentioned. In regard to this willingness to make large concessions and its cooperation in the release of Chiang Kai-shek, it is clear that the supporters of the Comintern had the upper hand in the party at this time.

The increasingly critical military situation between China and Japan accelerated the realisation of the cooperation between the two parties in the civil war. With their attack at the Marco Polo Bridge (*Lu-k'ou-ch'iao*) close to Peking, the invasion of Central China by Japanese troops began on July 7, 1937. This date is also very important for our analysis of the texts on dialectical materialism, since in July 1937 Mao is supposed to have delivered his famous lectures 'On Practice' and 'On Contradiction'.

Within only a few months, the Japanese had taken Peking, Shanghai and Nanking, forcing the national government to move its seat first to Wuhan and later to Chungking. Since the onset of the Japanese offensive the CCP and the Kuomintang had had intensive negotiations regarding the United Front, and in August 1937 the national government announced the renaming of the Red Army as the 'Eighth Route Army', so that it was formally incorporated in to the Chinese national army.[19]

8. 'EVERYTHING THROUGH THE UNITED FRONT' OR 'UNITY AS WELL AS STRUGGLE'

With the beginning of cooperation between the two parties, which coincided with the conclusion of the non-aggression pact between Moscow and Nanking, the CCP was faced with the question of what was to be its role within the United Front. It was inevitable that after the formation of the United Front, the conflict between those party factions more willing to compromise (mostly supporters of the Comintern, but also Chang Kuo-t'ao) and the faction less willing to do so should intensify.

Mao Tse-tung and Chang Wen-t'ien were supposed to have taken the following position:

The task of the CCP consists in fighting against Japan as well as the Kuomintang, whose character is and remains reactionary. Mao hoped that in the course of the war of resistance the Kuomintang would split into a pro-Japanese and an anti-Japanese wing, enabling the CCP to cooperate more closely with the anti-Japanese wing while simultaneously fighting the pro-Japanese wing, and then assuming the leadership of a reorganised United Front. The CCP therefore had to preserve its independence within the United Front, while extending its positions in every area. Mao also warned against too great a willingness to compromise *vis-à-vis* the Kuomintang, and demanded instead that the CCP should strive for an autonomous leadership role 'as well as an expansion of party power and especially that of the Red Army'.[20]

Mao considered the United Front with the Kuomintang merely as one stage in the national revolutionary war which, in the development of the revolution, by no means possessed an absolute character but rather a relative one. At this stage, the party was to use every opportunity – above all the war with Japan – to strengthen its position. The legalisation of the party; its freedom to organise and conduct propaganda throughout the country; its penetration of the Kuomintang, with the aim of splitting and weakening it while it was depleted of troops and personnel in the war against Japan – together these formed the long-term tactics which Mao hoped would prepare the groundwork for the CCP's assumption of the leadership of the United Front and thus make a victory over the Kuomintang possible.

These tactical considerations, which Mao supposedly expounded at the extended meeting of the CCP's Politburo, the Lo-ch'uan Conference of August 22, 1937, are indirectly confirmed by a report from November of that year, in which he commented: 'We have rejected the Kuomintang's demand that its members should be sent to the Eighth Route Army units as cadres, and have upheld the principle of absolute leadership of the Eighth Route Army by the Communist Party. We have introduced the principle of "independence and initiative [_tu-li tzu-chu_]" within the United Front in the revolutionary anti-Japanese base areas. We have corrected the tendency towards "parliamentarism" '.[21] Mao repeated several times the principle of 'independence and initiative'; it formed the central plank of his strategy regarding the United Front.[22]

In the same report he remarked upon splits in the CCP over the United Front and sharply condemned two tendencies in the party. Before the all-out Japanese attack on China, the main danger lay in 'left opportunism', the 'closed door policy' (_kuan-men chu-i_); thereafter the main danger became 'right opportunism' or 'capitulationism' (_t'ou hsiang chu-i_).[23] The attack on the 'closed door policy' was obviously aimed at the faction in the party which was against the United Front with the Kuomintang, whereas the accusation levelled against 'right opportunism' could only be applied to those parts of the party that were prepared to surrender 'independence and initiative' in the United Front with the Kuomintang, or were even ready to capitulate.

It was in this connection that Mao was concerned with the leadership question in the United Front: 'Will the proletariat lead the bourgeoisie in the United Front, or the bourgeoisie the proletariat? Will the Kuomintang draw over the Communist Party or the Communist Party the Kuomintang?'[24] In the report he confirmed that this question had already been posed, first in April in Yenan and then in August at the Lo-ch'uan Conference, thus bearing out our comments on his tactics regarding the United Front.

From the texts mentioned above, it follows there were clearly sharp disputes within the CCP over tactics, especially concerning the question of exactly how much 'independence and initiative' should be allowed in the Red Army and the party, of who should control the leadership, and of what relationship should develop between the areas controlled respectively by the CCP and the Kuomintang.

Wang Ming (_alias_ Ch'en Shao-yü) was the Comintern's 'Trojan horse' within the CCP. A close supporter of Stalin, he was looked upon as a rival and possible successor to Mao Tse-tung. Shortly after the 7th World Congress of the Comintern in 1935, he had already begun to criticise 'leftist sectarianism' in the party and demanded that the expropriation of those rich farmers and landlords who were taking part in the struggle against Japan be discontinued. This was a demand that would virtually have meant the end of the agrarian revolution, and thus it met with little enthusiasm in the party.[25]

In October 1937, Wang Ming returned to Yenan from Moscow, bringing with him new directives from the Comintern, which would soon find expression in the 'Declaration of the CCP on the Present Situation' of December 25, 1937. It is clear from this document that Wang Ming's faction was able to assert itself against the course being taken by Mao. In the 'declaration' much emphasis was given to the statement that the party is not only ready to 'save the native land from Japanese aggression, shoulder to shoulder and hand in hand with the Kuomintang, but it is ready to join with the Kuomintang in constructing the new China after the victory.'[26]

According to Wang Ming, the following guidelines were to apply to the United Front with the Kuomintang:

1. The consolidation and extension of the anti-Japanese, national United Front based on cooperation between the Kuomintang and the CCP; resistance against Japan above everything; everything must be subordinated to the United Front; all things must be channelled through the United Front; support to the Kuomintang leadership in the government and armed forces; common programme, common responsibility, joint consultation and reciprocal support, no power struggle for the leadership.

2. Strengthening a unified national defence government based on the national government (Kuomintang), but no reorganisation.

3. The strengthening and enlargement of the united army of national defence.[27]

Wang Ming placed the war of resistance against Japan 'above everything', in total conformity with Soviet foreign policy. Thus everything was to be subordinated to cooperation with the Kuomintang; all conflicts between them were to be avoided, since that would be a handicap in the struggle against Japan. Relations between the CCP and the Kuomintang should not be based on one controlling and subordinating the other, but on mutual respect, trust and support.

Wang Ming's tactics were clearly tied to recognition of the Kuomintang playing the leading role; this was to apply not only for the duration of the United Front but also after the war against Japan had ended. His ideas on military cooperation between the Red Army and the Kuomintang show this was not merely a negotiating ploy in his dealings with the latter. In his view, renaming the Red Army as the Eight-March Army and assigning it to the command of the Nanking government was simply the foundation and first step in drawing up an all-Chinese united army (*ch'üan chung-kuo t'ung-i ti chün-tui*). The formation of such an army, which would have meant fusing together the Red Army and the armies of the national government, was only possible if all regional and group interests of the individual parties and armies could be eliminated. The establishment of this 'united army' was for him a precondition for effective military resistance against Japan.[28]

To be more precise, Wang Ming's plans aimed at a complete fusion of both armies: they were to possess a 'unified command' (*t'ung-i chih-hui*), 'unified organisational structure' (*t'ung-i pien-chi*), 'unified discipline' (*t'ung-i chi-lü*), 'standardised weaponry' (*t'ung-i wu-chuang*), 'joint military planning' (*t'ung-i tso-chan chi-hua*) and 'joint strategy' (*t'ung-i tso-chan hsing-tung*).[29] At the same time Wang Ming demanded that the greatest strategic emphasis be placed on a conventional conduct of the war. As a prerequisite, he suggested increased training for the 'united army' in the strategy and tactics of modern warfare and military technology,[30] and, furthermore, the education of a great number of component cadres, who were also to be taught modern strategy and military technology. The backbone of this 'united army' was to consist of divisions armed with modern weapons.

9. 'INDEPENDENCE AND INITIATIVE'

Wang Ming's ideas, which he committed to writing in March 1938, were diametrically opposed to those of Mao Tse-tung. The former's suggested fusion of the Red Army and the Chinese nationalist army, and recognition of a leading role for the Kuomintang within the United Front, involved the danger that the Red Army's numerical inferiority might lead to it being swallowed up. Standardisation in all respects and an orientation towards modern military strategy and technology posed the threat of loss of 'independence', not only for the Red Army but also for those areas controlled by it, since its strength lay in its guerilla strategy.

At first it seemed as if the Wang Ming line would prevail in the CCP. Mao Tse-tung, who gave the report for the Sixth Plenum of the VI CC of the CCP in October 1938, supported the view of Wang Ming in his remarks: he explained that cooperation with the Kuomintang was long-term, and was not to be carried through with the intention of a renewed split and a new civil war after the victory over Japan. As to the question of 'independence and initiative', he pointed out that these had to be preserved, but that the term was a relative and not an absolute one, since absolute independence would endanger cooperation and benefit the enemy. The same was true of the relationship between the class struggle and the national struggle. 'It is an established principle,' he explained, 'that in the war of resistance everything must be subordinated to the interests of resistance.'[31]

Furthermore, Mao recognised the leading role of the Kuomintang in the United Front and, like Wang Ming, stressed the need for close and smooth cooperation between it and the CCP. However, it can be doubted whether his statements at the Plenum were sincere, and it is possible that he was merely paying lip-service to the Wang Ming line for tactical reasons. His report 'On the New Period' was not reproduced in full in the *Selected Works of Mao Tse-tung*, but only the seventh section, 'The Role of the Chinese Communist Party in the National War'.[32] The publishing committee responsible for Mao's works made a revealing annotation to this section; it was stated that Mao had spoken of the party's historical responsibility to be the leader in the war of resistance against the Japanese aggressors. Moreover, the plenum pointed out

45

'there had to be struggle as well as unity within the United Front, and that the proposition "Everything through the United Front" did not suit the Chinese conditions. Thus the error of accommodationism in regard to the United Front was criticised.'[33]

The publishing committee gives a further indication of the struggle. In its annotation to Mao's concluding speech at the 6th plenum on November 5, 1938, it writes as follows: 'At the same time the issue of independence and initiative within the United Front was one of the outstanding questions concerning the anti-Japanese United Front, a question on which there were differences of opinion between Comrade Mao Tse-tung and Comrade Ch'en Shao-yü. In essence, what was involved was proletarian leadership in the United Front.'[34] And a few pages later there is the comment: 'Comrade Mao Tse-tung had already settled the question of the Party's leading role in the war of resistance against Japan. But some comrades, committing right opportunist errors, denied that the Party must maintain its independence and initiative in the United Front, and so doubted and even opposed the Party's line on the war and on strategy.'[35]

These statements largely coincide with our analysis hitherto and make it seem that at that time Mao's comment on 'right opportunism' and 'capitulationism' most probably referred to the Wang-Ming line.[36]

The formulation 'Unity as well as struggle' was an appropriate transcription of Mao Tse-tung's United Front tactic. He proceeded on the assumption that the party should 'conduct a resolute and serious struggle on two fronts' against the bourgeoisie, especially the upper bourgeoisie: 'On the one hand, it is necessary to combat the error of neglecting the possibility that the bourgeoisie may join in the revolutionary struggle at certain times and to a certain extent. It is an error of "left" closed-doorism . . . to neglect the policy of forming a United Front with the bourgeoisie.'[37] On the other hand, he warned that the bourgeoisie would make every effort to transform the political and organisational independence of the proletariat and the CCP into an appendage of itself and its party. It would then betray the revolution at the point where the revolution and bourgeois interests came into conflict. 'To neglect all this is right opportunism.'[38] Hence the most important aspect of CCP policy, according to Mao, was that of simultaneously allying itself with the bourgeoisie while engaging in the struggle against it. This two-pronged strategy towards the Kuomintang meant in reality that the conditions created by the legalisation of the CCP were to be used to combat the Kuomintang ideologically and politically, to play off the individual factions against each other, thereby splitting the Kuomintang, to win certain of its factions over to one's own side and then destroy the remaining parts when the United Front came to an end.

The 'unification' of the two armies was thus understood by Mao not in a physical sense but rather as a division of labour, in which the troops of the Kuomintang were to fight a conventional war at the front while the Red Army spearheaded guerrilla operations behind enemy lines. In any case, the Red Army was to have its own structure and chain of command.

The subsequent course of the Chinese revolution and the Sino-Japanese war showed that Mao Tse-tung was able to enforce his tactic of the United Front. However, although the Red Army had been formally integrated into the Nationalist Chinese army, one could not speak of a 'united army' such as Wang Ming had in mind. Cooperation between the CCP and the Kuomintang and between their respective armies was marked by an insurmountable distrust on both sides, and the discord between them increased again after 1939. Mao was also able to assert himself *vis-à-vis* Wang Ming in strategic matters; instead of emphasising conventional strategy, the Chinese Communists relied on guerrilla tactics, especially behind enemy lines. With the help of the tactic 'unity as well as struggle', the Communists not only succeeded in preserving their military and territorial independence, but were also able in the course of the war to strengthen their regular troops tenfold and considerably increase the territory under their control[39] – a success they might not have achieved had the 'Wang-Ming line' been applied.

Wang Ming's influence, and hence that of the Comintern, diminished after 1939; however, Mao's victory over the Comintern supporters in the party resulted not only in their preservation of 'independence and initiative' in relation to the Kuomintang, but also meant the end of Comintern tutelage over the party as a section of the International. The CCP had begun to shed its garb of an agent of Soviet foreign policy and to develop and assert a policy that was independent of Moscow. Mao Tse-tung was the first Communist party leader to succeed in becoming emancipated from Moscow's hegemony over the international Communist movement.

This emancipation had its origin in such concrete matters as alliance policy and military strategy, and not ideology; it was a reaction to the existential threat, to which the CCP saw itself subjected both by the Kuomintang and by Japan. It was a 'balancing act'; a little too far to the 'right' or to the 'left', and there might have been unforseeable consequences. Too much readiness to compromise with the Kuomintang involved the danger of the party being absorbed by them; thus the party would have been sacrificed in order to defend the 'centre of the world revolution', something the Comintern expected from all its sections in view of the impending danger of war. On the other hand, rejection of the United Front would not only have pushed the Comintern too far but also probably led to further 'extermination campaigns', all of which would have meant the party losing those very advantages that would enable it to survive (e.g. the legalisation of its activities at the national level). Thus steps taken towards emancipation from the Comintern and a policy of independence were also steps leading to the CCP's salvation.

The explosive nature of this development was reflected in the sources, since by this balancing act the Comintern as well as the Kuomintang were to be kept in the dark as far as possible regarding the CCP's true intentions. Thus a special language came into being in which those intentions were formulated in such abstract expressions as 'everything through the United Front', 'unity as well as struggle' and 'independence and initiative'. The situation ruled out concrete prognoses concerning the CCP's goals *vis-à-vis* the Comintern and the Kuomintang to avoid those goals being jeopardised. The United Front's tactical discussions were thus conducted in what to outsiders was an abstruse linguistic grey zone, in which only the direction but not the goal was discernible. Where the statements of Mao Tse-tung were concerned, it was even partly contradictory, in that contradictory statements clearly had a tactical viewpoint. For the same reasons, the language was aimed at associative memory, at letting the listener sense the contents; this made it difficult to work out the various positions on the United Front question.

This type of language is continued in the 'philosophical' controversies, to which we now turn. In order to obtain a better understanding of the theoretical texts, it is therefore advisable to keep in mind the formulations we have just mentioned: 'Everything through the United Front', 'unity as well as struggle', 'independence and initiative', 'the leading role in the United Front', and their military-political basis and meaning.

Part III. THE CONTROVERSY OVER DIALECTICAL MATERIALISM

10. 'PHILOSOPHY' AND 'SCIENCE'

The relationship between philosophy and science had already featured in the controversies between the Mechanists and the Deborinists in the Soviet Union during the 1920s. The Mechanists had stressed the priority and autonomy of the individual sciences in relation to philosophy, while Deborin and his adherents persisted in their belief in the necessity of philosophy as the basis of all scientific conclusions. In their view the individual sciences needed a theoretical foundation to guard them against ideological errors and 'political betrayal'. 'When science itself is a philosophy,' wrote Deborin, 'when positive science must strive to liberate itself from every philosophy, then such a positivistic standpoint must inevitably lead to the negation of dialectical materialism in general, and the dialectic in particular.'[1] The link between the role of dialectical materialism to the domination of the proletariat made clear the social reference of this criticism of science. This proprietorial claim to truth in relation to the sciences had little to do with concern for the philosophy of dialectical materialism, but rather with fear of a possible erosion of the CPSU's dominant position. It was a fear expressed in Deborin's words that 'Mechanist' ideas would 'lead to the destruction of Marxism, to the capitulation of the proletariat to the bourgeoisie in the area of theory'.[2] The political capitulation of the proletariat would then be only a matter of time. After Deborin was 'purged' in 1930, his critics in Mitin's circle adopted the concept of the predominance of philosophy over the individual sciences; indeed they expanded it further to the extent that Soviet philosophy was to be placed unconditionally at the service of the party's political goals. Thus dialectical philosophy had finally become an ideological instrument for political domination.

The altercation among Chinese theoreticians over the relation of philosophy to science leads one to consider the political background in China as well. However, this was entirely different from that which pertained in the Soviet Union because the CCP, unlike the CPSU, was not in power but engaged in a civil war against the Kuomintang. The defence of the predominance of philosophy in relation to the individual sciences could hardly be taken as corresponding to a defence of the CCP's monopoly of power since it did not possess such a monopoly. Thus in examining the texts of the Chinese theoreticians, three questions are of central importance:

1. What were the supporters of 'philosophy' talking about when they stressed its predominance in relation to 'science'?
2. Which goals were the representatives of 'science' pursuing when they advocated the end of 'philosophy'?
3. Against whom did the two direct their criticism?

The examination of the texts that follow proceeds chronologically, according to date of publication, the works of Yeh Ch'ing being considered first. Quotation is extensive in order to give an impression (as most of the texts examined here do) of how an author writes a 'philosophical treatise', the sole purpose of which is to use a coded form to advocate or oppose particular political positions, which have no connection whatever with philosophy *qua* philosophy.

The Origin of 'Science' or the 'Annihilation of Philosophy'

Yeh Ch'ing (whose real name was Jen Cho-hsüan), the main adversary of Ai Ssu-ch'i, was born in Ssu-ch'uan in 1896. In 1920 he won a scholarship to France and became secretary of its CCP section but his political activities led to his deportation in 1925. He then went to the Soviet Union and studied for a short time at the Sun Yat-sen University in Moscow. Returning to China in 1926, he organised the CCP underground in Hunan, which fomented several small rebellions in Ch'angsha, P'ing-chiang and elsewhere. After being arrested by provincial officials, he left the CCP and began to work for the Kuomintang. In Shanghai, after 1929, he belonged to the circle of T'ao Hsi-sheng, Chu Ch'i-hua, Chou Fo-hai, Kuo Mo-jo, Lu Hsün and Mao Tun. He founded his own publishing house and began to publish in quick succession Chinese translations of the works of European philosophers, including La Mettrie, d'Holbach, Helvetius, Condillac, Diderot, the Greek philosophers Heraclitus, Democritus and Epicurus, and the Marxists Plekhanov, Deborin and Bogdanov. Simultaneously he founded two magazines: *Er-shih shih-chi* (The Twentieth Century) and *Yen-chiu yü p'i-p'an* (Research and Critique) which he used as a forum for his own philosophical ideas.[3]

Yeh Ch'ing maintained in his work *Che-hsüeh tao he-ch'u-ch'ü*

(Whither Philosophy?),[4] which appeared in 1934, that 'philosophy' is subject to the same law of evolution as everything else and is thus transitory. Here he relied on the article by the vulgar materialist Minin, 'Overboard with Philosophy',[5] which advocated the thesis that philosophy, including Marxism, was a remnant of bourgeois ideology. He referred at the same time to the biologist Enchmen, who took the concept *Weltanschauung* as merely an 'invention of the exploiters', and one which would disappear once the dictatorship of the proletariat had come to pass.[6]

Referring to Comte, according to whom the spirit of individuals as well as that of species first had to develop through a theological and then a metaphysical stage in order to reach the stage of positive science, Yeh explained his *che-hsüeh hsiao-mieh-lun* (Theory of the Annihilation of Philosophy) as follows. 'Philosophy' emerged from religion which in whatever manifestation – animism, ancestor worship, monotheism and so on – constitutes the earliest form of knowledge. On the basis of the then primitive relations of production, there could be no knowledge based on an understanding of nature; however, with the development of reason, human beings were no longer satisfied with traditional beliefs, but began to question the 'why' of things. This, Yeh says, was the beginning of 'philosophy'.

The content of 'philosophy' developed over a long period of time. The first forms were ontology (*pen-t'i-lun*) and cosmology (*yü-chou-lun*). Since humans were a part of nature, they began, after explaining nature, to try and explain human beings, and thus originated '*Lebensanschauung*' or 'life-view' (*jen-sheng-lun*). This was followed at the next level by a critique and examination of knowledge itself, and thus was developed the theory of knowledge (*chih-shih-lun*).[7]

According to Yeh, the contradiction between 'materialism' (*wei-wu-lun*) and 'idealism' (*kuan-nien-lun*) runs through the whole history of 'philosophy'. In the case of ontology, the contradiction lies in the fact that in 'idealism' the external world (*wai-chieh*) was only understood through the internal world (*nei-chieh*); the ideas were the essence and the cosmos merely a product of them.[8] In the case of 'materialism', on the other hand, the 'spirit' (*ching-shen*) was understood only as a function of 'matter' (*wu-chih*); it was the origin of the cosmos which would then have developed in a mechanistic and deterministic manner.

The same contradiction is found in the 'philosophy of life' and 'theory of knowledge'. Here, 'rationalism', according to which all knowledge has its origin in reason, is opposed to 'empiricism', whereby knowledge is based on experience and is merely a reflection of the external world. In the 'philosophy of life', 'idealism' stresses the spiritual, while 'materialism' stresses the material conditions of life. For Yeh, the contradiction between the two directions in 'philosophy' was decisive in the emergence of the 'sciences', whereby 'materialism' devoted itself to the 'external world'. After the natural sciences, the social sciences and finally the science of thought (*ssu-wei k'o-hsüeh*) developed.

Yeh concluded that since the emergence of the 'sciences', all investigations take place by means of scientific methods and, except for knowledge gained through 'sciences', there can be no knowledge. 'Philosophy' and religion have shown themselves incapable of creating true knowledge.[9]

However, for Yeh the 'annihilation of philosophy' was not a simple process, but rather the result of a dialectical process. In the period when 'philosophy' still determined knowledge, it already contained 'science' as a seed within it, and 'science' then gradually conquered all the fields of knowledge governed by 'philosophy'. First, 'religion' was conquered by 'philosophy' but because both of them still contained elements of 'idealism' and 'religion', 'science' was needed to give them the death-blow. In this process of development, 'the natural sciences stole the field of philosophy of nature from philosophy and the social sciences from the field of philosophy of life. Logic, ethics and psychology free themselves from philosophy and develop into individual sciences. Thus the field of philosophy was constantly shrinking.'[10] Yeh held that this development process went in accordance with the principle of dialectical negation, whereby 'science' preserves 'philosophy' and simultaneously negates it. 'Science' had taken over 'materialism', rejected 'idealism', preserved the dialectic of 'idealism' and thus developed 'materialism' to a higher level – to 'dialectical materialism' (*pien-cheng-fa wu-chih-lun*).[11]

Yeh regarded 'Dialectical materialism' as the highest form of scientific thought; however, this 'new philosophy' was no longer a 'philosophy' but only 'science'. What function, according to Yeh, was this 'new philosophy' or 'science' to have? 'Science', he wrote, becomes the judge of all things. All social activities and all intellectual products have become objects of 'science' and have entered the area of 'science'. In such conditions, nature, society and intellectual thought are all united with each other (*t'ung-i*) and form a large system. All abrupt or evolutionary processes in the cosmos follow exclusively 'scientific laws', and this is true for society and intellectual thought as well. The sudden change in society is the revolution, and what the revolution is to society so scientific critique is to intellectual thought: the two run parallel to each other: thus, 'science' has a revolutionary character. The targets of the scientific critique are the 'old ideas' and outmoded 'philosophies', their equivalent in the struggle against the 'old ideas' being the armed struggle against the ruling classes.

But against whom was this struggle now aimed? Yeh's critique was directed at Hu Shih, Chang Tung-sun and the scientists Lo Chia-lun, Ting Wen-chiang, Ch'ü Shih-ying, Jen Hung-chün and Kuo Jen-yuan, who, in his opinion, were in the 'service of capital'. They were all among the most important representatives and supporters of Western science and philosophy in China.[12] He accused them of clinging to 'philosophy', despite its being antiquated, and of justifying their adherence with the argument that 'science' must receive support from 'philosophy' in all problems which 'science' itself was incapable of solving. The systematic summation of the results of 'science' was supposedly possible only through 'philosophy'. The task of the individual sciences was analytical research, whereas that of 'philosophy' was to unite the individual sciences into a total knowledge and thus place them on a higher level of reason.[13]

Yeh referred to remarks by Chang Tung-sun and Wang Kuang-hung, who were of the opinion that 'philosophy' attempts to comprehend the 'essence' (pen-t'i), while 'science' only concerns itself with the 'appearance' (hsien-hsiang); 'philosophy' examines the whole, while 'science' deals with the particular.[14] However, Yeh asked, can 'philosophy' be a key to knowledge when 'science' can no longer find the answers? For him, since Hegel, 'philosophy' had been unable to provide a comprehensive, complete system. Empiricism, pragmatism, evolutionism and neo-positivism all developed from the 'sciences' and from the remnants of a collapsing 'philosophy'; how, on that basis, can 'philosophy' attempt to set up a system and a method?[15]

According to Yeh, only 'science' was capable of delivering the sole form of 'objective truth'. It had taken over all the tasks of 'philosophy'; even the critique of 'science' can no longer be derived from 'philosophy' but only from 'science' itself. When 'philosophy' was used as a critique, this meant, according to Yeh, that subjective standards of value were applied to objective decisions. What explained the attitude of those who supported 'philosophy' was simply that they were 'protecting their feeding dish' in advocating and preserving 'philosophy': they were merely concerned to perpetuate and defend the cultural wealth of those who replenished the 'feeding dishes' – namely the leading reactionaries.

Therefore Yeh criticised Chang Tung-sun and Hu Shih, among others, since they were propagandists of Western 'philosophy' in China and opponents of the theoretical struggle: 'The revolution of Chinese thought means to criticise them (Chang, Hu *et al.*).'[16]

Yeh was of the opinion that 'philosophy's' sole function was to protect the ruling classes; it was used by them as a weapon in the 'theoretical struggle'. He countered this by deeming 'science' to be the sole representative of 'objective truth', which had the task of overcoming 'philosophy'. Consequently, he wrote, 'the elimination of the remnants of "philosophy" goes hand in hand with the elimination of the rotten remains of society.'[17]

Yeh's criticism of 'philosophy' and advocacy of 'science' were seemingly aimed at the 'idealistic philosophy' of Chang Tung-sun and Hu Shih as well as the ruling interests on which it was supposedly based. The truth was that his comments served to establish his reputation as a competent authority on Western philosophy, especially Marxism, within leftist intellectual circles in China, above all in Shanghai. His sharp condemnation of 'idealism', contained in two other works,[18] was to place his Marxist outlook beyond all doubt, yet his criticism possessed even greater range and its main thrust was aimed in another direction: it was directed not so much against 'idealism' as against 'philosophy' as such, be it 'idealistic' or 'materialistic', and thus also against Marxism inasmuch as the latter was understood as a 'philosophy'. Rather later, this very point was to be contradicted by the Marxists.

'Materialism' and 'Idealism' or on the Way to Great Unity

Before attempting to explain the political importance of those works of Yeh Ch'ing we have been considering, his conceptions of the development of the relationships between 'materialism' and 'idealism' should be examined in more detail. Yeh treated this theme extensively in a number of articles written between 1935-6, which he published in 1936 as a collected volume entitled *Che-hsüeh wen-t'i* (Problems of Philosophy).[19]

Here Yeh again depicts the contrast between 'materialism' and 'idealism' as part of the development of 'philosophy' and 'science', leading to the negation of 'philosophy', and indeed of 'idealism' as well as 'materialism'. In order to give the appropriate theoretical emphasis to the struggle against 'Marxism' as a 'materialistic philosophy', he described in epic breadth, and free from the dictates of historical truth, the struggle between the two currents in 'philosophy' in such a manner that ultimately the unification of 'materialism' and 'idealism' and the 'annihilation of philosophy' would become inevitable.

For this purpose Yeh placed the start of the struggle between 'materialism' and 'idealism' in Greek antiquity. In the first phase of the contest, Thales, Heraclitus, Empedocles and Democritus stood, as 'materialists', against Plato, Socrates and Aristotle, the 'idealists'; the struggle continued with Aristippus of Cyrene and Epicurus being opposed to the stoic Zeno and the cynic Antisthenes. After several less important phases, Yeh arrives at the Middle Ages, where nominalists and realists, as adherents of 'materialism' and 'idealism', are in opposition: Roscellinus and Occam versus Anselm of Canterbury and Duns Scotus. In modern times, Bacon, Hobbes, Locke and Spinoza are named as adherents of 'materialism', while Descartes, Leibniz, Berkeley and Hume are seen as representing 'idealism'. Yeh then followed with the French materialists – de la Mettrie, Condillac, Diderot, Helvetius and d'Holbach – their counterparts being Kant, Fichte, Schelling and Hegel. The line continues with Feuerbach, Vogt, Büchner and Haeckel, and on the idealistic side with Schopenhauer and Lotze.[20] 'Philosophy' was, according to Yeh, thus split into two basically hostile camps from the outset. This tells one nothing about the differences between the two schools of thought and their adherents in antiquity and the Middle Ages. The sketch given of the history of philosophy has no more than a lexical character; it simply lists names and maintains that all philosophers and their schools can be categorised as either 'materialist' or 'idealist'.

However, Yeh eventually focussed on his actual theme: that the struggle between the two currents in 'philosophy' had led to several attempts to solve the contradiction between them. Here, Yeh differentiated between 'dualism' (erh-yüan-lun) or 'parallelism' (ping-hsing-lun), 'neutralism' (chung-li-lun) and the 'philosophy of identity' (t'ung-i che-hsüeh). In his opinion all these attempts had failed hitherto, a thesis supposedly proved by the history of 'philosophy'. According to Yeh, the attempts at solving the contradiction had begun with Plato and had reached their first climax with Descartes,[21] who considered both 'matter' and 'spirit' to be 'substances' (shih-t'i) which 'existed independently' (tu-li ts'un-tsai) of each other. Yeh pronounced Descartes' argument to be false, because 'matter' and 'spirit' were understood as 'existing parallel to each other' (ping-hsing) and not as 'connected with each other'(hsiang-chieh). This 'parallelism' of Descartes belonged, in Yeh's eyes, to the forms of 'dualism' in 'philosophy'.

Indeed, Yeh let things rest with this assessment, without examining

Descartes' philosophy. This was also true of the passages on Kant – who, he claimed, believed that 'experience' as well as 'reason' existed alongside each other (*ping-ts'un*) and that the origin of knowledge lay in 'experience' and 'reason'. The two could not exist without each other. If there is no experience, then reason remains an empty form and cannot become knowledge; without reason, experience is just disordered material.[22] Moreover Kant's 'dualism' was idealistic since, as Schelling was later to do, Kant assumed the existence of a being beyond the realm of knowledge. This, according to Yeh, was Kant's second form of 'dualism': the difference between 'phenomenon' and the 'thing in itself'. For Kant, knowledge could only provide evidence of a phenomenon, but had nothing to say about the nature of the 'thing in itself' represented by the phenomenon.

Schelling's 'philosophy of identity' was seen by Yeh as the third, miscarried attempt to solve the contradiction between 'materialism' and 'idealism'. According to Schelling, nature and spirit are derived from the highest origin, the 'absolute'. This is the cause of all duality: in it all things opposed become identical (*t'ung-i*) and therefore possess the same quality, and their differences are merely quantitative. In Yeh's view, Schelling's idealist philosophy unites 'materialism' and 'idealism', but at the expense of 'materialism'.[23]

Yeh was finally to conclude that 'dualism' (or 'parallelism') consists of the 'absolute opposition' of both sides (*chüeh-tui tui-li*), so that no relationship can exist between 'materialism' and 'idealism'. Although the right to exist is recognised on both sides – neither side denies the other – , the contradiction between them remains in place and unsolved. On the other hand, he saw the flaw of the 'philosophy of identity' in its concept of 'absolute unity' (*chüeh-tui t'ung-i*), in which the differences between 'materialism' and 'idealism' were not taken into account. 'Dualism' and the 'philosophy of identity' both still tend toward 'idealism'; they serve as a philosophical basis for religion and are thus unscientific. The 'relative unity' of 'dualism' and the 'absolute unity' of the 'philosophy of identity' have an additional disadvantage, in that both depict a condition of repose. This form of unity is therefore static and not dynamic, since there is no reciprocal relationship between the two sides of unity.[24]

For Yeh, the problem of 'neutralism' consisted in the fact that it seeks a third realm beyond 'materialism' and 'idealism'; but because there are only 'matter' and 'spirit' in the world, all things belong either to the one side or the other – there is no 'third' side. Everything which lies outside these two realms has to be 'spirit', and thus possesses a religious and not a scientific character.[25]

These three competing alternatives had, in Yeh's opinion, led to a dead-end in the history of 'philosophy'. As to which solution to the contradiction between 'materialism' and 'idealism' finally remained valid, he answered that, in trying to reach a decision, one must avoid the mistakes of the other attempts, especially those of Kant and Schelling; and only then would it be possible for the two currents in 'philosophy' to become truly unified.[26]

Yeh saw this unification in a comprehensive way. Since the contradiction ran through all areas of 'philosophy', so too would any solution have to do so. In the realm of cosmology, Yeh dealt with the unification of 'matter' and 'spirit' (*wu-chih, ching-shen*), 'mechanism' and 'teleology' (*chi-hsieh-lun, mu-ti-lun*) and 'determinism' and 'indeterminism' (*yu-ting-lun, wu-ting-lun*). In the 'philosophy of life' (*jen-sheng-lun*) it was imperative to solve the contradiction between nature and humanity, between necessity and freedom (*pi-jan, tzu-yu*), happiness and sorrow (*k'uai-le, k'u-hsing*) and heteronomy and autonomy (*t'a-lü-lun, tsu-lü-lun*). The 'theory of knowledge' was supposed to resolve the contradiction between 'experience' and 'reason' (*ching-yen, li-hsing*), 'perception' and 'thought' (*kan-chüeh, ssu-wei*), 'reality' and 'idea' (*shih-tsai, kuan-nien*) and 'nominalism' and 'realism' (*ming-mu-lun, shih-tsai-lun*).[27]

The method of unification was always the same, hence we will describe only the unification of 'matter' and 'spirit', which typifies all other branches of 'philosophy'. According to Yeh, the unification of 'matter' and 'spirit' assumed in advance that both categories existed in a unity and determined each other reciprocally. He then offered the following 'chain of evidence':

What, he asked, is 'matter'? Its first characteristic is that it exists independently of human knowledge. While the latter is 'subjective', 'matter' is 'objective', and furthermore possesses the two attributes of expansion (*kuang-yen*) and movement (*yün-tung*).

What is 'spirit'? Under it Yeh subsumed all terms such as 'soul' (*hsin-ling*), 'reason' (*li-hsing*), 'thinking' (*ssu-wei*) and 'subjective' (*chu-kuan*). Ideas, the product of thinking (unlike 'matter'), have neither 'form' (*hsing-t'i*) nor 'body' (*t'i-chi*), nor do they possess attributes such as expansion and movement.[28] Thus, one can see that 'matter' and 'spirit' are two opposing, contrasting concepts; and this contradiction is reflected in philosophers' minds as 'materialism' and 'idealism'.

How did it come about that 'matter' and 'spirit' existed in a single unity and determined each other reciprocally? If one studied the relation between 'matter' and 'spirit' more closely, Yeh wrote, one could ascertain that 'matter' existed at the beginning and that 'spirit' came later as the universe developed with the appearance of human beings. Consequently, in the beginning there were not 'words' but 'matter', and after a long period of development came the origin of the solar system, the earth and of the plants and fauna that exist upon it, among which human beings represented the highest stage of development. They were the only ones with the ability of conscious perception and thought; therefore it is only with their appearance that 'spirit' appeared. The development thus proceeds from 'matter' to 'spirit'; and in the course of that development, 'matter' has brought about 'spirit'. This was Yeh's reason for contending that the materialists should refrain from negating 'spirit' and 'idealism' respectively, but rather recognise that 'spirit' is a product of 'matter'.[29] Moreover, the existence of 'spirit' and 'idealism' was for Yeh proof of the correctness of 'materialism', since only through 'spirit' could the sciences – astronomy, physics, chemistry and so on – have been able to offer proof of the development of the universe from 'matter' to 'spirit'. Therefore, consciousness is evidence of the existence of 'matter', because without 'consciousness' human beings would not know of its existence.[30]

The principle by which 'matter' produces consciousness or 'spirit' can also, in Yeh's opinion, be reversed. After the appearance of humans in the development of the universe, that development did not cease: unlike the animals, humans constantly altered nature. Their method of working was based on ideas and concepts, which they then transformed into products. The production, exchange and distribution of raw materials, tools, products and consumer goods formed in turn the basis of economics, politics and society. They were at once a part of the still developing universe, whereby the production of 'matter' is a result of 'spirit'.[31] While, in Yeh's opinion, the theoretical natural sciences offer evidence of the process whereby as the universe developed, 'matter' brought about 'spirit', the applied natural sciences and social sciences are in turn proof that, in the course of further development, 'spirit' can bring forth 'matter': 'spirit' produced by matter becomes a force which, for its part, again produces 'matter'.[32]

With this description Yeh believed he had provided 'proof' of his contention that 'spirit' and 'matter' are reciprocally determined, one being only a function of the other, and vice versa. 'In this manner,' he wrote, 'we must recognise that both exist at the same time (t'ung-shih ts'un-tsai).'[33] However, 'spirit' and 'matter' exist not only as opposites but most particularly in a unity, and they unite and permeate each other completely in the development of nature.[34] For this reason, Yeh believed the idea that 'materialism' has attempted to destroy 'idealism' and vice versa, to be basically false. Instead, both currents should appreciate their reciprocal dependence and supplement each other.

According to Yeh, 'spirit' is 'sucked up' (hsi-shou) in the process of its unification by 'matter'. In this case, 'materialism' is transformed into 'science' and loses its character as 'philosophy'. The result of this process is the 'new materialism' (hsin-wu-chih-lun). This is then 'philosophy' in name only, because by now its content has made it 'science'. The former 'philosophical materialism' is incorporated into 'science'; it has become 'scientific materialism' and has thus lost its earlier 'independence' (tu-li-hsing). 'Idealism' suffers the same fate; it too has lost its character as 'philosophy' and forfeited its 'independence' through becoming unified with 'materialism' and through the incorporation of 'materialism' into 'science'.

Contrary to 'dualism', 'neutralism' and 'the philosophy of identity', which all necessarily lead to 'idealism', Yeh considered his suggested unification to have resulted in a 'monism', which is simultaneously 'materialistic' and 'scientific'. 'In this way the philosophical problem which originated through the contradiction between materialism and idealism is solved. After two thousand years of philosophical disputes we are now announcing the end. From now on there are no longer philosophical problems and consequently no more philosophical controversies . . . The solution to philosophical problems lies in the annihilation of philosophy.'[35]

The 'annihilation of philosophy' takes place according to the dialectical principle of 'thesis' (cheng) – 'antithesis' (fan) – 'synthesis' (he). As an example, Yeh cites Feuerbach's unification of mechanical materialism with Hegel's dialectic, which Marx completed to form dialectical materialism. 'Materialism' is the thesis, 'idealism' the antithesis, and, in the process of its unification, the mechanical aspect of 'materialism', as well as the idealistic aspect of the dialectic, are negated. With the synthesis of 'dialectical materialism', both 'materialism' and 'idealism' are destroyed as an independent 'philosophy'.[36]

'Science' as a New World-View or the Unification of the CCP and the Kuomintang

Yeh's remarks on the 'annihilation of philosophy' and his advocacy of 'science' seem to have been inspired by his belief in the omnipotence and superiority of scientific thought. Scholars such as Kwok and Brière have described Yeh as an independent materialist, an advocate of the old positivistic belief in science, to whom neither Marx nor God was sacred, and whose first principle was to accept only those assertations that had withstood all scientific criticism.[37]

If one considers the comments of Yeh Ching – as Kwok and Brière do – as philosophical contributions, one can add that 'science' appeared to Yeh as scientism, nourishing itself from the enthusiasm over the successes of Western science compared to the obvious inferiority of the traditional Chinese world-view. 'Science' replaced the traditional view of life and had a similar comprehensive character. The new world-view had a binding force for every area – for the cosmos, for society and for intellectual thought – as Confucianism had done formerly, but in contrast to Confucianism it was based on the laws of modern science. Through it, the lost unity between the micro and macrocosmos, between humans, society and the universe was reestablished on the basis of supposedly objective scientific laws. Yeh's comments were therefore part and parcel of the general belief in science which had been widespread among Chinese intellectuals since the 1920s. Belief in the 'omnipotence of science' (*k'o-hsüeh wan-neng*) inspired the geologist Ting Wen-chiang, the pragmatist Hu Shih and the anarchist Wu Chih-hui, as well as the advocate of Marxism Ch'en Tu-hsiu.[38]

However, such a philosophical-historical interpretation of the texts gives a false picture; it hides, rather than explains, what Yeh Ching, as well as his opponents, were trying to express. That Yeh's comments were lexical and superficial, and contained no exact definition of the concepts applied, is not hard to ascertain. His assertion that 'spirit' is a product of 'matter', and first occurred with the appearance of human beings in the universe, is neither conclusive nor logical, but merely an assertion. The thesis concerning the end of 'philosophy' also rests on shaky ground, as does his belief in 'science'. His 'philosophy' appears to be a congeries of assertions which he had borrowed from several descriptions of Western philosophy and formed into a unified system.[39] The lack of comprehension is especially clear in relation to idealistic philosophy: his comments on Kant are simplistic and the philosophy of Schelling and

Spinoza is portrayed in ways that betray ignorance of their works.

Thus it is pointless to use Yeh's texts for a serious comparison with the authors he mentions and to base an evaluation on such a comparison. It is more reasonable to try and ascertain Yeh's intentions, which led him selectively to construct the aforementioned world-view from elements of Western philosophy. Using this approach, only Yeh's conclusions are of interest, and not the logic of the preceding arguments. In all the texts evaluated in this study it appears that the sequence of thought in a text depends on, and is accommodated to, the conclusion which the author intends to reach. Thus the logic of the argumentation is determined by the conclusion and not vice versa, because behind it lies an intention which has nothing to do with the theme under discussion.

How then can one discover the author's intention? This, and hence the true meaning of the texts, emerges from a comparison of the conclusions in the text with the wider political struggles taking place at the time of publication, as we have already illustrated. The meaning of all 'philosophical' declarations lies not in the texts and in the thought-content of the concepts applied, but rather outside them. If this is true, then all the 'philosophical' concepts appearing in the texts are without content. Thus, since they do not possess any thought-content, I would like to see them understood as signs and symbols and not as concepts. 'Matter' and 'spirit', 'materialism' and 'idealism', 'philosophy' and 'science', 'objective truth' and so on – in other words, all the Chinese characters which the reader first identifies as philosophical concepts – are nothing more than symbols which the theoreticians relate to certain political parties, factions and positions, according to their own views. Hence the 'philosophical' assertions and conclusions in the texts reflect, in the manner of an analogue equivalent, nothing more than the political and, above all, the military-strategic intentions of their authors in the struggle against their political opponents.

What 'spirit' and what 'matter' were Yeh talking about? What was the meaning of Kant's 'dualism', Spinoza's 'neutralism' and Schelling's 'philosophy of identity'?

All Yeh Ch'ing's writings on the history of Western philosophy concerned relations between the CCP and the Kuomintang, between the Red Army and the Chinese Nationalist Army and the necessity for them to be united and the conditions by which this was to be achieved.

Yet nowhere in the texts we have examined so far is it possible to find a direct reference to the two parties – Communist and Nationalist; this could be evidence that Yeh is writing about the inter-party relationship and not about philosophy. Right up to the end he avoids making any reference to the question of the United Front. He expressed himself exclusively in terms of 'philosophy' when speaking of politics. The evidence for this can, of course, only be forthcoming when it is proved that all texts concerning 'dialectical materialism' in China are based on a structure in which every 'philosophical' assertion can be exactly related to a political position, faction or party.

We will first briefly summarise the assertions made by Yeh Ch'ing:

1. It is the fate of philosophy to be annihilated. This is true for both 'idealism' and 'materialism'.

2. In the process of withering away, 'philosophy' is increasingly being replaced by 'science' in the form of 'dialectical materialism'.

3. This results from the dialectical unification of 'materialism' and 'idealism'.

4. Through this unification the struggle between both currents in 'philosophy', which has lasted for more than 2,000 years, is finally resolved.

5. In the history of 'philosophy', all other attempted solutions have been condemned to failure. These include the 'dualism' or 'parallelism' of Kant and Descartes, the 'neutralism' of Spinoza, and Schelling's 'philosophy of identity'.

6. 'Matter' and 'spirit' determine and penetrate each other mutually (*hu-hsiang shen-t'ou*). They exist as opposites within a unity, whereby the contradiction between them is relative, whereas the unity is absolute.[40] It is therefore fundamentally false for one side to attempt to destroy the other by the solution of the contradiction. The recognition by both sides of this status quo is the prerequisite for the solution of the contradiction through unification.

Assuming we are able to confirm and re-confirm the thesis that the sole purpose of these texts is to provide analogies to contemporary political struggles, then Yeh's 'philosophical' statements yield the following political positions:

1. The struggle between 'materialism' and 'idealism in Western philosophy is analogous to the civil war between the CCP and the Kuomintang. Thus the terms 'matter' and 'spirit' are not used as philosophical concepts, but rather as linguistic symbols for the two parties and their respective armies. The description of the relationship between the symbols represents the relationship between the two parties at the time of publication.

2. The 'theory of the unification of matter and spirit' (*wu-hsin tsung-he*

lun) can thus only mean that Yeh is advocating the unification of both parties and of their armies.

3. Unification was to be implemented on condition that each side should recognise the right to existence of the other, and not, as in the past, strive for each other's 'annihilation'. The analogous equivalent to this suggestion was Yeh's comprehensive 'proof' that 'matter' and 'spirit' could, in principle, exist in unity and create each other. In concrete terms, his comments implied the CCP should abandon its attempts to overthrow the Kuomintang; as a corollary, the Kuomintang should cease its 'extermination campaigns' against the CCP.

4. The unification of the two parties and of their armies would result in each party and its military wing losing its individual independence. The form of their merger was characterised by a 'mutual penetration' of the formerly independent parties, the analogy of this political concept being Yeh's representation of 'dialectical materialism' as the result of the unification of 'materialism' and 'idealism'. He had written that the latter are destroyed as a 'philosophy' and lose their 'independence' (*tu-li hsing*) through the emergence of 'dialectical materialism'. The end of 'philosophy' in Western intellectual history, which Yeh proclaimed, meant nothing else but the end of the CCP and the Kuomintang as autonomous organisations.

According to Yeh, the end of 'philosophy' was also connected with the development of 'science'. Thus 'dialectical materialism' as a 'science' stood as an analogous equivalent of an umbrella organisation in which both parties and their armies were to be absorbed. Yeh Ching's advocacy of 'science', which negated 'philosophy', thus reveals political intentions which had nothing whatever to do with 'science' and 'philosophy'.

5. Yeh rejected all other means of merging the CCP and Kuomintang, something that can be deduced from his comments concerning the 'dualism' of Kant and Descartes, the 'neutralism' of Spinoza and Schelling's 'philosophy of identity'.

The 'dualism' of Kant and Descartes stood here as an analogy of the following position: between both parties there was cooperation – a sort of coalition, but not a unification – which would have led to the surrender of independence. Both parties remain separated, just as 'phenomena' and 'thing-in-itself' are separated in Kant's epistemology. Thus the contradictions between the two parties remained unresolved: the CCP and the Kuomintang exist in a Kantian and Descartesian 'dualism', independent yet in the closest proximity to each other, while they were to 'mutually penetrate' each other in the same way as, supposedly, 'matter' and 'spirit' do in 'philosophy'.

6. What is the position *vis-à-vis* Spinoza's 'neutralism' and Schelling's 'philosophy of identity'? According to Yeh, 'neutralism' presupposes there is a third position alongside 'materialism' and 'idealism'; however, there can be no such third position, because everything in the world belongs either to 'matter' or 'spirit'. It is possible that in this instance Yeh was thinking of the 'Third Force', those small parties founded by men like Chang Chün-mai and Chang Tung-sun, which attempted in vain during the Sino-Japanese war to build an independent position between the CCP and the Kuomintang.[41] But this 'Third Force' was too weak to absorb the CCP and the Kuomintang, and 'neutralism' as a possible solution was discarded.

7. Yeh considered that the weakness of the 'philosophy of identity' lay in its reduction of 'matter' and 'spirit' to mere characteristics of the 'absolute', in which both became identical. Since the 'absolute' was included in the realm of 'spirit' and was consequently considered to belong to 'idealism', the unification of both parties according to the precepts of the 'philosophy of identity' would have been tantamount to the CCP capitulating to the Kuomintang; 'matter' and the CCP were declared to be identical to 'spirit' and the Kuomintang respectively. Of course, the Chinese Communists could not be expected to accede to this demand and so Schelling's 'philosophy of identity' proved unsuitable as a solution.

Yeh's portrayal of the history of Western philosophy—from Thales, Heraclitus and Aristotle through Occam, Bacon and Locke to Kant, Hegel and later Einstein and Heisenberg—was based precisely on his political concepts and goals regarding the relationships between the CCP and the Kuomintang. To this end he had selected passages and sequences of thought from Western philosophy and constructed a unified system according to the principle of the analogous equivalent. He thus disguised his concepts whereby the CCP and Kuomintang should combine in a 'philosophically' disguised form.

Comte's doctrine of the three-stage development of consciousness, from religion through philosophy to science, served Yeh merely as an analogy to his belief in the necessity of each party losing its independence in the course of attaining unification. The philosophy of Kant, Spinoza and Schelling served him as an example of how not to obtain this unification. He had, in this instance, arranged all the 'philosophical-historical' details in his texts in such a way as to ensure the structure of its arrangement was congruent to that of the political struggles and his political position.

What Europe's philosophers had thought and argued about for 2,000 years could now finally be resolved: the contradiction between 'matter' and 'spirit' was to find its negation in the unification of the CCP and the Kuomintang.

'Report on a Journey to the Tip of a Cow's Horn' or the 'Scientific' and the 'Philosophical' Concept of Matter

Along with Yeh Ch'ing, Ai Ssu-ch'i, who was born in Yunnan in 1910 and whose real name was Li Sheng-hsüan, was the best-known theoretician of dialectical materialism in China. He never possessed a power-base within the party but was reputed to be the most important authority on questions of cadre education and ideology. His career began as the co-publisher of the magazine *Tu-shu sheng-huo* (Study and Life) in Shanghai, with which the authors Ch'en Po-ta, Ch'en Chih-yüan, Hu Sheng and Hsüeh Mu-ch'iao were also involved. Ai first came to prominence as the author of *Che-hsüeh chiang-hua* (Talks on Philosophy), which appeared in *Study and Life*; they were later published in January 1936 as *Ta-chung che-hsüeh* (Philosophy for the Masses) and went through a total of thirty-two editions in succeeding years.[41] It is this work which made his name as a Marxist philosopher and on which his reputation rests today.

In October 1935 Ai joined the CCP on the recommendation of Chou Yang and Chou Li-po. When the Sino-Japanese war broke out in July 1937, Ai went to Yenan and taught at the Anti-Japanese Military-Political Academy (*K'ang-ta*), becoming one of Mao's closest collaborators over questions of ideology. He held a number of influential positions, among them that of General Secretary of the Central Research Institute of the CCP Central Committee and of deputy publisher of *Chieh-fang jih-pao* (Liberation Daily), the most important organ of the CCP. After 1949 he taught as a professor at the Institute for Marxism-Leninism in Peking, the pre-eminent institute for the education of party cadres, and from 1951 was deputy chairman of the Chinese philosophical society.

Ai Ssu'ch'i is widely regarded by scholars such as Brière, Kwok and, more recently, Fogel as China's leading populariser of the philosophy of Marxism. In my opinion the prime example of this so-called popularised Marxist philosophy, *Philosophy for the Masses*, has as little in common with a philosophical treatise as does Yeh's *Whither Philosophy?* It does indeed provide an introduction to the basics of dialectical materialism – as Brière and Fogel rightly point out – but it is also remarkable for its communication of political problems, which lie beyond every philosophical approach; it belongs rather to the realm of the parable. As with Yeh Ch'ing, the 'philosophical' terminology consists merely of empty formulae and is the analogous equivalent of the author's political ideas regarding the United Front.

In 1986, the *Jen-min jih-pao* (People's Daily) published an article on the occasion of the fiftieth anniversary of the publication of Ai's *Philosophy for the Masses*.[42] The article claims that Ai thought one of the main reasons for the success of his book was its correct party line regarding the United Front with the Kuomintang. This statement confirms our central thesis, since on no page of *Philosophy for the Masses* can one find the term 'United Front', but only discussions about 'materialism and idealism', 'theory of knowledge', 'formal and dialectical logic' etc. *Philosophy for the Masses*, which is among the few standard works of early Chinese Marxism, could hardly have been understood by the 'masses', since a real understanding could only be based on an exact knowledge of internal party struggles.

In the context of the struggle over 'philosophy' and 'science', we are interested here only in the book's first two chapters, in which Ai Ssu-ch'i described, in broad terms, the differences between 'materialism' and 'idealism.' The other chapters on the 'theory of knowledge' and the basic rules of dialectical materialism will be dealt with below.[43]

Ai Ssu-ch'i explained to his readers that 'philosophy' was not something mysterious, but rather an everyday concept which could prove useful in resolving personal as well as social problems. It shed light on the causes of the problems; it was helpful, *inter alia*, in the struggle against 'exploiters'; and it offered an opportunity for 'self-liberation'. With these and similar introductory remarks about the practicability of 'philosophical' reflection, Ai then led his readers on to the theme of 'materialism' versus 'idealism'. Here he came to his central thesis: 'materialism' and 'idealism' are the two 'camps' in 'philosophy' which have fought each other constantly over time and stand 'eternally in contradiction' to one another. Every 'philosophy' can be traced back either to 'materialism' or to 'idealism', and it makes no difference which one is being referred to, or how it is described.

The contradiction between the two 'camps of philosophy' extends into every area. Not only do 'materialism' and 'idealism' struggle eternally with each other, but so too do 'perceptual' and 'theoretical' knowledge, 'formal' and 'dialectical' logic, 'subjective' and 'objective', 'analysis' and 'synthesis' etc.[44] Accordingly, all themes are split up into opposites; however, they constitute a unity, the decisive factor in this unity being the absolute opposition between the two sides of a contradiction.

Unlike Yeh Ch'ing, up till 1936 Ai Ssu-ch'i stressed in his 'Talks on Philosophy' the irreconcilability of the two sides of a contradiction; for him there could be no question of recognition and a possible unification: 'idealism' was a diseased state which had to be combated. He designated 'feudal philosophy' a mortal enemy of 'materialism', the 'vitalism' of the Kuomintang theoretician Ch'en Li-fu as fascism,[45] and was also of the opinion that pragmatism was a dangerous 'philosophy'.[46] Any compromise between 'materialism' and the various directions of 'idealism' was fundamentally excluded.

In such a context, how would the relationship between 'philosophy' and 'science' be resolved? In his 'Talks on Philosophy' Ai had initially not touched on this theme. Because of Yeh Ch'ing's sharp criticism of 'philosophy' (and thus of 'materialism') and his prediction that 'philosophy' would eventually be annihilated and replaced by 'science', Ai was compelled to revise 'Talks on Philosophy', in answer to Yeh:

At the present time, where sciences are very developed, where there are natural sciences, social sciences and a science of thought, one can explain all things on earth through the use of science. Consequently there are people who maintain that one should annihilate philosophy (hsiao-mieh) and simply replace it with science. That is a mistake . . . every science has a specific realm; however, it is the task of philosophy to assimilate general knowledge from all realms.[47]

According to Ai, 'science' only investigates the laws within its respective realm. On the other hand, 'philosophy' analyses 'general laws' and thus stands essentially above 'science'.

With this supplement to 'Talks on Philosophy' Ai Ssu-ch'i made it clear that he had seen through the manouevre against 'materialism' contained in Yeh Ch'ing's thesis, which was aimed at the CCP. However, his most successful rebuttal of Yeh's theory of the 'unification of matter and spirit' and of the 'annihilation of philosophy' was his 'Report on a Journey to the Tip of a Cow's Horn'.[48] Here, in the form of a parable, he explained the difference between the 'philosophical' and 'scientific concept of matter'. The 'travel report' first appeared in the column 'Scientific Conversations' in the Tu-shu sheng-huo and was later also included as a supplement in Philosophy for the Masses.[49]

In this work, Ai described how two friends changed themselves into flies and flew together inside the horn of a cow in order, on their way to the tip of the horn, to explore the essence of matter. During the flight, they establish that, along with solid and visible matter, of which, for example, the cow's horn consists, there is also a further type of material in the form of small, invisible particles, which, as they travel, constantly bounce against the flies' bodies in a very unpleasant fashion: these are the molecules which make up the air. In the hope they can discover the essence of the material in the molecules, the friends change themselves from flies into molecules. But they notice, to their disappointment, that even now they do not seem to form the essence of matter, which consists rather of atoms, which themselves consist of even smaller particles, namely electrons. The two travellers then conclude finally that matter seems to consist of electrons.

To make a more precise investigation of these smallest building-blocks of matter, the two travellers decide to change themselves from molecules into electrons. As they shrink more and more, they eventually reach the tip of the cow's horn and there make a strange discovery: that some electrons obviously have the property of wanting to unify themselves with others. When such a unification occurs, it is as if two bombs have collided. An invisible beam of light is then created, with the result that the two unified particles are annihilated (*hsiao-mieh*). One of the travellers concluded from his observation that matter obviously does not exist at all, since all solid matter can be traced back to the smallest particles, the electrons, and these, in the case of unification with other particles, are annihilated in the collision and the ensuing radiation. However, the other traveller, who takes the position of dialectical materialism, believes that matter simply passes through different states: solid, gaseous and finally that in which it dissolves into rays of light. He thus concludes that the 'scientific concept of matter' recognises matter as having a solid form, but ultimately contains the seeds of its own annihilation. By contrast, the adherent of 'dialectical materialism' and the 'philosophical concept of matter' does not see in its transformation into radiation the destruction of matter, but only a change in its state, through which it can pass. He closes with the warning: 'In the study of philosophy, one must differentiate this point very carefully, otherwise one will get caught up in the intrigues of idealism.'[50]

Nuclear fission was first discovered some time after this 'travel report' of 1935, but it is clear that Ai Ssu-ch'i had some theoretical knowledge of atomic physics. However, his concern was less with the essence of matter than with the 'intrigues of idealism': for him the 'scientific concept of matter' was an 'idealistic' concept, since it meant that in 'unification' matter is 'annihilated'. Thus Ai unmasked the coded thesis of Yeh Ch'ing, whereby the CCP and Kuomintang were to unite, as an 'intrigue of idealism' which possibly had the aim of the 'destruction of matter' – or of the CCP. Thus the 'tip of a cow's horn', where the particles united and 'matter' was annihilated, was politically a very dangerous dead-end for the adherents of the 'philosophical concept of matter'.

Transformations have a long tradition in Chinese literature, whether it be the seventy-two transformations of the monkey-king Sun Wu-kung in *Hsi-yu-chi* (The Pilgrimage to the West),[51] or the *Liao-chai chih-i* (431 Strange Tales recorded in the studio of contemplative leisure) by P'u Sung-ling, or numerous other novels and fairy-tales.[52] The same phenomenon can be found in European literature – e.g. Swift's *Battle of the Books* and *Gulliver's Travels*.[53] However, the heroes of these two political parodies were unable to transform themselves into atoms and electrons like Ai Ssu-ch'i's two travelling 'investigators of nature' – natural science had not yet developed that far – but only into spirits or animals and vice versa.

After the publication of his 'Travel Report', Ai Ssu-ch'i took a stand concerning the relationship between 'philosophy' and 'science' in two further articles defending the importance of 'philosophy' against Yeh Ch'ing.[54] 'It is not correct,' he wrote, 'to preserve, as before, a philosophy or metaphysic that goes beyond science, but it is also wrong to reject the knowledge of philosophy absolutely, so that it will no longer possess its own special sphere and object. This is also a mistake of mechanism. What is the actual importance of philosophy? The old pure philosophy, which goes beyond science, must of course be negated, but this has nothing whatever to do with Yeh Ch'ing's theory of the annihilation of philosophy. Yeh Ch'ing dissolves the whole of philosophy into individual sciences. In his opinion, it no longer possesses an independent territory (*tu-li ling-yü*). When the theories of all the individual sciences are combined, according to Yeh, materialism emerges . . . On the contrary, dialectical materialism does not allow philosophy to be absorbed in the individual sciences, but preserves its independent territory and the object of philosophy.'[55]

In Ai's opinion, the objects of 'philosophy' are the general developmental laws of nature, society and thought. These laws take the research of the individual sciences as a basis, but 'they can, on the other hand, direct the research of the individual sciences.'[56] Ai Ssu-ch'i criticised Yeh Ch'ing in this vein as a supporter of Deborin and Bukharin, accusing him of advocating their views in his works.[57] Yeh Ch'ing was later labelled a 'Deborinist'. This was a mistake, for Deborin had always defended 'philosophy' against the 'sciences' and stressed its leadership role (see above). It can thus be concluded that Ai Ssu-ch'i had not read Deborin's works but had merely accepted his overall condemnation by Mitin.

The opinion, expressed by Ai, that 'philosophy' should direct the research of 'science' is certainly worthy of discussion and could even be used as a theme for a philosophical seminar; however, if the participants were to limit themselves to this question, they would miss the basic point. Ai's statements are indeed very general, but it is possible to understand precisely their essential meaning. Ai had distinguished between two types of 'philosophy': the 'old philosophy' and the 'philosophy of dialectical materialism'. In his opinion, the 'old philosophy' should be 'negated'; but the latter was to preserve its 'independent territory' and 'direct the individual sciences'. This was a very clear political declaration: the 'negation' of the 'old philosophy', i.e. of 'idealism' and 'feudal philosophy', stood for the destruction of those social forces – the landlords and the new Chinese bourgeoisie – which were attached to it in the sense of a very limited understanding regarding the Marxist relation between basis and superstructure. The 'independent territory' of dialectical materialism is to be taken literally though (this formulation will surface quite often in the course of our study). It stands, on the one hand, for the territory controlled by the CCP, and, on the other hand, for the party's organisational independence. In this context we would like to recall that the Kuomintang had demanded the abolition of the independent territory under CCP control as a prerequisite for national unification (cf. Part II).

Thus in all his texts Ai Ssu-ch'i warned that unification with the Kuomintang would mean the loss of the CCP's independence, just as Yeh Ch'ing had portrayed it in his works, using the coded example of the annihilation of 'philosophy'. Guidance of the 'individual sciences' only makes sense from this point of view when, after the negation of the 'old philosophy' (i.e. the destruction of the social forces mentioned), society would be led by the only independent force still in existence, namely the CCP.

The claim to political control, expressed in the 'philosophical works' of Ai Ssu-ch'i, underwent a tactical modification in the autumn of 1936.

While, up to August 1936, Ai had portrayed 'philosophy' as being divided throughout the cosmos into irreconcilable and eternal opposites, he suddenly discovered in October of that year a certain preference for 'old philosophy'. In two articles he expressed his views on the question of cooperation between adherents of every philosophical direction, with the goal of 'saving the nation',[58] and demanded a 'united cultural front'.

It does not matter if there are elements of capitalist, feudalistic culture, pragmatism or socialism, it is only important that what develops from them is useful and advantageous, in which case they will be given an open welcome in the movement.[59]

In contrast to his earlier condemnation of every current of 'idealism', Ai now described 'idealism' as the 'theoretical basis' of the war of resistance:

The demands of life are material demands of the nation. If in this connection vitalism develops, it can become the theoretical basis of resistance and salvation . . . In China we must mobilise the whole strength of the nation, including the forces of philosophy, throughout the war of resistance. We need no one who suppresses others, but rather the unification of all forces. Everyone must develop his best qualities and use them for the people as much as he is able. Those who believe in materialism can go hand in hand with vitalism, and those who believe in vitalism should not be considered as enemies by the materialists.[60]

Thus an offer of cooperation was made to the former 'mortal enemy'. The occasion for this new evaluation of 'idealism' was the CCP's change in tactics regarding the United Front, as noted above, especially in the form expressed by the resolutions of August 25 and September 17, 1936.[61] In connection with the offer of a United Front to Chiang Kai-shek contained in those resolutions, the CCP began, with the writings of Ch'en Po-ta, Ai Ssu-ch'i and Chou Yang, a campaign among the country's intellectuals called the 'New Enlightenment Movement' (Hsin ch'i-meng yün-tung). Its aim was to strive for a national United Front in politics as well as in cultural matters.[62] This offer of cooperation within the framework of patriotic competition between 'feudalistic' and 'capitalistic' culture, between 'pragmatism' and 'socialism', was also to affect all other areas of Ai Ssu-chi'i's 'philosophy' – the relation between 'perceptual' and 'theoretical' knowledge as well as that between 'formal' and 'dialectical' knowledge, of which more later.

Ai's critics now accused him of having changed his 'philosophy of opposites' (tui-li che-hsüeh) into a 'philosophy of alliance' (lien-he che-hsüeh). The first of these principles contained the absolute negation of one side of the contradiction and was thus merely a reflection of the relationship between the CCP and Kuomintang before the establishment of the United Front. Hence one can hardly term this 'philosophy', and much less 'dialectic philosophy'. The *lien-he che-hsüeh* apparently meant suspending absolute opposition, since it called for fair and equal cooperation with the former enemy. However, if one was loathe to place oneself at the mercy of one's opponent in such an arrangement, it was necessary to solve the question of what were the long-term goals of this cooperation and of who was to assume leadership in the United Front. Consequently, as has already been shown, the problem of the United Front leadership was to become the most contentions issue in the struggle within the CCP.

Henceforth the problem was reflected in all the 'philosophical struggles', which constantly revolved around the question of whether 'philosophy' or 'science', 'matter' or 'spirit', 'materialism' or 'idealism', etc., should assume the leadership.

The Leading Role of the CCP or on the Solution of the Crisis in the Natural Sciences

On September 1, 1936, Ch'en Po-ta intervened in the discussion about 'philosophy' and 'science' in an article which appeared only a few days after the CCP resolution of August 25 offering a United Front with the Kuomintang and a willingness to compromise, a fact which revealed the guiding role of the Comintern.[63] Although Ch'en Po-ta is considered to have been one of the initiators of the 'New Enlightenment Movement', which called for cooperation with all directions of 'idealistic philosophy', he argued in the article that the 'philosophy' of 'dialectical materialism' should strive for the leadership role.

Ch'en first accused Yeh of having completely misunderstood the relationship between 'philosophy' and 'science'. For him, 'philosophy' was indispensable, while 'science' was just a part of 'philosophy', which included all the 'sciences'. According to Ch'en, 'science' had indeed made itself independent of 'philosophy' over the course of time, but 'philosophy' still contained the knowledge of 'the general laws of nature', 'of society and intellectual thought'. Although there was a separation of 'philosophy' and 'science', 'philosophy' embraced the results of the sciences in every epoch. According to Ch'en, summarising and systematising scientific theories necessitated a reconciliation between 'philosophy' and 'science': 'If the modern sciences did not receive the aid of the philosophy of dialectical materialism, they could not solve the crisis of the natural sciences. That is the opinion of most progressive natural scientists.'[64]

For Ch'en, this supposed necessity of the existence of 'philosophy' was proof that not only was Yeh's 'theory of the annihilation of philosophy' false but that, on the contrary, the role of 'philosophy' had to be strengthened. Yeh's assertion that Hegel was the last great philosopher was considered by Ch'en to disparage Marx and Engels, who, in his opinion, had preserved the dialectic of Hegel through the negation of idealism and thus created the system of 'new materialism'. He accused Yeh of doing the opposite – of preserving the idealism of Hegel while rejecting the dialectic: 'Yeh Ch'ing's theory of the annihilation of philosophy is nothing more than an attempt to revive the idealistic system.'[65] Furthermore, Ch'en believed 'dialectical materialism' should remain unequivocal in its commitment to the individual sciences. Here he adopted the argument in Soviet philosophy against the mechanical materialists, who had questioned the authority of philosophy in relation to the individual sciences on the basis of a vulgar materialism and positivism.

Yeh's observation that philosophy belonged to the 'rubbish heap of history' because its knowledge was inexact was countered by Ch'en thus: 'In my view, philosophy is by no means just a pile of inexact knowledge, but rather a real and objective reflection.'[66] Certain subjective outward appearances should not, in his view, obscure the fact that the existence of the 'new materialism' was substantiated by its being a reflection of objective nature. His criticism of Yeh culminated in the accusation: 'The intention to eliminate idealism and materialism means the elimination of the active class struggle; it means making materialism dependent on idealism; and it means making the exploited dependent on the exploiters. Why does Yeh Ch'ing toy with the intention? It is because his interests are identical to those of the exploiters.'[67] This last accusation levelled against Yeh Ch'ing indicates that Ch'en's remarks on 'philosophy' and 'science' must also have had a political meaning.

If one is to place Ch'en's criticism of Yeh in relation to the discussion over the United Front, then one can outline his political views as follows:

Contrary to Yeh, Ch'en insisted 'philosophy' was independent of 'science', and fundamentally rejected its 'annihilation'. In concrete terms, this could only mean he was warning of the CCP's possible loss of independence should it join in a United Front with the Kuomintang. According to Ch'en, it was imperative that the role of 'philosophy' should be strengthened in order to master the 'crisis' of 'science'. This passage indicates that Ch'en not only advocated that the CCP retain its independence, but insisted on its assuming the leadership within the United Front.

For the CCP, the United Front might possibly mean having to delay, if not surrender the realisation of its social-political measures and goals, since the Kuomintang would make that a condition of their cooperation. Despite his offer of cooperation in the 'New Enlightenment Movement', Ch'en Po-ta was obviously not yet prepared to accept this when he wrote that the 'elimination' of 'materialism' and 'idealism' would mean the end of an 'active class struggle'. The 'class struggle' and thus the struggle against the Kuomintang was to be continued during the period of cooperation.

Thus in his article Ch'en Po-ta was as little concerned with 'exact knowledge', 'philosophy', 'science' or the 'reflection of the objective world' – to say nothing of the 'solution of the crisis in the natural sciences' – as Ai Ssu-ch'i had been concerned with the problems of atomic physics in his 'Report on a Journey to the Tip of a Cow's Horn'. Describing the relationship between these terms merely served as a pretext for expressing his ideas (or those of his faction) on the CCP's role within the United Front.

However, one question was notable by its absence in Ch'en's writings: he did not address the fundamental relationship between 'materialism' and 'idealism' in history, and whether the two are 'absolutely' unreconcilable opposites, a position Ai Ssu-ch'i had supported in his articles up till the autumn of 1936, when he switched over from 'philosophy of opposites' to the 'philosophy of alliance'. Ch'en only gave his views on the role of the 'philosophy' of 'dialectical materialism', so one can conclude that in general he endorsed the plans for a United Front, but was not ready to support the extensive concessions to the Kuomintang contained in the resolution of August 25. The quintessence of his 'philosophical' contribution was rather that there should be a United Front with the Kuomintang – but without equality between the parties; the CCP should have the leading role and continue its struggle against the Kuomintang.

Who Determines Who? or 'Spirit' and 'Matter'

The transition from the 'philosophy of opposites' to the 'philosophy of alliance' met with criticism from a group of theoreticians, whose pseudonyms concealed the identity of Lu Lung-chi, Ai Sheng and T'an Fu-chih. Ch'en Po-ta characterised them as 'literary Pharisees' because they alleged that he and Ai Ssu-ch'i were transforming Marxism into a 'philosophy of alliance' and 'patriotism' (ai-kuo che-hsüeh).[68] They adopted a position in their articles which indicates they were opponents of the United Front with the Kuomintang, and saw in it the betrayal of Communist principles.

On September 15, 1936, Lu Lung-chi published an article entitled 'On Spirit and Matter'[69] in which he stated unequivocally that 'the two directions in philosophy, "materialism" and "idealism", were opposed to each other from start to finish, and find themselves engaged in struggle where it is impossible for them to reach a compromise [che-chung] or a reconciliation.'[70] Throughout the history of 'philosophy' all attempts to let the two directions coexist alongside each other (ping-ts'un) and to make use of their reciprocal advantages and thereby end their struggle, had been unsuccessful. He considered the reason for this to be that 'materialism' and 'idealism' were founded on two irreconcilable world-views which reflected the class contradiction in society.

Lu worked on the assumption that the struggle between 'matter' and 'spirit' could not possibly stop at the present time, but that on the contrary it would enter a 'new, complicated stage'; everyone speaking now of conciliation, he wrote, would weaken the will to resist the enemy. Anyway, the history of 'philosophy' offered evidence that the tendency towards conciliation (t'iao-he-p'ai) between 'matter' and 'spirit', especially the 'dualism' of Kant, had constantly been defeated. He went on to criticise Yeh's assertion that 'matter' brought forth 'spirit', which in turn would bring forth 'matter'. For Lu, 'thought' was solely a function of 'matter' developed at its highest form; thus it was not 'spirit' and hence 'idealism' that could transform society but rather 'materialism'.[71] He demanded that 'spirit' in Yeh's definition should never be allowed to determine 'matter', but only the reverse.[72]

Lu saw Yeh as an 'idealist' who came in the guise of 'materialism', an enemy who stood behind rather than in front of one and who caused unrest in his own ranks. Yeh's 'philosophy' served merely to use the weapon of 'dialectical materialism' against itself.

What was this criticism supposed to mean? It is improbable that Lu associated the words 'spirit' and 'matter' with the corresponding Western concepts. The words were not defined, but only juxtaposed with each other as labels, and the relationships between them were described. The article itself remains meaningless if it is considered as a philosophical statement and not in conjunction with the political context. In the former case it appears absurd, for what can be the meaning of the statement that 'spirit' should never be allowed to determine 'matter'? However, if one links 'matter' to the CCP and 'spirit' to the Kuomintang, then the formulation has a meaning: for Ai Ssu-ch'i, Ch'en Po-ta and Lu, but not for Yeh, the CCP and the Kuomintang stood irreconcilably opposed to each other. Reconciliation between the two parties was excluded not merely for the present but also in the future. Moreover, Lu pointed out that the struggle between them was entering a 'new, complicated level', and that the contrasts between them would increase rather than decrease. Thus with the comment that 'spirit' should never be allowed to determine 'matter', he rejected any subordination of the CCP to the Kuomintang. This suggests that Lu associated himself with the wing of the party opposed to cooperation with the Kuomintang.

Two and Three Make Five or the Difference between Dialectic and Algebra

In April 1937 Ai Sheng published a much sharper, highly polemical criticism in *A Critique of Yeh Ch'ing's Philosophy*.[73] This work, like Ai Ssu-ch'i's *Philosophy for the Masses*, was a collection of articles written since the autumn of 1936. Like other critics before him, Ai Sheng objected to Yeh Ch'ing's assertion that it was the fate of 'philosophy' to suffer annihilation. In his view, 'philosophy' and 'science' supplemented each other:

Science investigates concretely the developmental laws of the objective universe, while philosophy investigates the general laws of movement in nature, society and intellectual thought. Science delivers to philosophy the material on which it writes, and philosophy in turn enriches the content of science through the individual sciences. Afterwards, it negates the sciences.[74]

Ai Sheng sought to refute Yeh's assertion by citing the following examples: when science negates its own laws by creating new laws, when a society based on private property is replaced by a new society, then this does not mean that science is negated as society is. Philosophy works in the same way; thus 'idealism' and 'mechanism' are negated by 'materialism' and 'dialectical materialism' respectively. Here annihilation befalls 'idealism' and 'mechanism' but not the 'philosophy of dialectical materialism'; the latter is rather the upshot of this negation. In

Ai Sheng's view, instead Yeh attempts to destroy all 'philosophy' and simply 'crush' the 'new philosophy' in the bud instead of encouraging its growth.[75] When the realms of 'science' are constantly expanding and deepening, then a concentrated investigation is necessary – a general, overlapping and comprehensive theory and rule. 'Therefore, science cannot replace philosophy!'[76]

Ai Sheng also criticised Yeh's portrayal of the origin of dialectical materialism. Yeh had written that Marx's greatest service was in having united Hegel's dialectics with materialism, to which Ai responded as follows:

Yeh assumes that Marx has drawn the dialectic out of Hegel's philosophy and fused it with materialism . . . Such a unity, however, is not a development of the contradiction, not a negation of the negation, but rather a compromise [che-chung] and conciliation [t'iao-he] . . . According to Yeh, the combative dialectical materialism had transformed itself into a mixture, into a peaceful dualism. It is an absolute, metaphysical concept of combat.[77]

Hitherto Ai Sheng's criticism had differed very little from that of other theoreticians; for example, his formulations were almost identical to those of Ai Ssu-ch'i and Ch'en Po-ta. The difference first became clear as he began elaborating the relationship between 'materialism' and 'idealism' and thus assumed the position which Ai Ssu-ch'i had advocated up till the autumn of 1936. In his view 'matter' and 'spirit', and 'being' and 'spirit' should first be conceptually clarified:

Materialism maintains that 'matter' comes first and 'thought' afterwards, and that the former determines the latter. On the other hand, idealism asserts that 'spirit' existed before 'matter' and determines it . . . Both these large groups in philosophy stood opposed to each other from the beginning, and in the struggle between them no compromise [che-chung] or conciliation was possible. Although many people believed that the two groups could coexist with each other . . . and that the contradictions and struggle between them could be eliminated, they repeatedly suffered defeat, because idealism and materialism are based on two world-views, between which there can be no peace or compromise.[78]

The 'conceptual clarification' exhausted itself in this passage. However, it becomes clear that Ai Sheng clung, in contrast to Ai Ssu-ch'i and Ch'en Po-ta, to the irreconcilable nature of the contradiction between 'materialism' and 'idealism'; in other words, he rejected any compromise between the CCP and the Kuomintang. In almost the same words as Lu Lung-chi, he said that the struggle between the parties was entering a new phase: 'Its form is becoming more and more complicated,' he wrote, 'and therefore there could be neither inaction nor compromise in the present period.' The contradictions and thus also the 'philosophical struggles' were visibly growing in intensity. However, the main targets of the 'philosophical struggle', according to Ai Sheng, were not the 'idealists', who understood themselves as such, but those 'idealists' passing themselves off as 'materialists':

At present there are many in the camp of idealism who scream that no one else besides themselves understands anything about the dialectic. On what grounds? They are idealists through and through, but they wear the clothes of the new materialism. Such people exist not only in Russia, like Bogdanov, but they also exist in our China . . . They join in our front and work by means of deception and dulling the senses. Therefore, our present foes are those who stand behind us and not those who stand before us. Only when we have eliminated them can we take the next step.[79]

Ai Sheng demanded that the false clothes be stripped from these 'wolves in sheep's clothing', as he called them, to reveal their true features. One of them was Yeh Ch'ing who, on the basis of his works, was falsely dubbed the greatest of the 'new materialists'. Ai Sheng compared Yeh Ch'ing's role in 'philosophy' with that of Plechanov and Bodganov;[80] like them he too used the method of conciliation to induce the two mutual enemies of two thousand years 'to drop their inherited hostility, live with the hate they feel in their bones, and look at each other without mistrust and with a handshake'.[81] For him, Yeh was a 'mediator' (t'iao-he-che), comparable to the mayor of a country town, who compounded disagreements between the 'local tyrants' and 'corrupt gentry' in the country (t'u-hao lieh-shen) on the one hand and the poor people on the other. It was his function to paper over the contradictions between these groups; thus there was no difference between Yeh and such a mayor.[82]

Yeh's dialectic, whereby the two sides in a contradiction supplement each other (pu-tsu), and their negation only consists of getting rid of the reciprocal shortcomings as the thesis and anti-thesis are unified, was compared by Ai Sheng to the 'method of addition and subtraction' in algebra (chia-mieh-fa). He accused Yeh of wanting to add 'matter' and 'spirit' according to the rule: 2 plus 3 equals 5; he added together thesis (cheng) and anti-thesis (fan) to make a synthesis (ho).[83] However if, like Yeh, one places things in succession with equal weight and thus distorts the dialectical method in algebra, then one resolves the warring contradictions and pursues a compromise between them.

The term 'chia-mieh-fa' had a dual meaning in this connection. It stood for an alliance of two parties according to the principle of addition; however, the character 'mieh' pointed to the possible consequence of such an alliance, because it means 'subtraction' only in a figurative sense – its real meaning is 'obliterate', 'destroy' or 'annihilate'. Yeh Ch'ing had also used the character in this sense when he wrote of 'the annihilation of philosophy'(che-hsüeh hsaio-mieh). Thus Ai Sheng's little example of calculy was a clear indication that in the 'unification of matter and spirit' (i.e. of the CCP and the Kuomintang) there the threat was not so much that of the 'annihilation of philosophy' but rather of the destruction of the CCP. This danger emerged from a mathematical comparison of the respective troop strengths of the Red Army and the National Chinese Army. If the unification of the two armies was accomplished by the Red Army surrendering its independence, this would probably spell the end of the Communist movement in China. 'Where does the philosophy of Yeh Ch'ing lead to'? asked Ai Sheng finally. He answered: 'It leads back to idealism.'[84]

On the Meaning of Battle Flags or the Difference between Alliance and Identity

Along with Lu Lung-chi and Ai Sheng, it is especially in the articles of T'an Fu-chih that opposition to a United Front with the Kuomintang can be detected. His writings began to appear in the autumn of 1936 and were published in a collected volume entitled Che-hsüeh p'i-pan-chi (Philosophical Critiques) by the same publishing house and at the same time as the work of Ai Sheng.[85] These circumstances point to these publications being coordinated and having a common goal, namely to counteract the CCP's increasing readiness to cooperate with the Kuomintang.

While T'an Fu-chih characterised Yeh Ch'ing as an 'idealist', he admitted that both Ai Ssu-ch'i and Ch'en Po-ta still stood firmly by 'materialism', with a tendency to lean towards Yeh Ch'ing's position. T'an divided the development of Ai Ssu-ch'i's 'philosophy' into two phases: in the first it had been a 'philosophy of opposites' (tui-li che-hsüeh), in which Ai had represented all the realms of 'philosophy' as having fallen into absolute opposition and 'materialism' and 'idealism' stood opposed to each other in an 'eternal struggle'. T'an referred especially to Ai Ssu-ch'i's Philosophy for the Masses, which, he wrote, was still inspired by an 'audacious leftist spirit'.[86] Because Ai's new publications were connected with the 'New Enlightenment Movement', T'an feared that Ai would move too far to the 'right'. The offer of cooperation between the two 'mortal enemies', 'materialism' and 'idealism', now introduced a second phase and, according to T'an, marked a decisive shift in the work of Ai Ssu-ch'i from the 'philosophy of opposites' to the 'philosophy of alliance' (*lien-ho che-hsüeh*).

Where, he asked, was the partiality of 'philosophy' of which Ai had constantly spoken? He regarded the 'new philosophy' of the United Front as the negation of all that Ai had written hitherto. It was no longer based on the principle of the unity of opposites, but represented a pause for rest and a compromise.[87] On the other hand, T'an considered 'materialism' an intellectual weapon of the oppressed, not as the 'intellectual helper of the tiger', which fawns upon 'idealism'. The contradiction between the two directions in philosophy reflected for him merely the contradiction between the working class and those who did not work. However, when the contradictions intensify, he wrote, one cannot demand the 'great unity of all parties and groups' (*ko-tang ko-p'ai ta-lien-hua*) without surrendering the partiality of 'philosophy'.[88] Ai's 'philosophy' was, therefore, a 'patriotic philosophy', but not 'new materialism'.[89]

T'an directed the same accusations at Ch'en Po-ta's article '*Hsin che-hsüeh che ti tzu-chi p'i-p'an*' (Self-Criticism of a New Philosopher),[90] in which Ch'en, like Ai, had suggested cooperation with 'idealistic philosophy'.[91] T'an also accused Ch'en of having urged the 'great unity with idealism' and of wanting to bring the contradictions in 'philosophy' to a halt. Ch'en's synthesis (*he*) of thesis and anti-thesis in the dialectical process was only an alliance, and not the result of the dialectical negation whereby Ch'en had also transformed dialectical materialism into a 'philosophy of alliance'. Still, this was not enough: Ch'en and Ai were both in the process of moving from the 'philosophy of alliance' to a 'philosophy of unity (or identity)' (*t'ung-i che-hsüeh*), thus moving even closer to the position of Yeh Ch'ing. 'Whoever strides through the phase of alliance will surely land by unity, because alliance is the first necessary stage for unity.'[92]

What does this warning mean? T'an, who generally formulated his thoughts much more clearly than Yeh Ch'ing or Ai Ssu-ch'i, suddenly described the difference between the two types of 'philosophy' very concretely and thus divulged the true meaning of his article: in an alliance, 'every group and every party still has its own battle flag, its forces still stand side by side. But the "unity" is not unity but rather "identity", i.e. everything is one. In unity there is only one battle flag and the troops are not allowed to have different colours, i.e. there will not be peaceful co-existence among the forces of all parties and troops, but only a unified system. And as for the contradiction, well, of course, it no longer exists.'[93]

Thus the struggles over 'matter' and 'spirit' dealt with a problem that was of decisive importance for the future of the CCP: the relationship between the Red Army and the National Chinese Army in a possible United Front against Japan. As has been described above, the basic problems here were the form in which the Red Army would become integrated, the question of its independence, the acceptance of Nationalist Chinese officers, and common action under the command of Chiang Kai-shek.

T'an's attitude here was clear: he spoke out against an alliance of the two military forces, in which two autonomous armies would have continued to coexist alongside each other. And above all he was also against a unified national army, in which the Red Army would be absorbed and thus destroyed. The 'philosophy of alliance' stood for the first form of military cooperation, while the 'philosophy of unity' or the 'unification of matter and spirit' stood for the second form, in which all the troops would be fused into one unit.

'Point Towards the East and Talk From the West' or Tentative Theses

From the texts so far examined one can draw the following conclusions and presumptions. Of the three questions which we asked at the start of this chapter, the first two – concerning the true meaning of the terms 'philosophy' and 'science' – have already been answered. The third question – against whom was the criticism from both sides directed? – can only be answered on the basis of the texts examined in the form of a hypothesis.

1. Yeh Ch'ing's works concerning 'philosophy' and 'science' appeared to be attacks on 'idealism'; however, they were basically a criticism of Marxism as a 'philosophy'.

2. Yeh's 'philosophy' was criticised by all the theoreticians: by Ai Ssu-ch'i and Ch'en Po-ta as well as by Ai Sheng, T'an Fu-chih and Lu Lung-chi. All of them saw the danger to the Communist movement in his *Wu-hsin tsung-ho lun* (Theory of the Unification of Matter and Spirit).

3. Ai Sheng, T'an Fu-chih and Lu Lung-chi were opponents of a

United Front with the Kuomintang and therefore they criticised not only Yeh Ch'ing but also Ai Ssu-ch'i and Ch'en Po-ta, because they had shown a readiness to cooperate with the Kuomintang. Nevertheless, in their criticism of Yeh, Ai and Ch'en insisted on the 'independence of philosophy' and indirectly advocated a leading role for the CCP in the United Front. It concerns a position, which will crystallise more and more strongly in the following chapters.

4. All of Yeh Ch'ing's critics related his statements to the CCP and made him the main target of their criticism. This can only mean that if Yeh's theories had not reflected a conflict within the party, no one would have been upset by them.

5. Thus one can obviously presume that the true object of the criticism was not Yeh Ch'ing but those factions of the CCP which advocated extensive cooperation with the Kuomintang: the faction around Wang Ming combined with the supporters of the Comintern line, but also those around Chang Kuo-t'ao's faction. The explanation that the criticism is linked with the Comintern line is particularly supported by the fact that Wang Ming's plans provided for a national army, to be formed from the unification of the Red Army with the Nationalist Army, and for a unified command structure, training, discipline, armaments, logistics, etc. (see also chapters 10–16).

6. If we are able to confirm this supposition in the following chapters, we shall have an explanation for an essential aspect of the development of dialectical materialism in China: that dialectical materialism adopted from the Soviet Union served the Chinese Marxists, especially the supporters of the 'Mao Tse-tung line' as a 'philosophical weapon' in their struggle against the United Front policy of the Comintern.

7. The opponents of the Comintern's United Front policy availed themselves of a covert, two-pronged approach: while they wrote abundantly about 'philosophy' and its importance for 'science', they were in fact merely thinking about the CCP's interests, which they saw as being jeopardised by the policy of the Comintern. They set up Yeh Ch'ing, who was outside the party, as an opponent and defamed him as a 'Deborinist' and 'Bukharinist', while in reality their target was an opponent within their own ranks. Thus their criticism accorded to the principle, 'Point to the east and talk of the west' (*chih-tung shuo-hsi*); it also applied an old strategy from Strange Tales Recorded in the Studio of Contemplative Leisure, mentioned above: 'Point to the baobab tree and curse the mulberry tree' (*chih-sang ma-huai*).

8. For the reader of the Marxist texts, it is hard to imagine that hiding

behind the two concepts of 'spirit' and 'matter', over whose contents whole generations of European theologians, philosophers and scientists had racked their brains without achieving a tangible result, there should be nothing more than two opposing armies in the Chinese civil war. It seemed even less plausible that the suggested unification of these armies should result in the final – and, for the observer, very surprising – solution to the problem of 'matter' and 'spirit'.

However, one cannot exclude the possibility that the Chinese dialectical materialists wrote articles without employing the analogical equivalent, and in which Western concepts were not misused to represent intra-party struggles. At this point the theory of knowledge should be examined.

The Marxist theory of knowledge, which we consider in the next chapter, has a central place in the ideology of the Chinese Communists, for whom Mao Tse-tung's work 'On Practice' was of supreme importance. The general understanding of the theory of knowledge is that it serves to establish whether, and if so how, knowledge is possible at all. Seen in this light, it is unsuited for political struggles. To write about the nature of knowledge and thereby mean a certain military strategy has nothing to do with the theory of knowledge; such contrasted concepts are mutually exclusive. Such a 'theory of knowledge' is the opposite of what it pretends to be, since it masks what it is supposed to explain.

No one seriously will claim that Kant's *Critique of Pure Reason* was merely a political parable, in which he described the relationship between the 'thing in itself' and the 'phenomenon' in analogy to the relations between Frederick the Great and Maria Theresa, and the Russian attempts at mediation during the War of the Bavarian Succession in 1778–9.

When we examine the works by Chinese theoreticians on the 'theory of knowledge' we must bear in mind the possibility that they too are merely analogic equivalents for intra-party conflicts, reflecting in particular the struggles over the Comintern's efforts to bring the CCP and the Kuomintang to the negotiating table in the face of the Japanese threat. If we can confirm this supposition, the question arises whether Chinese Marxism really possesses a theoretical base, whereby the name of Marxism can be justified.

11. 'PERCEPTUAL' AND 'THEORETICAL' KNOWLEDGE

Chaplin and Hitler or the Relation between 'Perceptual' and 'Theoretical' Knowledge

We saw in the last chapter how Chinese theoreticians represented the relationship between 'philosophy' and 'science' as analogous to their conceptions of the United Front between the CCP and the Kuomintang. In this chapter we will elaborate this pattern of analogous thought, using as an example the theory of knowledge of dialectical materialism in China.

The treatises of Ai Ssu-chi'i, Yeh Ch'ing and Mao Tse-tung concerned with the theory of knowledge do not discuss problems relating to that theory, but merely the United Front in the form of an analogical equivalent. The terms for 'knowledge', 'process of knowledge', 'perceptual' and 'theoretical' knowledge, 'subjective' and 'objective', 'analysis' and 'synthesis', 'objectivity' and 'universal knowledge' etc. are, as before, not concepts, but merely symbols. Thus they have no intellectual content such as is found in Western concepts, but stand for concrete political and military-strategical positions.

Our discussion in this chapter is concerned with texts by Ai Ssu-ch'i and Yeh Ch'ing regarding the theory of knowledge. Because of its importance in the struggle within the CCP, 'On Practice', in which Mao Tse-tung also devotes himself to the theory of knowledge, is treated in another chapter.

In *Philosophy for the Masses* Ai Ssu-ch'i introduces the following simple model of the process of knowledge. The starting point of all knowledge is perception. The subordinate objects of the external world are reflected in the consciousness, comparable to the image on a photograph, when a picture is taken. The objective existence of sugar, for example, corresponds in substance to the subjective form of the perception 'sweet'. The objective essence of a thing – in this case sugar – is thus already given.[1] This type of knowledge is 'perceptual' knowledge (*kan-hsing jen-shih*).

The materialistic theory of knowledge is based on reflection, but it receives only a part, and not all, of the objective environment through perception; and in this it differs from the knowledge of picture-taking, since 'perceptual' knowledge only imparts the external appearance of a thing.[2]

However, if one wants to go beyond this level of knowledge, one needs the help of 'theoretical' knowledge (*li-hsing jen-shih*—in the *Selected Works* of Mao the same characters are partly translated as 'rational knowledge'). Just what is 'theoretical' knowledge? On the basis of their 'cognitive faculty', human beings are able to understand and organise the contents of 'perceptual' knowledge. Thus many things, which according to Ai seem to be the same on the basis of 'perceptual' knowledge, are in truth different; for example, 'perceptual knowledge tells us that both Charlie Chaplin and Adolf Hitler have a small moustache, and that consequently the same person is meant. Theoretical knowledge tells us, on the contrary, that Chaplin and Hitler are two separate people. The first is the "King of Comics", the latter is a fascist dictator.'[3]

Conversely, 'perceptual' knowledge can perceive external things as different, while 'theoretical' knowledge can establish the opposite, namely that both are the same. Although a group of comics are all different externally, 'theoretical' knowledge can ascertain that they are all comics. 'What appears as unity to perceptual knowledge is recognised as diverse by theoretical knowledge, and what is diverse for perceptual knowledge becomes uniform for theoretical knowledge. To see the unity in diversity and the diversity in unity is the contradiction in human knowledge . . . That is the contradiction between perceptual and theoretical knowledge.'[4]

The two types of knowledge find themselves 'in an eternal struggle with each other', and in the history of philosophy two directions – 'empiricism' (*ching-yen-lun*) and 'rationalism' (*li-hsing-lun*) – have based themselves upon them and act like a pair of 'wrestlers', each of whom has only one object: the defeat of the other.

'Perceptual' knowledge and its advocates, the 'empiricists', can only reach subjective knowledge of the objective environment, which 'theoretical' knowledge and the 'rationalists' do not take into account, since it is empty, and more than a subjective illusion. Thus the 'empiricists', who do not proceed beyond subjective perception, represent only a subjective standpoint, which depends on their situation and place in society. As an example, Ai Ssu-ch'i names the 'exploiters' and the Japanese imperialists, whose ideas are no more than a reflection of their subjective situation. No less 'empirical' for him are those who experience the exploitation and imperialist aggression as 'perceptual knowledge', without drawing theoretical consequences or changing their situation.

The 'rationalists', by contrast, renounce 'perceptual' knowledge. As an example of this, Kant advocates the view that one cannot know the 'thing in itself' (*wu-tsu-t'i*). He thus acts like one who describes a walnut and maintains that since one cannot perceive the inside of the nut, one therefore cannot know what it contains and what it is in itself. On the contrary, according to Ai, one only needs to bite open the nut to know what the nut is 'in itself'.

After this representation of the relationship between 'perceptual' and 'theoretical' knowledge, Ai Ssu-ch'i turns to 'practice' (*shih-chien*). Since neither type of knowledge furnishes objective truths, the only criterion of truth is 'practice'. It is a method of action in which 'perceptual' knowledge is taken as a basis. This contains a subjective truth, from which 'theoretical' knowledge is obtained. However, only the application of 'theoretical' knowledge through the changing of the objective environment, i.e., through social practice, can lead to objective knowledge. In this case 'perceptual' knowledge is always subjugated (*ch'ü-fu*) to 'theoretical' knowledge.[5]

The development of knowledge is comparable to a constant approach to 'absolute truth'. In this process, each particular item of knowledge is at first relative. This relative knowledge, in turn, changes through 'practice' the 'perceptual' knowledge from which a new – even higher – 'theoretical' knowledge is obtained, which again transforms the 'perceptual' knowledge, and so on. Hence, the development of knowledge resembles a spiral leading up to absolute knowledge. Consequently, a part of the absolute truth is already contained in the relative truth of an item of knowledge. The 'unity' of 'theory' and 'practice' on the basis of the contradiction between 'perceptual' and 'theoretical' knowledge is now, according to Ai, the core of the theory of knowledge in dialectical materialism.

I know of no text in Chinese Marxist literature which provides clearer insights into this theme than those just mentioned. Even Mao Tse-tung's 'On Practice' is in many places similar to the dicta of Ai Ssu-ch'i, which seemed to have been used as a model. The simplicity of the description suggests that Ai was not aware of the basic problems of the theory of knowledge. His presentation was an abridged version of the discussion on 'theory and practice' in the Soviet Union at the beginning of the 1930s, which had been a part of the polemic against Bukharin and Deborin.[6] However, while the dialectical theory of knowledge in the

Soviet Union was still treated, as Gustav Wetter shows, in detail if already one-sidedly, its basic characteristics would ultimately become lost in the Chinese discussion.

In October 1936, a few months after the change in the Comintern's United Front strategy, Ai Ssu-ch'i again took up the theme of the theory of knowledge in his work *Ssu-hsiang fang-fa lun* (Methodology of Thought).[7] Earlier, in *Philosophy for the Masses*, he had juxtaposed the terms 'perceptual' and 'rationalists' with 'exploiters' and Japanese imperialists. Thus the way was open to make the whole theory of knowledge an analogy to political questions. The various elements of the theory of knowledge had now become weapons in the struggle over the United Front; in the first pages of his 'Methodology', Ai make it clear that he was concerned with correcting 'false thinking' within the CCP: 'We want to discuss at this point how thinking starts off on the wrong track, and which methods we must use to change it.'[8] Moreover, he recommended the use of his 'Methodology of Thought' as a basis for the evaluation of existing opinions within the CCP on the United Front![9] He then depicted this by the example of the relationship between 'subjective' and 'objective' and that between 'analysis' and 'synthesis'.

'Subjective' and 'Objective'. Ai Ssu-ch'i first explained the two 'concepts' as follows:

Subjective and objective [*chu-juan, k'e-kuan*] are two opposing concepts . . . Subjective means relating to oneself, whereas objective is everything which lies outside oneself. If, for example, an organisation [*t'uan t'i*] wants to carry out a task, it needs the power to be able to do so. This power can be designated subjective power. Everything lying outside the organisation we designate as objective environment.[10]

The 'subjective' aspect of an organisation consists of its ideals, its will, its opinions, and its power. The 'objective' aspect is made up of the material environment.

Ai distinguished between two forms of 'false thinking': the 'over-emphasis of the subjective' (*chu-kuan t'ai ch'iang*) and 'absolute objectivism' (*chüeh-tui ti k'e-kuan chu-i*). In his view, 'over-emphasis of the subjective' necessarily goes with neglect of the 'objective' aspects; it means exaggeration of the spiritual and destruction of the material. These are the characteristics of idealism and, according to Ai, those who act thus will certainly fall into the 'slough of idealism'.[11] On the other hand, 'absolute objectivism' is basically a feature of 'mechanism'. Its advocates, unlike the 'subjectivists', possess no individual opinion, which means that when they encounter resistance they immediately give up and become inconstant in their attitude. However, this peculiarity is found not only in individuals: 'organisations and states have this peculiarity as well. For example, if conditions are unfavourable, they reject the standpoint of the organisation and capitulate to hostile forces.'[12] Ai saw the most important characteristic of 'absolute objectivism' as being the attitude of 'swimming with the stream', i.e. 'to forget one's own standpoint and strength completely and instead exaggerate all the forces that surround one. . . . '[13] 'Absolute objectivism' was a variety of Mechanism: the former proceeds from the assumption that what is objective is important, but neglects the role of consciousness: 'It only knows that consciousness is a property produced by matter, but it does not know that this consciousness can also exert a counter-reaction against matter.'[14] Thus the Mechanistic thought of Bukharin shows a clear tendency towards submission (*ch'ü-fu*) and compromise (*che-chung*).[15]

What does 'counter-reaction' (*fan-tso-yung*) of the consciousness against matter mean here? Ai characterises the relations between 'consciousness' and 'matter' without 'counter-reaction' as 'absolute objectivism' and 'mechanism', since both tended towards 'compromise' and even 'capitulation' to the enemy. The terms for 'consciousness' and 'matter' thus did not have a philosophical meaning, but rather a military one: namely, that 'consciousness', or the 'subjective forces' of the individual organisation, respectively (and here this could refer only to the CCP), faces 'matter', or the hostile forces. Thus the 'counter-reaction of the consciousness' means that Ai advocated advancing against the hostile forces, not yielding to them.

To this interpretation one could object that Ai may merely be using the image of 'subjective forces' and the 'objectively hostile environment' as an example to illustrate his description of the relationship between 'consciousness' and 'matter', but was actually speaking on the two 'concepts'; he would thus have used these illustrations in the legitimate and even desirable process of popularising philosophy. However, this is at odds with the argument I have been propounding: that the relationship between the 'subjective forces' and their 'hostile environment' is not in any way used as an example to explain the relationship between 'consciousness' and 'matter', since the former terms have nothing to do with what we understand by the latter two terms. Their emptiness is especially evident from the way they are applied for different purposes. In the discussion on 'philosophy' and 'science', the term 'matter' was the analogous equivalent of the CCP, while 'spirit' was the term used for the Kuomintang. In the texts we are dealing with here, 'matter' is far from being equivalent to the CCP, but stands instead for the hostile forces surrounding the CCP. On the other hand, 'consciousness', previously classified as 'spirit' and thus as the Kuomintang, now appears as an equivalent of the CCP. Thus 'consciousness' and 'matter' are arbitrarily exchangeable terms, no more than symbols attached exclusively to the political ideas of certain groups, factions, and parties, and suit no other meaning.

Ai Ssu-ch'i then described how the 'counter-reaction of the consciousness against matter' was to take place, or in other words, how the CCP was to act towards the Kuomintang. On the question of resistance to the enemy, he continued, the 'Mechanists' saw only the enemy's weapons and compared these to their own, thus completely failing to consider the role of the 'will of the masses to resist'. They thus overrated the opposition and believed that surrender to the enemy was the only possible course. 'That is the mistake of exaggerating objective things and underestimating subjective things.'[16]

Of which enemy was Ai Ssu-ch'i speaking? Japan, the Kuomintang, or both? The accusation that the 'Mechanists' in the party had a tendency to compromise indicates that the enemy concerned was the Kuomintang, since the Comintern faction was not interested in a compromise with Japan – on the contrary – but rather in one with the Kuomintang. Thus, Ai's remarks concerning the relation between 'subjective' and 'objective' would have referred only to the relation between the CCP and the Kuomintang. He made the accusation that the 'Mechanists' would reject the 'standpoint of the organisation' (i.e. of the CCP) and, faced with the military superiority of the opponent, wanted to 'capitulate to the hostile forces'.[17] But for the 'Mechanists' the enemy was not the Kuomintang but Japan, and they saw the unification of the Red Army and the Chinese Nationalist Army as providing the best conditions for an effective resistance against the foreign aggressor. Against the conventional military strategy which the unification implied, Ai-Ssu-ch'i opposed the 'will of the masses to resist', i.e. the strategy of a people's war, whereby the Mao Tse-tung faction hoped to expand its bases and consolidate its independence from the Kuomintang. It is thus clear that portraying the relationship between 'consciousness' and 'matter' was an analogy to the disagreements over which military strategy would be used against the Kuomintang as well as against Japan.

The 'counter-reaction of consciousness against matter' is equated by Ai to the 'will of the masses to resist' against the enemy's weapons. The characters for 'subjective' are the symbols for the active forces of the organisation which are ranged against the enemy. The 'philosophical' equivalent of the hostile forces is once again represented by the characters for 'objective'.

Ai Ssu-ch'i now confronted both forms of 'false thinking': the 'absolute objectivism', which overrated the Kuomintang, and 'subjectivism', that faction which overestimated its own strength and was therefore against a United Front; he did so with the 'new' or 'dialectical materialism' which assumes the unity of contradiction between 'subjective' and 'objective'. It takes the exact measure of the hostile forces surrounding it, but does not underrate its own strength, which it is able to use against the enemy. Ai converts this attitude into the following 'philosophical' statement:

The new materialist takes objective things as a basis . . . Consciousness is a product of matter but it has at the same time an effect that is against matter. Consciousness and matter actually form a unity, however, they also stand simultaneously in contradiction to one another and are directed at each other.[18]

The unity of 'subjective' and 'objective', and of 'consciousness' and 'matter' thus represents the unity of the CCP and the Kuomintang through the further continuation of the contradiction between them. The attitude of the CCP towards the Kuomintang now forms the decisive point in this unity. Ai explained the false attitude – the suspension respectively of the contradiction and the struggle against the Kuomintang in the United Front – by the example of the 'mechanistic theory of knowledge':

The mechanistic form retains knowledge when the external world is reflected in the consciousness, and neglects the independent force of the process of knowledge in the consciousness itself. The subjective form of knowledge does the exact opposite . . . Our thinking and its content are a reflection of the world around us in our consciousness . . . However, if one considers the [subjective] consciousness merely as an organ of perception at which something is tossed from outside, then one is completely immovable and cannot initiate the slightest counter-reaction against what is external. This type of opinion is mistaken in the same way as the mechanistic materialism mentioned above, which stressed the objective too much and completely neglected the role of the subjective.[19]

Ai compared this form of knowledge to a mirror. It was not an 'active' and 'lively' knowledge, but rather 'passive', a pure reflection of the environment in the subject; and with this picture he made clear how he assessed the Comintern's policy: namely, that the struggle against the Kuomintang should be abandoned in favour of a United Front. Instead of this 'passive knowledge' (corresponding to a passive attitude towards the Kuomintang) he now demanded 'subjective activity' in the 'process of knowledge' (corresponding to a continuation of the struggle against the Kuomintang) – how what has been recognised by the subject reacts to the object in order to transform it. For him, this was the true essence of the 'new' materialism.

'The process of human knowledge of the world can in no way only proceed from the object; in practice it proceeds from the subject as well.'[20] Thus if, according to Ai, 'subjective activity' in the form of 'practice' is synonymous with the behaviour of the 'subjective forces' towards the enemy, then this means in plain language that the party should not be passive and ready to compromise with the Kuomintang within the United Front. If it failed to continue with the struggle against the Kuomintang in this period, or to apply the strategy of the people's war, then it would be pursuing a 'Bukharinistic' and 'Mechanistic' policy of compromise.

There is yet another equivalent between the 'process of knowledge' and the United Front. As has been described above, the Comintern insisted the United Front should not exist for a limited time only, but that the two parties should continue to cooperate after the victory over Japan. By contrast, Mao's faction considered the United Front as being limited to a fixed period.

Ai Ssu-ch'i made this difference plain by the example of the infinity of the 'process of knowledge'. In this case, the 'process of knowledge' as a whole is an analogy for the Chinese Revolution, in which the period of the United Front is merely one of relative calm. Just as 'knowledge' constantly progresses, so too does the revolution. The 'process of knowledge' is not disrupted by an individual 'item of knowledge' any more than the Chinese Revolution is disrupted by the United Front. And just as every individual item of knowledge is 'relative', so too is the United Front. The latter behaves towards the Chinese Revolution as 'relative' knowledge does towards 'absolute truth' in the 'total process of knowledge'. The 'absolute' in 'relative knowledge', to which Ai and only a few months later Mao referred, meant merely the continuation of the revolution within the United Front.

We will return later to the relation between 'absolute' and 'relative'. All we have shown here is that the characters for 'perceptual' and 'theoretical' knowledge, and 'subjective' and 'objective' stand as symbols for the political forces in the United Front, and the whole 'theory of knowledge' reflects the strategic concepts of the 'Mao Tsetung line'.

It is in this connection that the symbols for practice (*'shih-chien'*) attain their own importance: 'practice', the method for realising a goal, as it should be translated, is the next link in the chain of analogy. The unity of 'theory and practice' on the basis of the continuing contradictions between 'perceptual' and 'theoretical' knowledge, between 'subjective' and 'objective, stands for the continuation of the struggle against the Kuomintang within the United Front. Furthermore, 'practice' means in military terms that with the mobilisation of the masses, i.e. by a people's war, the enemy can be defeated. For Ai Ssu-ch'i, *'shih-chien'* thus means a position opposed to the Comintern policy, which advocated peaceful cooperation with the Kuomintang and placed the main emphasis on conventional strategy.

'Analysis' and 'Synthesis'. Ai Ssu-ch'i's remarks on 'analysis' and 'synthesis' were a variation on the theme of 'perceptual' and 'theoretical' knowledge. In his view, both were parts of the process of knowledge. In this context, 'analysis' means that one proceeds from concrete perception, step by step, to the discovery of abstract concepts, laws or rules. With 'synthesis' one seeks the explanation of concrete things, proceeding from general rules.[21]

It is unclear from the text whether Ai really wanted to discuss inductive and deductive methods, but this is not important for the true meaning of his statements. The symbols for 'analysis' and 'synthesis' can be replaced at any time by those for 'inductive' and 'deductive', without this resulting in any change in the statement's content.

Ai now described the role of the bourgeoisie in the United Front, using the example of the relationship between 'analysis' and 'synthesis'.

To establish the present level of development of Chinese society, one must first analyse all the individual elements – feudalism, capitalism, imperialist aggression etc., then compare all the elements and finally study the relations between them. After that, one must establish which of them is the most important, and in so doing one realises that Chinese society is by its nature feudalistic. In this process of understanding, one analyses the abstract and simple determinants from the concrete and complicated appearances. The path taken here is thus basically one of analysis.[22]

Proceeding from this 'analysis', one now comes, according to Ai, to the following conclusion: since China is still by its nature feudalistic, it must develop into a bourgeois democracy at the next stage of development; thus the bourgeoisie would have to play a special role. The advocates of a 'synthesis' would have a different opinion, maintaining that China is half-feudalistic and that capitalism cannot develop freely because of the forces of imperialism. Thus the bourgeoisie cannot also assume the role of a 'motor of development'; rather this role devolves on the 'working masses' of the lower classes. Ai considered as equally one-sided the ideas whereby the capitalist elements in Chinese society already held a position of leadership, the society thus being basically capitalist and not feudal.

In Ai's view the error in all these opinions was that 'some people' would forget the 'synthesis' during the 'analysis', and vice versa. Whoever, in carrying out the 'analysis', comes to the conclusion that China is feudalistic, has analysed the individual elements in complete isolation and forgotten the 'synthesis'; and whoever believes that the bourgeoisie cannot be a bearer of social development because of imperialist aggression, also pursues the 'synthesis' in isolation without heeding the analysis. That the working masses had to be the exclusive bearers of social development was, for Ai, as false a concept as the opinion that the bourgeoisie was of no use at all for the development of China.[23]

What was Ai Ssu-ch'i driving at? The declaration that China was feudalistic meant that the next level of social development had to be bourgeois democracy. But that meant that the leading forces of society were the representatives of the bourgeoisie, namely the Kuomintang. The other view, that China was a half-feudalistic country, denied every function of the bourgeoisie, particularly the Kuomintang, since capitalism could not develop freely.

Ai Ssu-ch'i now chose the middle way between these two positions: in face of the danger, he wrote, in which China found itself due to imperialist aggression, the bourgeoisie alone could not assume the 'task of the times', but 'it can also become a force of resistance against the violent aggression of the enemy.'[24] With this he turned against the opponents of the United Front as well as those advocating a leading role for the Kuomintang in the war against Japan. He characterised the two sides as 'mechanistic'; they proceeded, respectively, 'isolated' by the 'analysis' as well as by the 'synthesis', engaging themselves either for the bourgeoisie as the main bearer of social progress or for the working masses as its exclusive support.

However, according to Ai, the dialectical materialist pays attention' to the unity and connection between analysis and synthesis; he who uses analysis or synthesis as an ''independent'' method, sees things rigidly and in isolation as in the metaphysical method.'[25] Ai's 'unity of analysis and synthesis' thus meant that the 'working masses' were not to lead the struggle without the bourgeoisie, but the bourgeoisie were also not to assume the leading role in this struggle, but merely 'also become a force of resistance against Japan'. This in essence was nothing other than the claim of the CCP to leadership in the United Front with the Kuomintang, and Ai Ssu-ch'i's 'theory of knowledge' served to legitimise this claim *vis-à-vis* the Wang-Ming faction as well as the opponents of the United Front within the party.

How Red is a Mandarin Orange? or the Reconciliation between 'Perceptual' and 'Theoretical' Knowledge

We now turn to Yeh Ch'ing's 'theory of knowledge'. We have already shown that Yeh used the three-tier law of Comte and the theses of Minin and Encmen as examples, in order indirectly to demand the dissolution of the CCP.

What concepts did he now have regarding the 'theory of knowledge' and what did he aim to achieve with its presentation? In his work *Che-hsüeh wen-t'i* (Problems of Philosophy) he dealt first with the relationship between 'experience' and 'reason' (*ching-yen, li-hsing*).[26] For Yeh, 'experience' was a direct, inductive and immediate form of knowledge, gleaned from objects or phenomena. Thus it was, not an essential part of the human capacity for knowledge, but rather it delivered the external material for human knowledge.

What was 'reason' (*li-hsing*)? According to Yeh, it was, in relation to sensory perception, the ability to engage in logical deduction, to differentiate between good and bad, and, in relation to rational comprehension, it was the ability to produce the highest thoughts, such as the concepts of the soul, God and the world. 'Experience' and 'reason' were in constant opposition to each other, the former lying beyond 'knowledge' and the latter within the capability for 'knowledge'. Hence, 'experience' was the successor whereas 'reason' had a prior existence. 'Experience' provided the raw material for 'reason'.[27]

In Yeh's theory of knowledge, two contradictory directions

(*liang-p'ai*) had crystallised. These were 'empiricism' and 'rationalism', which proceeded respectively from one of the two starting-points of knowledge. 'Empiricism' maintained that all knowledge stemmed from experience and that no knowledge could exist without there being a prior experience. All concepts, ideas and notions originated first from experience. On the other hand, 'rationalism' insisted that there was knowledge before any experience, that thoughts and ideas did not come from the external world, but were already present in the human capacity for knowledge. Hence, in research, 'empiricism' used the method of 'induction' (*kui-na-fa*) and 'rationalism' that of 'deduction' (*yen-i-fa*); 'induction' derives general rules from phenomena while 'deduction' explains the characteristics of phenomena from general rules. Because of this attitude, 'empiricism' and 'rationalism' were contradictory to each other.[28] Such was Yeh Ch'ing's 'theory of knowledge'.

Yeh had, as he himself writes, taken the definition of the concepts 'experience' and 'reason' from a work by V. Egger to which the present writer unfortunately could not gain access. However, despite the ideas Yeh had adopted from Egger, the outline of his statements become clear immediately one has grasped the basic elements of his 'theory of knowledge' and the relationship between 'experience' and 'reason', which he advances as the expression of a particular political goal. This goal becomes plain in those passages where Yeh deals with the solution of the contradictions regarding the 'theory of knowledge'.

How, Yeh asked, could the historical contradictions between 'experience' and 'reason', between 'empiricism' and 'rationalism', be resolved? Contrary to Ai Ssu-ch'i, he suggested uniting them – just as he had already wanted to unite 'idealism' and 'materialism' so as to resolve their contradictions.[29] That Ai Ssu-ch'i had also spoken of the 'unity of perceptual and theoretical knowledge' is not in question, but – and here was the decisive difference – the contradiction between the two forms of 'knowledge' was to persist. In the 'process of knowledge' (*jen-shih kuo-ch'eng*) the negation of one side of the contradiction was to occur through 'practice'; one could not, *pace* Ai Ssu-ch'i, speak of a reconciliation of both sides of the contradiction and their fusion into a unity.

But how was the unity of 'experience' and 'reason', 'empiricism' and 'rationalism' to come about? For Yeh, the prerequisite was the recognition that 'experience' and 'reason' were, respectively, essential parts of the whole. 'In no case,' he wrote, 'can one negate either of the two.'[30] Here one can already anticipate Yeh's intention, namely a peaceful unification of the two political camps, which would supplement one another in their unity and thus avoid mutual destruction.

But if Yeh wanted the two political camps to be unified, then he had to prove in his 'theory' that 'experience' and 'reason' were two parts of 'knowledge', inseparable and mutually dependent – they should not be allowed to 'negate' each other. Hence his 'proof' was not the result of a logical-discoursive contemplation of problems relating to the theory of knowledge, but was pieced together by analogy to political conceptions, the material for it being sought, on this basis, from Western texts on the theory of knowledge.

In the following passage we see clearly how a political opinion can be expressed by the consideration of something apparently as unimportant as a mandarin orange! With the 'substantiation' that knowledge is impossible without the unity of 'experience' and 'reason', Yeh informed his readers that he considered it a mistake for the CCP and the Kuomintang to exist independently; instead, he advocated their merging into a United Front:

I would like to use an example here, to show that both reason and experience are founded in reality. For example, I take a mandarin orange and ask you, what is it? You will necessarily answer: that is a red, round fruit. In rationalism 'one', 'red' and 'round' are general concepts, which existed prior to your knowledge of the mandarin orange. When one speaks of the 'colour red', we know only red paper, red flowers and red materials, but up till the present one has never seen the colour red. Can one, therefore, dispense with the recognition of general concepts, which lie prior to the experience? . . . Empiricism assumes that the general concepts 'colour red', 'one piece', 'round form' and other concepts are based on experience. For example, the colour red only has existence when an organ of vision is present. Those born blind do not know that it is. That is a good proof that the colour red exists in the external world and certainly not in the internal. Therefore, whatever does not exist in experience is also not present in reason. So is it not correct to say that empiricism and rationalism are both right? In no case can we negate one of them. That is why, in the history of philosophy, every attempt no negate either empiricism or rationalism has failed.[31]

As one can see the logic of this argument leaves much to be desired. The most striking things about this text are Yeh's assertion that both sides are 'logically' correct and his conclusion that both are right. He says first that 'empiricism', whereby there can be no concept without experience, is right, and then says that 'rationalism', which maintains the exact opposite, is correct too. Yeh does not devote a single line to the logical contradiction between the two assertions; clearly it does not disturb him, since he goes on to a corresponding analogy.

Since 'empiricism' and 'rationalism' stood for real, existing political forces, Yeh did not use his argumentation to show – logically and without contradiction – which 'theory of knowledge' was now correct – something the Western reader would expect. Rather, he explained that both types of 'theory of knowledge' were correct because he wished to express the right of both political forces to exist. His 'logical' argumentation was thus subject to a certain concrete aim and not to the principle of freedom from contradiction; thus what the Western reader may perceive as a contradiction, in this analogous intellectual construction, emphatically had its correct and also its logical place.

Because, according to Yeh, 'empiricism' and 'rationalism' are both in the right, they could not have any relationship to each other in which one would try to 'negate' the other, because 'complete knowledge' of something is possible only through the unity of 'experience' and 'reason'. Whoever wants such 'complete knowledge' must advocate a solution of the contradiction between 'empiricism' and 'rationalism' – by way of their unification. Only a unification in which one does not 'negate' the other can guarantee that there is a 'universal, objective knowledge'. This 'universal, objective knowledge', of course, has nothing to say to us about what we understand as knowledge, but stands for a certain combination of political and military forces.

Yeh now warned, in the process of unification of 'empiricism' and 'rationalism', against relapsing into the error manifested in what we already know as 'dualism' (*erh-yüan-lun*). What does 'dualism' mean here? As described above (pp. 79ft.), the texts of T'an Fu-chih had shown that unification between the Red Army and the Chinese Nationalist Army was rejected by all theoreticans by reference to the model of Kant's 'philosophical dualism', even if for very different reasons. When Yeh wrote of the danger of 'dualism' through the unification of 'empiricism' and 'rationalism' it is clear that here too he thought not so much of 'philosophy' as of the relationship between the parties and the armies. Kant's concept, in his theory of knowledge, concerning the supposed inability of doing away with the separation between 'phenomenon' and the 'thing in itself'[32] was characterised by Yeh as a negative example of 'dualism'. In reality, however, Yeh only repeated his opposition to a coalition between the CCP and the Kuomintang in which the two sides would end their hostilities and co-exist peacefully and independently. His 'unification' of 'empiricism' and 'rationalism' was, instead, to be 'monistic': the two parties and their armies were to surrender their independence and unite into a form of organisation that would be more a fusion, perhaps comparable to the first United Front of 1924–7, in which the Communists joined the Kuomintang while retaining their CP membership.

The characters for 'practice' ('shih-chien') can also be derived from this concept of Yeh Ch'ing. Unlike Ai Ssu-ch'i, for whom 'practice' was a means of 'negating' the (hostile) environment and who thus, like Mao later, insisted on contradiction in unity, Yeh regarded 'practice' in the 'process of knowledge' as being possible only through the unification of 'experience' and 'reason', in the sense that the two sides 'penetrate each other reciprocally' while giving up the attempt to 'negate' each other. Consequently he wrote: 'Practice is the unification of empiricism and rationalism . . . empiricism – rationalism – practice.'[33] In this way, according to Yeh, the contradiction in 'philosophy' could finally be resolved. He recommended the same solution for the contradictions between 'inductive' and 'deductive' methods (kui-na-fa, yen-i-fa) and between 'perception' and 'thought' (kan-chüeh, ssu-wei).[34] In each of these cases he stressed that they formed an inseparable unity in the 'process of knowledge', and that only 'practice', as the unification of all these paired aspects of the 'process of knowledge', would permit the 'great leap forward' (ta-yüeh-chin) in knowledge.[35]

If one focuses on this concept of 'practice' in connection with the United Front and the war against Japan, 'practice' as a 'great leap forward' thus means that the unification of the CCP and Kuomintang, as well as their armies, could lead to the 'great leap forward' in the struggle against Japan. However, Yeh neglected to point out another possible consequence of suggested unity: that the incorporation of the CCP into the United Front and a fusion of the two armies would mean that the CCP, because of its inferior numbers, would lose its independence, leading probably to the end of the Communist movement in China. This is what fired the resistance of Ai Ssu-ch'i: he insisted on a 'practice' which would guarantee the CCP's independence within the United Front, and simultaneously offered the precondition for assuming leadership in the United Front.

The discussions on the 'theory of knowledge' and on 'empiricism' and 'rationalism' showed the same features as the struggles over 'philosophy' and 'science' and over 'materialism' and idealism'. All the terms were arbitrarily interchangeable and thus void. Efforts to arrive at objective knowledge and the critical evaluation of all subjective factors did not have an important place in the thought of the Chinese theoreticians, which tended in the opposite direction: philosophical thought was an expression of a completely subjective partiality, and of political interests. The concept of objectivity in the scientific sense was quite foreign to the theoreticians, although they continually used the terms for objectivity and science. Analysis of the texts of 'formal logic' and 'dialectical logic' in which the military aspect of dialectical materialism in China appeared more clearly, substantiates this assessment.

12. 'FORMAL' AND 'DIALECTICAL' LOGIC

On Questions of the Military Balance of Power or the Negation of 'Formal Logic'

The struggle over the two types of 'logic' is the most extensively documented, and obviously aroused the greatest passion. Indeed for Ch'en Po-ta, the 'struggle' between 'formal' and 'dialectical' logic was a 'struggle between life and death', a statement the later history of the Chinese revolution was certainly to prove correct.

The struggle between the two types of 'logic' can be divided into two phases, and this chronological division coincides with the change in the United Front policy of the Comintern, which for the first time officially found its expression in Wang Ming's article of May 1936, 'The Struggle over the Anti-Japanese Popular Front in China'. In it, as explained above, Wang Ming had advocated the thesis that the anti-Japanese United Front should, from that time on, include the Kuomintang and Chiang Kai-shek, and we shall see that this political transformation was to be of great importance for the history of 'formal logic' in China.

As before over the question of 'philosophy' and the 'theory of knowledge', there was a parallel to the Soviet Union in regard to 'logic'. There Mitin and the dialectical materialists, in their struggle with the 'mechanists' and Deborin, had rejected 'formal logic' as 'metaphysical' and demanded its replacement by 'dialectical logic'. Classical formal logic rests on three principles: identity, contradiction and the excluded third. An object can only be identical to itself (A equals A); consequently it cannot be identical to another object (A does not equal Not-A), and because A is either *equal to B* or *not equal to B*, there cannot be a third.[1]

However, according to the view of dialecticians taking Engels and Lenin as their authority, formal logic was only capable of recognising solid, unchanging objects which it considered to be isolated and independent of each other. It was not able to grasp the interdependence of objects, the relation between them, as well as their transformation. Mitin and Aizenberg, therefore, confronted 'formal logic' with 'dialectical logic', the most important part of which was the law of unity and the simultaneous struggle of opposites. In accordance with Lenin, they demanded that the laws of the dialectic in the objective world should be the same as those of the theory of knowledge.

If 'dialectical logic' was now the only correct form of thought with which to grasp the objective world, what then was to happen to 'formal logic'. Thus one's attitude on 'formal logic' became the criterion by which it could be established if one were a correct dialectical materialist or not. Mitin and Aizenberg thus criticised the mechanists, especially Plechanov, for wanting to reconcile 'dialectical' with 'formal logic' and give the latter its own independent area, instead of rejecting it.[2] Plechanov had only barely accepted 'formal logic' as a moment in 'dialectical logic', when he wrote: 'Just as rest is a special case of movement, so thought, according to the rules of formal logic [the 'principles' of thought], is a special case of dialectical thought.'[3]

In constrast, the dialecticians argued that as one cannot consider alchemy a subordinate moment of chemistry or astrology as a subordinate moment of astronomy, so in the same way 'formal logic' has no place in 'dialectical logic'.[4] The criticism of Plechanov and the mechanists, who wanted to reconcile 'formal' with 'dialectical logic', was also aimed at Deborin who, like Plechanov, had also neglected to reject 'formal logic' and instead attempted to reconcile both forms of 'logic'.[5] Mitin and Aizenberg made clear their total rejection of 'formal logic'. For them there could not be a 'sublimation', nor could it form a supplement to 'dialectical logic'; it was incompatible with 'dialectical logic' and therefore could not co-exist with it.[6]

As I have shown above, the controversy between the 'dialecticians' and the 'mechanists' was part of a struggle which Stalin was leading against the party's 'rightist deviationists' Bukharin, Rykov and Tomsky, and the 'Menshevik idealism' and 'Trotskyism', of which Deborin was considered to be the apostle. The 'reconciliation' between 'formal' and 'dialectical logic' was here synonymous with Bukharin's position on the kulak question, whereas the 'rejection' of 'formal logic' demanded by the 'dialecticians' meant not only the liquidation of the kulaks through the collectivisation movement, but also the elimination of the group around Bukharin.[7] One repurcussion of this 'theoretical' struggle was the banning of 'formal logic' from all textbooks and university curricula. Only after 1946, with the weighty sanction of a resolution of the CPSU Central Committee, was logic once more rehabilitated and introduced into schools and universities.

The Chinese theoreticians of that time derived their knowledge of logic from the works of Mitin and Aizenberg, which Ai Ssu-ch'i had translated. Although a large number of Western works on logic had appeared in Chinese at that time, including John Stuart Mill's *Logic* (translated by Yen Fu in 1902), and in the 1920s Dewey's pragmatic methods and the mathematical logic of Bertrand Russell[9] were discussed, none of this was to be found in the works of the Chinese Marxists. They relied exclusively on Soviet models, from which it can be concluded that they had no knowledge of the development of logic in European and American philosophy and science. A slight exception has to made for the works of Yeh Ch'ing, whose knowledge of the French language enabled him to quote from French philosophical texts and the works of Marx and Engels, while Ai Ssu-ch'i, who knew Russian and Japanese (and supposedly German), quoted only from Russian sources in his writings on dialectical materialism. Still, it was not the aim of Chinese theoreticians to occupy themselves with questions of logic; for them, the terms 'formal' and 'dialectical logic' were merely symbols which helped them – like their Soviet colleagues – to designate, protect or combat political positions.

In his work *Philosophy for the Masses* Ai Ssu-ch'i first presented the three laws of 'formal logic' and then spoke of the relationship between 'formal' and 'dialectical logic':

We want to compare it [formal logic] with mobile logic [i.e. dialectical logic], so as to investigate which of them has value. We have already announced the death penalty for formal logic and stressed how great is the supernatural power of the first law of dialectical logic, the law of the unity of contradictions. We have, furthermore, stressed how little formal logic corresponds to reality and how it tends to make people laugh.[10]

However, he continued, among the advocates of 'formal logic', there were also those who argued under the guise of 'dialectical logic'.

One cannot, of course, contradict mobile logic (*fan-tui*), yet nor can one either overturn formal logic (*t'ui-fan*). Mobile logic controls the territory (*ti-p'an*) of movement and development as well as their reciprocal relationship, whereas formal logic controls the static, individual and independent territory. This argument is advocated by many people in China – without regard to foreign lands. For example, one of them is Yeh Ch'ing. Is this opinion correct? Our answer is: No . . . we already have a mobile logic of high format, and therefore we do not need a formal logic. Up till now, formal logic has been abolished and negated [*fou-ting*] by mobile logic. Anyone who still considers formal and dialectical logic to be equal wants to turn back the wheel of history, or at least to compromise with those forces which would turn back the wheel of history.[11]

When the article appeared in July 1935, Ai's position on 'formal logic' was unequivocal: it was worthless, whereas mobile 'dialectical logic' was of 'supernatural power', and a compromise between the two was to be fundamentally rejected. But his later essays on the relationship between 'formal' and 'dialectical logic' show obvious differences from the passages just quoted, revealing that his attitude to 'formal' logic had changed along with the party's new line regarding the United Front.

As mentioned above, the CCP had renewed its offer of a United Front in a letter to Chiang Kai-shek on August 25, 1936, but it did so in a way that corresponded to Comintern policy. Because of the concessions to the Kuomintang which the letter contained, there followed a violent intra-party debate. The 'Resolution on the New Situation in the Movement to Resist Japan and Save the Nation and on the Democratic Republic' of September 17, 1936, emphasised the leading role of the CCP in the United Front and the maximum consolidation of Red power and the Red Army. At the same time, it stressed the securing of the party's political and organisational independence as the basic prerequisite for victory in the United Front.[12] Against this background and during the very same period (autumn 1936), Ai Ssu-ch'i transformed his ideas on the relationship between 'formal' an 'dialectical logic'. Whereas, in *Philosophy for the Masses* and up to the end of 1935 Ai had spoken of the uselessness of 'formal logic' and had rejected every compromise between it and 'dialectical logic, he now took the following position:

1. The rejection of 'formal logic' is not a simple negation, but includes the preservation of its positive aspects as well. 'Formal logic' is absorbed (*hsi-shou*) by 'dialectical logic', and in that process its positive aspects are sublimated and its negative ones are negated.

2. 'Dialectical logic' must possess the leadership in the period of transition.

3. 'Formal' and 'dialectical logic' must not be considered as equal, and not as mutually independent 'territories' (*ti-p'an*).

4. An independent 'territory' of 'formal logic' is inadmissible.

5. Rather the unity between 'formal' and 'dialectical logic' is characterised by a 'reciprocal infiltration'(*hu-hsiang shen-t'ou*), whereby 'dialectical logic' assumes the leadership, and not by a mechanical alliance (*chi-hsieh ti chieh-he*).

6. The mechanical alliance of both logics is nothing less than a compromise (*che-chung*).[13]

If, Ai continued, the two areas of logic could not 'penetrate one another' (*hu-hsiang ch'in-fan*), then they would stand 'equal in relation to each other' (*tui-teng*) and one would 'consider them equal' (*t'ung-teng k'an-tai*).[14] However, 'dialectical logic' was to 'absorb' (*hsi-shou*) and 'digest'(*hsiao-hua*, literally 'transform by destruction') 'formal logic', thus sublimating its positive aspects and annihilating its negative ones. Ai also tackled the theme in his work *Methodology of Thought* (October 1936). He asked what position metaphysics and its method, 'formal logic', have in Chinese society, and whether indeed it is necessary at all:

Some people assert that one must preserve a place for formal logic in our present society and that many things still have to be investigated which cannot be governed [*kuan-hsia* = to administer, to have rule over, to govern] by dialectical logic; therefore, one should allow formal logic to continue its existence. These thoughts are not infrequently found among people who consider themselves to be dialectical materialists.[15]

Ai admitted that one needs 'formal logic' at the first levels of research,

. . . but this type of thought is false in practice. It is a mistake that comes from not understanding the true essence of metaphysics. Therefore, it is not metaphysics, because it differentiates things analytically and separately and because, after analysing them, it considers the separate parts as isolated and immovable and forgets the relationships between them, as well as the change and movement . . . The dialectical method, on the other hand, preserves the active relationships of all parts and is thus able to perceive the future development of things.[16]

According to Ai, metaphysics was an obstacle to active thought, and its method should therefore not be accorded a special place in society.

We will begin the analysis of these passages by studying the characters used by Ai Ssu-ch'i. The phrase '*ti-p'an*' is translated in most dictionaries as 'sphere of influence', 'territory under one's control'[17] or 'territory occupied by force'.[18] Indeed, one can translate '*hsing-shih luo-chi ti ti-p'an*' in a figurative sense as the 'field of application of formal logic', i.e. in the sciences, but I intend to show that the 'field of application of formal logic' meant the territory controlled by the Kuomintang. In turn, the 'field of application of dialectical logic' corresponded to those areas under CCP control.

The characters '*kuan-hsia*' in relation to 'formal' or 'dialectical logic', which are translated as 'administer, govern or rule', are further evidence that this concerns areas of political and military control rather than areas of intellectual thought. The formulation '*hu-hsiang ch'in-fan*' (= reciprocal encroachment) corresponds to this too; the last two characters in particular evoke military associations: '*ch'in-fan*' is a forceful violation of the rights or territory of others. How these violations occur is shown clearly by the characters '*shen-t'ou*', which mean 'penetrate' or 'infiltrate'. A military unit which has the task of infiltrating enemy territory is called in Chinese 'shen-t'ou pu-tui' and the tactic used is known as 'shen-tou chan-shu'. The aim of this 'infiltration' is made clear by the characters 't'ui-fan' (= overthrow), which are used in political texts in connection with the forceful overthrow of feudalism, imperialism and bureaucratic capitalism (t'ui-fan ti-kuo chu-i, feng-chien chu-i ho kuan-liao tzu-pen chu-i).

Ai Ssu-ch'i thus almost exclusively used expressions with a military and administrative connotation in describing the relationship between 'formal' and 'dialectical logic'. The use of these terms is sufficient indication that he was not referring to problems of logic, but to military and political problems. If one were to interpret his texts on logic from this perspective, then he made a significant political statement in 1935. Using the example of the 'absolute negation' of 'formal logic', he explained that a United Front between the CCP and the Kuomintang could not be considered, since that would be tantamount to a compromise with those forces that wanted to 'turn back the wheel of history'. This attitude corresponded to the United Front tactic of the CCP as well as to that of the Comintern at that time.

In 1936, Ai Ssu-ch'i had taken into account the Comintern's revised tactics which aimed at the inclusion of the Kuomintang in the United Front and even considered allowing it the leading role. He now recognised the right to existence of 'formal logic' and even admitted that in the past it had certain achievements in philosophy and science to its credit. However, in the autumn of 1936 he objected emphatically to 'formal' and 'dialectical logic' having equal status and advocated a leading role for the latter. In doing so he contradicted Wang Ming's line; he had not forgotten that the CCP, despite its equal status within the United Front, should recognise the leading role of the Kuomintang. On the other hand, using the example of the 'dialectical negation' of 'formal logic', Ai made it clear that the CCP must have the leading role. The decisive point, however, was the development of the relationship between the two parties in the United Front period. Within the United Front, in Ai's words, 'dialectical logic' was to 'absorb' and 'digest' 'formal logic', and reciprocal penetration or infiltration ('hu-hsiang shen-t'ou') was to serve as a means of attaining the goal of the final negation of 't'ui-fan', i.e. the overthrow of 'formal logic', or, in other words, the Kuomintang.

The epistemological discussion by Ai Ssu-ch'i of questions of logic thus had an interesting military-strategic implication: namely, the infiltration of areas then under Kuomintang control by existing Chinese Communist guerrillas or those that were still to be created, with the order to 'absorb' (*hsi-shou*) the opponent and finally to 'digest' (*hsaio-hua*, i.e. destroy) him. The last point will repay differentiation. In a general sense, 'absorb' and 'digest' meant that the Chinese Communists should continue the struggle against the Kuomintang during the United Front period in order to create all the preconditions, by the end of the war against Japan, for the elimination of Kuomintang control. But this necessitated a certain tactical approach, for which the Chinese dialectical materialists use the word 'sublimate'. Sometimes only phonetically translated, it is often rendered with the characters '*yang-ch'i*', meaning that, by being negated, the positive aspects of an object are 'raised' (*yang*), while on the other hand its negative aspects are 'rejected' (*ch'i*).

The principle of dialectical negation, conceived first by Hegel and now an essential part of dialectical materialism, was applied to Chinese conditions by Ai Ssu-ch'i in an astonishingly pragmatic way. The 'sublimation' or 'preservation' (*yang-ch'i*) of the positive aspects of 'formal logic' could – by equating 'formal logic' with the Kuomintang – only mean that the Chinese Communists should make the effort, in the process of infiltration, to 'absorb' the 'positive aspects' of the Kuomintang – its anti-Japanese and progressive wing as well as its troop units (e.g. Chang Hsüeh-liang's forces) – i.e. to detach it and draw it over to the CCP and, with the expanded power-base that resulted, to 'negate' the 'negative aspects' of the Kuomintang, such as its pro-Japanese and reactionary wing.

The Hegelian concept of 'sublimation', the essence of his dialectical philosophy, to Ai meant nothing less than the 'rolling up' of the opposing military forces, and thus became transformed in Chinese dialectical materialism in to a political and military strategem.

Retreat is Attack or the 'Law of Identity'

The military importance of the discussion of 'formal' and 'dialectical logic' is revealed in another of Ai Ssu-ch'i works, in which he gives concrete examples for the explanation of both forms of 'logic'.[19] Here he demonstrates undisguisedly that 'formal' and 'dialectical logic' are merely – to use a concept of dialectical materialism – 'reflections' of opinion in the CCP concerning the correct military strategy and the United Front tactic. Kant, Hegel and the philosophers of Greek antiquity are again quoted and cited as principal witnesses to the correct or false line of the CCP during the civil war.

Ai Ssu-ch'i described the various positions within the CCP first by the example of the basic laws of 'formal logic':

> The law of identity [*t'ung-i-lü*] is a rule of the abstract, absolute unity; it sees in identical things only the aspects of absolute identity, recognising this aspect alone and disregarding its own contradictory and antagonistic aspects. Since an object can only be absolutely identical to itself, it cannot therefore be identical to another aspect. One expresses this with the formula: A is not Not-A, or A is B, and simultaneously it cannot be Not-B . . . For example, 'retreat is not attack' (A is Not-A), concentration is limitation of democracy (A is B), one cannot in this case simultaneously develop democracy (simultaneously 'not is Not-B'). In this definition, an object (conception, thing, etc.) is confronted absolutely with another object, which lies beyond the actual object, a consequence of which is that an object (A) and the others (Not-A) have no relations at all with each other . . . The law of identity thus only recognises abstract identity, and the law of contradiction only recognises an absolute opposite.[20]

The unifying of several objects identical to themselves was, according to 'formal logic', merely a combination or addition of absolutely independent and unconnected objects (*tu-li wu-kuan-lien ti tung-hsi*). There could be no struggle between them, since struggle would already have meant a relationship. 'But,' Ai discovered, 'without a struggle there is no driving force of the movement.' Therefore, such a unification would mean a state of rest.[21]

Ai then turned to the third law of 'formal logic':

> Then the law of identity only recognises an absolute confrontation. The law of the excluded third specifies: either there is an absolute identity (A is B) or an absolute opposition (A is not B); an object cannot be simultaneously identical and at the same time be antagonistic. For example, 'concentration' [*chi-chung*] is either limited democracy or unlimited democracy; it cannot at the same time be limited and a developed democracy. A government in which the people participate is either a democratic organ or it is not a democratic organ. It cannot be simultaneously democratic and insufficiently democratic. Therefore, the law of the excluded third only recognises opposition or unity, and struggles against the 'unity of opposites' [*tui-li ti tung-i*]. This meant that it ['formal logic'] and the dialectic are diametrically opposed.[22]

What did Ai Ssu-ch'i intend to express with his explanation?

1. What is the meaning of 'Retreat is not attack'? As we will see in more detail below, this formulation referred to the strategical principles

of the long-protracted war, but in particular, it could also refer to the discussion of the strategic significance of the provincial capital, Wuhan. The Comintern, together with the Wang-Ming faction, attached great importance to the defence of Wuhan against the advancing Japanese forces in the autumn of 1938. A successful defence of the city would mark a turning-point for the counter-offensive; therefore Wang Ming advocated protecting Wuhan with all available forces.[23]

For Mao Tse-tung, by contrast, the defence of Wuhan had no special meaning. Instead, he advocated surrendering the city and building up the anti-Japanese resistance in the countryside. Ai Ssu-ch'i thus defended Mao's tactics, in that he dismissed the phrase 'Retreat is not attack' as 'formal logically'. To consider the 'retreat' from Wuhan solely as a retreat or non-attack corresponded, according to Ai, to the first law of 'formal logic' and was in no way seen as 'dialectical'. On the other hand, Ai wanted to show that the retreat was at one and the same time both a retreat and not a retreat, since it prevented an unnecessary waste of forces against a superior opponent and instead prepared for the future attack from rural base areas. The retreat thus contained an attack.

2. The explanations of 'democratisation' and 'concentration' were also a criticism of Wang Ming's concepts of setting back 'democratisation' in favour of the 'concentration' of all political and military forces, and of attempting to commit the CCP exclusively to the support of the national government. Behind this was hidden the consideration that a possible 'democratisation' of Kuomintang control could lead to an impairment of the military effectiveness of the United Front. Ai criticised this view as 'formal logically', because 'democratisation' and 'concentration' were seen as mutually exclusive contradictions: 'If we thus say: during the war against Japan, everything must be concentrated and united, but that at the same time as much democracy as possible must be developed, that is, according to the rules of formal logic, unreasonable, i.e. illogical.'[24] However, according to Ai, that was true only for the rules of 'formal' not of 'dialectical logic'.

Ai Ssu-ch'i thus marked down Wang Ming as a 'formal logician' and political opponent. In no instance did he include him among the representatives of the 'dialectic' because, according to 'dialectical logic', 'democratisation' and 'concentration' were not mutually exclusive but rather represented unity. Ai thus argued in support of Mao Tse-tung's position since Mao had often insisted that the 'democratisation' of all areas of the state by the Kuomintang was essential for the concentration of all forces in the struggle against Japan.[25]

3. However, Ai Ssu-ch'i made a further observation concerning the relationship between the CCP and the Kuomintang by speaking of the 'unification of several objects identical to themselves' and by characterising them as a 'formal-logical' combination of independent, mutually unrelated objects, which thus represented a state of rest. The 'formal-logical identity' served him as an example of how the relationship between the two parties should *not* be constituted. The United Front was not to be a condition of repose, but the very reverse: the 'struggle' was to form the 'driving force' (see above). This was a clear rejection of the concept of the Comintern faction within the United Front which wanted to suspend the struggle against the Kuomintang.

Through the example of the 'law of identity', Ai also grappled with the question of how far the CCP could acquiesce in the Kuomintang's demand to base itself on the 'Three principles of the people'(*san-min chu-i*), without endangering the independence of the CCP. The Kuomintang had made it a prerequisite for the establishment of the United Front that the CCP should declare itself in favour of the 'three principles' of Sun Yat-sen, as already described. The reaction to this demand within the CCP was varied, and Ai then evaluated the individual reactions in a 'formal-logical' manner:

Since the law of identity only recognises the absolute aspect of identity, one can maintain in the United Front that all parties and factions have now already given up their independence and have only one goal; consequently many people say that the CP has given up Marxism. Since, on the other hand, the law of contradiction only recognises the absolute opposite, some people advocate the view that every party and faction must retain its own independent programme and organisation.[26]

Ai characterised the adherents of the first view as 'right deviationists' and those of the second as 'left deviationists'. He accused the 'right deviationists' of advocating the support of the 'three principles' and of wanting to prescribe this position for the party in order not to endanger future cooperation with the Kuomintang. The 'left deviationists', on the other hand, made the mistake of seeing a departure from Communism in support of the 'three principles' and in insistence on nothing but an individual, independent programme. Both groups—the 'right' and 'left deviationists' – are, according to Ai, 'formal-logical' in their thought; they consider only one aspect of the whole, and make that absolute. They both make the mistake of 'formal logic', which includes only the 'external part' of what 'simultaneously exists (*ping-ts'un*), but not the diverse connections of the 'internal parts'. 'Formal logic' recognises only attack and/or retreat, only concentration and/or democracy, only the 'three principles of the people' and/or communism. However, it is not capable of comprehending the existing relationships between these respective pairs of objects.

'Left and right deviationists' now stand in opposition to the 'dialecticians'. The latter, according to Ai, think it necessary to support the 'three principles'. However, they do not make the mistake of trying to prescribe it for the party, and they certainly do not surrender Marxism, but instead consider the execution of the 'three principles' merely as a prerequisite intermediate step on the way towards Communism. Ai then combined this middle position between the two wings in the CCP – the readiness to accept Kuomintang demands with the maintenance of long-term goals – with the formulation 'dialectical logic', which sees the identity of an object as well as its opposite in unity:

Unity is unity, but unity must also have as a basis the independence of every party. Centralised state power is centralised state power, but a united, effective concentration of forces to the maximum extent must be established on the basis of democracy. The two opposing sides penetrate each other . . . If one were to write this as a formula, it would be: 'A is A and at the same time Not-A'. Or, 'Affirmation is rejection, rejection is affirmation'.[27]

Thus, in concrete terms, 'dialectical logic' can be explained thus: the United Front is accepted and at the same time rejected, in that the struggle against the Kuomintang is to be continued within the United Front.

Ai's criticism of the 'right deviationists', whom we had characterised as advocates of 'formal logic' and as 'compromisers', was not without historical irony: he made the same accusation against the China policy of Stalin which Stalin's 'philosophers' had directed at Bukharin against the background of the kulak question—of wanting to reconcile opposites and make compromises. Obviously, Ai did not think it the right time to accuse the supporters of the Comintern, and thus Stalin too, of 'Bukharinism', 'Mechanism' and 'Deborinism' over the United Front question. In view of Stalin's recent liquidation of the 'right deviationists' in the CPSU it would hardly have been diplomatic to do so. Hence criticism was directed against Yeh Ch'ing, the 'Chinese Deborin', behind whose 'mechanistic dialectic' there lay, one suspected, a strategy of encouraging the CCP to join the Kuomintang in the United Front against Japan and thus to benefit Soviet security interests in the Far East.

The reception of Soviet dialectical materialism in China thus developed in a way which the 'fathers' of this 'philosophy' probably did not anticipate. 'Dialectical materialism' became a weapon against those from whom it had once been accepted, and against those who supported it in one's own party.

The 'Slough of Idealism' or the Reconciliation between 'Formal' and 'Dialectical' Logic

The 'Chinese Deborin', Yeh Ch'ing, devoted many articles to the relation between the two types of logic, and published them in 1937 in a collected volume entitled *Lun-li hsüeh wen-t'i* (Problems of Logic).[28] In it he defended 'formal logic' against the attacks of the 'dialecticians' and attempted to prove the former was an integral part of 'dialectical logic'. For him the laws of identity, contradiction and the excluded third were indispensable for intellectual thought. The most developed form of 'logic' was indeed 'dialectical logic', knowledge of which was essential for the study of 'the processes of movement of matter'. But at the same time one should not relinquish 'formal logic', which was instead to form the basis of 'dialectical logic'.[29] Yeh Ch'ing also constantly characterised himself as an advocate of dialectical materialism, but his form of the negation of 'formal logic' was less far-reaching in its consequences than that of Ai Ssu-ch'i, as this quote from Yeh Ch'ing indicates: 'In regard to inductive [formal] logic, one must reject its mechanistical character, but preserve its essential content to form the basis of dialectical logic.'[30]

What was to be the result of the negation of 'formal logic'? Like Ai Ssu-ch'i, Yeh also characterised the political situation with the proposition that in the 'present period' there existed two types of 'logic', which contradicted each other:

The present problem of logic is the relation between formal and dialectical logic. This problem reads exactly as follows: Which of the two types of logic is correct and which is false? Which is replaced by the other? How do the relationships between them appear? Which should we support and which should we fight against? . . . How are the contradictions between them to be solved?[31]

Yeh concluded there were two ways of resolving this contradiction. The advocates of one view accepted only 'dialectical' and rejected 'formal logic', while their counterparts admitted only 'formal' and rejected 'dialectical' logic. Both views, according to Yeh, were false in that they merely attempted to resolve the contradiction between the two types of 'logic' by means of 'formal logic' and proceeded from the assumption that 'dialectical' and 'formal logic' could not be united with each other.[32] The opponents of 'formal logic' applied 'dialectical logic' only externally, for the simple rejection of 'formal logic' was, by its nature, also 'formally logical'. Thus, according to Yeh, the views are indeed different, but the method of solving the problems remains the same. The only way of resolving contradictions was now the unification of both the two forms of 'logic'. He justified this as follows:

We should recognise the true essence of formal and dialectical logic. Its origin and development are by no means accidental. The early dialecticians and formal logicians all strove for truth. Therefore, it is unreasonable that the dialecticians should negate or reject the formal logicians, and vice versa. For both have their aspects of inadequacy. While the formal logicians reject the contradiction and lay the stress on the individual and repose, the dialecticians for their part recognise the contradiction and lay the stress on relationships and movement. However each grasps only one aspect, which is at once their strength and their weakness. Should our knowledge be satisfied with just one aspect? No, we want universal knowledge. Thus there is only the method of reciprocal support, in what we unite the two.[33]

Yeh now referred to the law of the 'unity of opposites', whereby unification was to resolve the contradictions between two theses; only thus could the positive features of both be preserved and their negative aspects excluded. In Yeh's view, 'dialectical logic' demanded of itself such a form of unity, since it always assumed the 'unity of opposites'.[34]

What exactly was Yeh Ch'ing trying to say? We can start from the assumption that the 'universal knowledge' of which he spoke was not his actual goal, as he had already shown in connection with his 'theory of knowledge'. He was referring rather to the two parties, the CCP and the Kuomintang. The two were to unite, each thus eliminating the deficiencies of the other and instead supplementing each other reciprocally. He also advocated a peaceful framework for the United Front, with neither party harbouring the intention of 'negating' the other. Yeh had already suggested this method of resolving contradictions in the relationships between 'idealism' and 'materialism' as well as between 'rationalism' and 'empiricism'; as in the aforementioned cases, the 'dialecticians' again reacted with sharp criticism of the unification of the two 'logics'.

On several occasions, T'an Fu-chih and Ai Sheng warned that Yeh Ch'ing was an 'idealist' who came in the 'mask of a dialectical materialist' in order to pull the CCP into the 'slough of idealism'. Yeh denied that his form of unification involved a 'compromise' (*che-chung*) or 'harmonious conciliation'; instead it was a process of 'absorbing' (hsi-shou) the 'formal' by the 'dialectical logic'. The course of history, he wrote, indicated that 'dialectical logic' and 'materialism' would finally emerge successful. And as he had already shown in his 'theory of knowledge' – with the example of the mandarin orange – the necessity (as he thought) of the unification of 'rationalism' and 'empiricism', he now produced 'proof' of the necessity of unification between 'formal' and 'dialectical logic'.

He maintained that the unity of the two 'logics' already existed in theory, but had not been completed in practice because those concerned had lacked insight.[35] Yeh explained to his readers that, in the process of intellectual thought, the two 'logics' determined each other reciprocally and presupposed each other's existence. The one could not exist without the other: 'Formal logic rejects contradiction . . . However, the laws of identity, contradiction and the excluded third have contradiction as their prerequisite . . . If there is no contradiction, why does one need the law of contradiction?'[36] And the law of identity, too, whereby an object can be identical only to itself, was based on the recognition of contradiction, because being finally presupposed not-being. Thus Yeh concluded: 'While the laws of identity, contradiction and the excluded third exclude contradiction, they all assume it as a starting-point, in that they simultaneously reject it.'[37]

It was the same with 'dialectical logic', for it worked on the understanding that it could only be correct when it recognised and applied the laws of 'formal logic'; namely, it recognised contradiction, but could not do without the law of contradiction, which it rejected. 'Dialectical logic' assumed that 'a thesis is a thesis, an antithesis an antithesis, and synthesis just a synthesis, that quantity equals quantity and quality equals quality etc . . . thus all represent a clearly limited area and cannot be mixed with each other.'[38] Thus thesis A is just thesis A, or it is not. The same goes for the antithesis, it is it, or it is not it. But this means, in Yeh's view, that 'dialectical logic', in which thesis and antithesis are grasped as a contradiction, can only state what is a thesis and what is an antithesis with the help of the laws of 'formal logic'. From this Yeh concluded: 'Dialectical logic therefore rejects contradiction in that moment where it recognises it.' And this led him to an assessment which was to have far-reaching political implications: 'The construction of dialectical logic thus takes place formally-logically.'[39]

With this Yeh believed he had 'proved' that the two 'logics' determined each other reciprocally and depended on each other. That he had mixed formal-logical contradiction, which existed in intellectual thought, and a real contradiction such as can exist in society, was unimportant to him; it would only have been a problem had it disturbed the sophistry of his argument, since he merely wanted, as in the case of the mandarin orange, to 'prove' that the CCP and the Kuomintang determined each other reciprocally, formed a unity in themselves and were not to 'negate' each other within the unity.

Once Yeh believed he had found for his readers the unity of the two 'logics' and thus, theoretically, of the two parties, he came to speak of its application in 'practice'. His description of 'practice' within the United Front contained four important terms: 'consider two opposing objects as equal' (*tui-teng k'an-tai*); 'define borders and control,' i.e. the control of territories separated from each other (*fen-ch'iang ehr-chih*); 'dualism' (*ehr-yüan lun*), 'eclecticism' or 'readiness to compromise' (*che-chung chu-i*).

With the sophistry of which he had just given proof, Yeh now attempted to side-step the accusation of his opponents that he wanted a compromise with the Kuomintang.

If one considers formal and dialectical logic as equal [*tui-teng k'an-tai*], as controlling areas separate from each other [*fen-ch'iang erh chih*], then that means dualism [*erh-yüan lun*], eclecticism [*che-chung chu-i*] and harmonious conciliation. However, this type of unity is not a dialectical unity. Dialectical unity requires an object, which leads and absorbs the other.[40]

The leading role in the unity should thus be assumed by 'dialectical logic'. An equal position for each party, even the separation of their areas of control, is out of the question. This 'dualism' meant 'compromise' for Yeh in that he would allow both parties to continue to exist and thus the existing situation too, but only with the proviso that the civil war was to end and each side would promise not to undertake anything to jeopardise the other side's control of its own territory. Each party would then wield independent control over its territory.

But had not Ai Ssu-ch'i also spoken of the necessity of 'dialectical logic' assuming the leadership in the unity? Had he not argued against 'dualism', 'eclecticism' and against compromise? What, then, were the differences between Ai and Yeh?

When Ai Ssu-ch'i spoke of 'dialectical logic' he meant the CCP and its leading role in the United Front. He rejected Kant's 'dualistic philosophy' because he hoped that through the 'reciprocal penetration' or infiltration (*hu-hsiang shen-t'ou*) of the parties and their territories the

Kuomintang could be overthrown if the CCP succeeded in maintaining its independence and adroitly extending its position. Yeh Ch'ing, however, considered the CCP as merely a component of 'dialectical logic', its second part being 'formal logic' – the Kuomintang. Only the unity of the two parts could bring about the realisation of 'dialectical logic' and thus of the supposed 'universal knowledge'. His idea of the 'materialistic elimination' of 'dualism' in 'logic', as in 'philosophy', was therefore a challenge to the CCP to disband and relinquish its independence and area of control in favour of a fusion with the Kuomintang – a call which he did not mention openly at this time (March 1937).

The characters for *tui-teng k'an tai* ('consider as equal') we find in the texts by Yeh as well as by Ai and later on by Mao; and *fen ch'iang erh-chih* ('control areas separate from each other') is to a certain degree the Chinese 'definition' of the Western concept of 'dualism'. What Western philosophy represents as the duality of two opposing or equal areas of being – matter and consciousness, body and soul, the 'thing in itself' and the 'phenomenon' etc. – becomes, with the Chinese theoreticians, the duality of two military and political areas of control. And if Kant's dualistic philosophy, with its differentiation between the 'thing in itself' and the 'phenomenon', is cited as an unfavourable example of a thought tending towards political and military compromise, this raises the question whether the Chinese Marxists not only made a fundamental misunderstanding in their reception of Western intellectual thought, but also whether their intellectual predisposition was such that they were able to receive Western ideas only in a formal way, going on to make an analogous application of what they received.

The concept of 'eclecticism' (*che-chung chu-i*) suffered a similar fate to that of 'dualism' in the course of its reception. The first two characters, '*che-chung*', can also mean compromise; accordingly, *che-chung chu-i* means the principle of finding the middle way. For the Chinese theoreticians, therefore, 'philosophical eclecticism' is a term for a political or military compromise; its advocates are respectively 'eclecticians' and 'compromisers' (*che-chung chu-i che*).

Yeh's suggestion for resolving the contradiction between 'idealism' and 'materialism', 'reason' and 'experience', 'rationalism' and 'empiricism', and 'formal' and 'dialectical logic' meant the result was to be found in the unification and not in the struggle of the respective opposites. 'Dialectical materialism' was thus the result of the unification of 'idealism' and 'materialism'; 'universal objective knowledge' originated from the unification of 'reason' and 'experience', and 'dialectical logic' from the unification of 'formal logic' and 'dialectical logic'. The 'leading role' in the unity was thus a political force, which originated from the fusion of the two parties. But it is impossible to deduce from Yeh's works whether he thought of an alliance between the CCP and the left wing of the Kuomintang. The fact that, as a former cadre of the CCP, he had close contacts with left-wing Kuomintang members in Shanghai (see above, p. 50) lends weight to this interpretation. The 'leading role' of 'dialectical logic' would therefore mean that, in the event of such a unification, the left wing of the CCP as well as the pro-Japanese wing of the Kuomintang would be eliminated. Yet, this hypo-thesis hardly seems possible in view of the hardened fronts between the parties caused by the civil war.

It appears to the present author that Yeh Ch'ing's goal was not the unification of the two parties, but something more ambitious. His representation of 'dialectical materialism' served the purpose of urging the Chinese Marxists to abandon their struggle against the Kuomintang as a direct consequence and requirement of the materialistic dialectic, and of inducing them to surrender their independence and perhaps even disband their party in order to unite with the Kuomintang. We have already pointed out that a possible consequence of such a form of unification was the end of the Communist movement. The goal of Yeh Ch'ing's 'theory of unification' (*tsung-he-lun*) was therefore not unification in itself, but rather a trap to bring about the destruction of the CCP. This was the 'slough of idealism' of which Ai Ssu-ch'i, T'an Fu-chih and others had spoken, and into which the CCP was to fall.

In 1939, two years after the publication of his work *Problems of Logic*, Yeh Ch'ing joined the Kuomintang, and in the ensuing period developed into the chief propagandist of the 'Three People's Principles' (*san-min chu-i*), the ideology of the Kuomintang. As early as March 1938 he had published an article openly expressing the true goal of all his 'philosophical' unifications: the dissolution of the CCP. On the one hand, the CCP had insisted that in the struggle against Japan the Red Army was to remain under absolute party control, but it had also declared its readiness to accept the position of the Kuomintang, the 'Three People's Principles' and Chiang Kai-shek. Yeh then asked which arguments the party could use to justify independent operations and sug-gested it would do better to dissolve itself and accept the leadership of the Kuomintang.[42] One cannot exclude the possibility that Yeh had been working for the Kuomintang prior to 1938, and that his works on 'dialectical materialism' were a form of psychological warfare against the CCP on its behalf.

Yeh's 'philosophical' proofs concerning the necessity of 'unity' were no less equivocal than those camouflaged Marxist concepts of his adversaries Ai Ssu-ch'i, Ch'en Po-ta and their friends on the relation between 'perceptual' and 'theoretical knowledge' and between 'formal' and 'dialectical logic'. The rhetoric of both sides was aimed at the destruction of the other, whether it be the CCP or the Kuomintang; and the 'unity' sworn to by both sides was to be used by each as a means of realising its goals. The Japanese threat was merely an excuse for Yeh to demand of the CCP a form of 'unity' that would have been equivalent to capitulation, while Ai Ssu-ch'i saw in the war against Japan and the fictitious 'unity' between the CCP and the Kuomintang the chance of ultimate victory over the latter.

On this occasion Yeh Ch'ing's tactical approach was very adroit. He not only posed as a well-read 'dialectical materialist' and quoted extensively from the works of Engels, especially his *Dialektik der Natur* and *Ludwig Feuerbach and the Outcome of Classical German Philosophy*, in order to prove there could be no justification for reading the negation of 'formal logic' into the original texts,[43] but also called into question the whole basis of his adversaries' knowledge of questions of Marxism-Leninism, and discredited them for being followers of Moscow. This was an astute move, because Ai Ssu-ch'i and Ch'en Po-ta, as we have seen, were anything but adherents of the Comintern.

Yeh wrote that the 'new philosophers' (Ai Ssu-ch'i and others) were orientating themselves exclusively on the then dominant direction of Soviet philosophy, the 'textbook group' (*chiao-k'e-shu-p'ai*). They had no independence whatever in regard to 'philosophy', and indeed he said their publications were all copied from two Soviet works: Mitin's *Dialectical Materialism* and Aizenberg's (Ai-sen-pao) and Sirokov's (Hsi-lo-k'e-fu) *Course of Instruction in Dialectical Materialism*. Their works were nothing but propaganda, Yeh added: 'They do not contribute to understanding, but merely repeat blindly.'[44]

While Yeh presented the 'new philosophers' as virtual 'Russian Marxists', who merely parroted what was written in Moscow – a view which can be seen as superfically correct –, he alleged they were the representatives of Soviet interests within the CCP. From his knowledge of the works of Ai Ssu-ch'i and Ch'en Po-ta, he must have known precisely that they used Soviet dialectical materialism to legitimise their concepts of the United Front *vis-à-vis* the Comintern representatives within the party. Yeh, for his part, recommended his 'dialectic' as the true Chinese form of Marxism, free of Soviet influence and based on original sources, and his imputation that the 'new philosophers' merely followed the Moscow line was designed to weaken their position in the struggle with the Moscow faction and so strengthen the latter. The Comintern's concepts regarding the United Front were of considerably more service to the goals of the Kuomintang, which sought to destroy the CCP, than was the United Front strategy of Mao Tse-tung. One can therefore understand Yeh's caustic criticism of the 'new philosophers' at the end of his comments on 'formal' and 'dialectical logic':

The level of Chinese culture distinguishes itself by the fact that there is not the slightest talent for individual research. In conveying what is modern culture, one exclusively follows others. This is valid for individual as well as socialist culture . . . These people do not use original sources, but rather adhere to Soviet literature. They pay no attention to original sources, probably because the revolution in the native land of Marx and Engels was not successful . . . Such people are nothing more than machines without heads. We should not criticise them, but merely regard them with pity.[45]

A Table has Four Legs or From Contradiction to the Opposite

Yeh's criticism could indeed be applied as much to him as to the 'new philosophers'. His own system of 'philosophy' was not distinguished by the originality which he himself demanded. His comment that 'dialectical logic' was to be constructed 'formal-logically' and 'formal logic' was to form the basis of 'dialectical logic', was naturally an affront to the 'new philosophers', and was violently criticised by them, especially by Ch'en Po-ta, who suspected not merely a 'philosophical' train of thought behind this structure of two 'logics', but also some clearly 'insidious intentions'. Everyone, he wrote, knows that the 'struggle between both logics is a life and death struggle.'[46] He accused Yeh of considering 'formal' and 'dialectical' logic as equal, but he added that the two 'logics' could never be one and the same, no more than 'exploiter' and 'exploited'. Whoever placed the two 'logics' on an equal footing also endorsed the view that 'the exploited work together with the exploiters', which was 'the true intention of all the philosophical works of Yeh Ch'ing'.[47] This was a frank and honest statement which revealed that the Chinese theoreticians, despite all their enthusiasm for materialist dialectic and the persuasiveness with which they advocated it, were well aware that they were essentially dealing with something entirely different.

If there was a hidden intention behind Yeh Ch'ing's 'philosophical works' of bringing about cooperation between the two parties and hence the destruction of the CCP, what was the intention of 'dialectician' Ch'en Po-ta regarding the United Front? He wrote:

While Yeh Ch'ing equates dialectical logic with formal logic, he intends to wrench the weapon of revolutionary consciousness away from the Chinese people; his plan is to snatch from the Chinese people the theoretical weapon with which it organises the United Front for the defence of the homeland and struggle.[48]

Ch'en's dialectic obviously obeyed laws of its own: the organisation of the 'United Front for the defence of the homeland' presumed that one was against cooperation in such a United Front. However, if one was for cooperation, then one was at the same time against the United Front. His 'dialectic' thus signified a United Front without cooperation, according to the 'law' set down by Ai Ssu-ch'i: A is A and simultaneously not-A (cf. p. 112, above). 'We can ascertain,' he concluded, 'that dialectical and formal logic cannot exist as equals under heaven, but that the former constantly overcomes the latter, and always replaces the latter.'[49]

Ch'en gave his opinion of the United Front no less forthrightly when he turned to the laws of 'formal logic'.

We know that dialectical logic contains affirmation and at the same time negation. However, the dialectical affirmation has nothing in common with the law of identity of formal logic. Thus, for example, the Ch'ing dynasty was replaced by the Chinese Republic after the Hsin-hai revolution. But this Chinese Republic was not a republic, because the people of this state had no republican power. It was merely a dictatorship of the Northern warlords. But according to the law of identity of formal logic, the Chinese Republic is just the Chinese Republic.[50]

He also attempted to refute the 'law of the excluded third' of 'formal logic': if one applied this law, then the revolutionary movements in China in the 1930s were the same as either the Hsin-hai revolution or the revolution of 1925-7; but, according to Ch'en, both analogies were erroneous. In this he was certainly correct, only it was just as true that this example had nothing to do with the law mentioned above. What Ch'en really wanted to express was rather the following. The United Front, as a revolutionary movement, should be neither a 'bourgeois' movement, as in the Hsin-hai revolution, nor a new version of the United Front of 1924-7.[51] According to Ch'en, 'formal logicians' were those who wanted a 'bourgeois' United Front, or a United Front with the conditions of 1924-7, which had ended in devastating defeat for the CCP. And so as 'social conditions' had changed in the mean time, he rejected a new version of this type of United Front.

Ch'en considered 'dialectical logic' to be the only correct method of analysing the contradiction and its 'complicated connections', 'formal logic' being completely unsuited for this task. What did he understand by contradictions? According to Ch'en, there was nowhere on earth that was not subject to the dialectic. For example, China was a half-feudalist and half-colonial society, full of contradictions between landowners and farmers, capitalists and workers, and between imperialists and the Chinese people. He then became more specific:

A table contains a contradiction. It has table-legs and a table-top. Without the contradiction of table-legs and table-top there can be no table. The table-top is the centre. It is limited simultaneously by four sides. Without this centre, the table-top has no limitation, and vice versa. This too is a contradiction. The table also has a drawer. It is directed outward as well as inward. Without this contradiction of the two directions, there would be no drawer. Now let us take a fountain-pen. It has a point and it has a rear part, each of which shows in a different direction. That is a contradiction. The fountain-pen also has an external case, which covers its inner emptiness. This too is a contradiction. Without it there can be no fountain-pen.'[52]

This was too much even for Yeh Ch'ing. 'That is child's opera dialectic,' he raged.[53] And it gave him useful additional proof that the 'new philosopher' Ch'en Po-ta understood absolutely nothing of 'materialistic dialectic'.

Was this really true, or had Ch'en Po-ta perhaps meant something different? We do not know whether he expressed his views on 'contradictions' elsewhere. Still, the reader should not feel disappointment at this curiously naive way of explaining the most important aspect of dialectical materialism. Ch'en's article clearly worked on two levels. On the one hand, he advocated the primacy of 'dialectical logic' over 'formal logic' and thus a form of the United Front in which the Kuomintang finally would be overcome by the CCP. On the other hand, a few lines further on he represented the contradictions, by the example of the table, as opposites which complemented each other, and without which the entirety of an object would not be possible. After all, a table cannot stand without legs. How can this contradiction be resolved?

Perhaps the date when Ch'en's article was published is revealing. It appeared on September 1, 1936, and it was during the period between August 25 and September 17, 1936, that the concessions to be accorded to the Kuomintang were revised, and the independence of the CCP, of the Red Army and especially the CCP's leading role in the United Front were again determined by resolution.[54]

A few days before this resolution, on September 10, Ch'en Po-ta published in the magazine *Tu-shu sheng-huo* an article entitled 'Self-Criticism of a New Philosopher and Suggestions for a New Enlightenment Movement',[55] in which he demanded that the 'new philosophers' should enter into a great coalition (*ta-lien-he*) with all other schools of philosophy for the salvation of democracy and the homeland. On the other hand, the 'new philosophers' were to insist unremittingly on their 'own standpoint' (*tzu-chi ti li-ch'ang*), but they were also to give up the 'closed door policy' (*kuan-men chu-i*) and bind themselves closely to all 'patriotic forces', 'rationalists' and 'democrats' in order to 'defend the homeland' and develop the 'people's consciousness'.[56] Ch'en's article thus had a dual purpose. The party was certainly not to be so ready for compromise that it would relinquish its 'own standpoint' and thus its independence – this was directed at the address of the Comintern faction. But, at the same time, neither was it to insist on the 'closed door policy', like the opponents of the United Front.

Thus there was a political connection between the articles of September 1 and 10 respectively. In the first article, Ch'en wrote of the long-term strategy towards the Kuomintang, according to which 'formal' and 'dialectical logic' (Kuomintang and CCP) could never co-exist as equals, but 'formal' would always be replaced by 'dialectical logic'. With this, Ch'en advocated the CCP's claim to leadership as had been officially designated by the resolution of September 17. Here the leading role of 'dialectical logic' paralleled the leading role of 'philosophy' versus 'science' mentioned above. At the same time Ch'en suggested a 'great coalition' of all 'patriots', 'democrats' and 'rationalists'. He drafted the 'philosophical picture' for this coalition from the example of contradictions, which are united in a table or in a fountain-pen. These contradictions seemingly had the character of 'peaceful opposites', without – as Ch'en stressed – requiring the 'new philosophers' to abandon their independent standpoint. It would thus seem that this connection between the CCP's claim to leadership and the simultaneous offer of peaceful cooperation, was a tactical approach by Ch'en to each of the two wings of the party as well as to the participants in the future 'grand coalition'.

It could be argued that we have exaggerated the importance of the description of 'contradictions' as 'peaceful opposites' from Ch'en's example of the table, and that perhaps he considered the phenomenon of the table for itself without thinking of politics. We ourselves advocated this point of view till it transpired that Ch'en's table had a function similar to that of Yeh Ch'ing's mandarin orange.

The Division of Heaven or the Developmental Process of Matter

Ch'en's short passage about the contradictions having been transformed into peaceful opposites had clearly served to awaken distrust in those who were against a United Front with the Kuomintang and were concerned to maintain the independence of the Red Army as a guarantor of the continued existence of the Communist movement.

Ch'en's remarks on the essence of a table were by no means seen as unpolitical or even as 'children's opera' by T'an Fu-chih. On the contrary, T'an saw something 'very dangerous' hiding behind this type of 'dialectic'. He wrote, regarding the 'table', that Ch'en Po-ta transformed the developing contradictions into 'peaceful opposites', which co-existed with each other in 'equality'. Where, asked T'an, is the 'novelty', the 'movement' to which the struggle of the contradiction gave birth? And he scoffed: 'I fear that the novelty consists of Ch'en Po-ta sitting on his table and writing a criticism against Yeh Ch'ing with his fountain-pen.'[57]

However, enough of polemics. Even if we still suppose that Ch'en only wanted to express himself in a naive fashion on contradiction, or was only capable of doing that – we do not assume that he did so, because the chronological parallel to the discussions within the CCP is too striking – it is possible to establish that every statement was immediately given a political construction and understood as an analogy. Just as Ch'en suspected 'insidious intents' in the works of Yeh Ch'ing, T'an feared that Ch'en was only too ready to transform the struggle of the contradictions into peaceful coexistence, and thus compromise with the enemy. And, as in the struggle over 'philosophy' and 'science', he again accused Ch'en of being on the way to surrendering the 'partiality of Marxism'.[58] From this it is apparent how politically explosive the description of a 'table' can sometimes be.

In his aforementioned work of May 1937, T'an also dealt with the relationships between 'formal and dialectical logic'; he divided them into three groups:

1. the absolute opponents of 'dialectical logic',
2. the adherents of 'dialectical logic' who considered the two types of 'logic' to be absolutely incompatible, and
3. the compromise faction, that of the 'eclecticians' (*che-chung-p'ai*). They criticised the 'formal logicians' as well as the 'dialecticians', provided that each excluded the other. They argued that both 'logics' were necessary, the first because the 'moved matter' faced something which is 'at rest', and the second because all 'objective things' are 'in movement'. And if one wants to clarify the meaning of 'being in a fixed period', one is less able than ever to relinquish 'formal logic'. Hence this faction was of the view that 'formal and dialectical logic' must 'co-exist'(*ping-li ts'un-tsai*) within a 'fixed period', with each having its own 'territory' (*ling-yü*).[59]

T'an confirmed, in his explanation of this thesis, that *ling-yü*, the territory of the respective 'logic' in question, could mean nothing other than the area under the military control of the CCP or the Kuomintang respectively. The 'fixed period' in which the two 'logics' were to co-exist was a paraphrase for the period of the United Front. He described his own ideas regarding the United Front very vividly:

Do we advocate that formal logic should make itself comfortable in an armchair? Do we advocate that the world should be equally divided, with formal logic receiving one half of heaven and dialectical logic receiving the other half? No, we oppose that. Can the contradictions between formal and dialectical logic be mediated at all? Can they be melted together in one pot? We are of a completely different opinion from those who speak of conciliation.[60]

According to T'an, 'formal logic' must therefore not be allowed to keep a 'half of heaven' and exist independently, since – such was his 'philosophic' argument – the 'fixed period' (the United Front) was merely one 'side of the total developmental process of matter' (probably, the Chinese revolution). The correct way to treat 'formal logic' was that it should definitely be negated after a period of 'sublimation'; it had to be 'digested' (*hsiao-hua*) and rejected: 'The result is dialectical logic, which has overcome and negated formal logic, whereby the latter no longer possesses an independent function.'[61]

In the writings of T'an Fu-chih, as in those of Ai Ssu-ch'i, it is apparent the 'dialectical materialists' did not possess a concept of matter. The 'being of the total developmental process of matter' which concerned T'an, was no more than an analogy for the Chinese revolution. The formulation was as devoid of genuine intrinsic substance as Ai

Ssu-ch'i's description of the 'total process of knowledge', which was also no more than a symbol for the duration of the Chinese revolution. And the 'fixed period' had, in relation to the 'total developmental process of matter', the same meaning as Ai Ssu-ch'i's 'relative knowledge' in relation to 'absolute truth': i.e. both formulations stated that there was talk of the United Front only as a period in the total process of the Chinese revolution.

T'an Fu-chih thus rebutted the 'right opportunists' as well as Ch'en Po-ta. He then summarised his strategy unequivocally and definitively:

On every territory where formal logic is to be found, we must take the standpoint of dialectical logic in order to conquer and negate formal logic. In no case can we stand at a random border and have the plan to unite the two or bring about conciliation between them since this conciliation means 'co-existing' [*ping-li ts'un-tsai*], 'live together in peace'[*hsiang-an*] and 'control territories separated from each other' [*fen-ch'iang erh chih*].'[62]

Two Types of Tactics or the 'Laws of Logic'

The texts of Ai Ssu-ch'i, Ch'en Po-ta, Yeh Ch'ing and T'an Fu-chih on logic are notable, like all those we have considered so far, in that they betray a lack of knowledge of Western philosophy. They represent in themselves a self-sustained group of 'empty formulae'. These 'empty formulae' were utilised for political purposes in a remarkably casual way. One prerequisite for this seems to be that Western philosophy and its concepts were not accepted insofar as their contents were concerned. But its formal, purely linguistic reception also reveals errors, which increased the vagueness regarding Western concepts, encouraged their inappropriate use and thus altered their meaning.

The law of identity is translated in Chinese as *t'ung-i-lü*, with *t'ung-i* meaning 'equal', 'similar' or 'the same'; but the concept of identity is not conveyed directly through the Chinese characters in this translation, and there remains a difference between 'equal' and 'identical'. The logic of identity has hardly played a role in Chinese philosophy (see below, p. 188); in other words, the importance of Aristotelean logic could not have been known to the Chinese Marxist theoreticians, since, except for the Soviet commentaries, they had not concerned themselves with works on logic.

The law of contradiction is translated as *mao-tun-lü*, in which *mao* means 'lance' and *tun* 'shield'. The military connotation of this character is clear, even if, as Lippert proves, *mao-tun* can also be found in the early

Meiji period as a technical term in formal logic meaning 'contradiction'.[63] However, as in the first law, one is safe in presuming that the formal-logical contradiction was not particularly important to the theoreticians as a part of the logic of identity.

The military connection seems more important. The struggle between 'materialism' and 'idealism' always had a military character, as when Ai Sheng wrote:

In the course of the struggle, the progressive side does not only use its weapons. The conservative side too learns to reproduce the weapons of its enemies in order to use them for defence. At the same time it attacks the enemy with them. One characterises this method as 'attacking the shield of the philosopher with the lance of the philosopher'.[64]

The formal-logical contradiction is indeed represented here, but it is understood only in a military or socio-political sense, as the texts have indicated.

The third law of formal logic, that of the excluded third, becomes even more obscure in its Chinese translation: *chü-chung-lü*. *Chü* means 'reject', 'resist'; *chung* is the character for 'middle', and *lü* for law. Literally translated, *chü-chung-lü* thus means 'the law of rejection of the middle'; but the character *chung* (middle) can be misleading in this connection, for the 'excluded third' must by no means be the middle between A and B.

In the process of being transferred to political relationships, the third law acquires a very concrete meaning, namely that of a middle position between the CCP and the Kuomintang. Alternatively, it served, when applied to the struggles in the CCP itself, to delineate two positions: first, the rejection of the United Front, and secondly 'everything through the United Front'. A middle position, similar to that of the 'dialecticians', was thereby 'excluded'. Thus the vagueness of the translation, and the lack of concern with formal logic in Western philosophy, may together be responsible for Chinese theoreticians understanding the three laws of formal logic and applying them according to their political positions, a process which culminated in the following definitions of the three laws:

1. The law of identity meant that in a political or military situation a standpoint would be made absolute. There would be either total adherence to the struggle against the Kuomintang and rejection of any cooperation, or absolute affirmation of unity with it. 'Only struggle' was just as much a product of 'formal logic' as 'only unity', and

consequently Ai Ssu-ch'i characterised the 'left deviationists' as well as the 'right deviationists' as 'formal-logical'.

2. The law of contradiction meant that one political standpoint excluded the other. 'Struggle' could only be 'struggle'; it could not at the same time be 'unity'. It was the same with 'retreat' and 'attack', 'democratisation' and 'concentration of forces'.

3. The law of the excluded third meant that a middle position, which, for example, could include 'struggle' as well as 'unity', was impossible.

In addition the Kuomintang was regarded, in its own way, as just as 'formal-logical' as all the other political forces which tended towards 'idealism' and not towards 'materialism'.

'Dialectical logic' now offered a way out of this 'formal-logical' dilemma in which the CCP found itself. Ai Ssu-ch'i's interpretation of 'negation' offered the possibility of suspending each of the two sides in its own absoluteness and of striving toward unity, which then interrupted the 'formal-logical' contradiction. The formulae of 'unity and the simultaneous struggle of the opposites', of 'democratisation' as a prerequisite for the 'concentration of forces', and of 'retreat' as a prerequisite for 'attack' were all representative of this development. Only the formula of 'unity and the simultaneous struggle of the opposites' untied the Gordian knot. The 'as well as' did not exclusively mean either 'struggle' or 'unity' and thus submission to the Kuomintang, but rather kept open the option of the future 'negation' of the opponent. It also embodied a necessary adjustment to the contemporary demand to form a United Front with him.

The characters for 'dialectical logic' thus stand for the core of Mao Tse-tung's strategy and the CCP faction which was unwilling to surrender the party's claim to leadership in the Chinese revolution, and which saw in the war against Japan – through a two-pronged strategy of struggling against the Kuomintang while simultaneously cooperating with it – the chance of the CCP eventually taking power in China.

13. TWO TYPES OF SICKNESS

What was the function of the attack by Japanese imperialism on China in this 'philosophical' puzzle? How was the war against Japan to be inserted into the 'materialist dialectic', into the formula of 'unity and the simultaneous struggle of the opposites'? The answer may be found in analysing the discussion on the relationships between 'absolute' (*chüeh-tui*) and 'relative' (*hsiang-tui*) as well as between 'internal causes' (*nei-yin*) and 'external causes' (*wai-yin*).

The representation of the relationships between 'absolute' and 'relative' was begun by Ai Ssu-ch'i in typical fashion. He answered a reader's letter in the magazine *Tu-shu sheng-huo*.[1] (Yeh Ch'ing was in the habit of saying of these readers' letters that Ai wrote them himself in order to have the correct questions for his answers.) Where, asked Ai, is the meaning of 'absolute' and 'relative' to be found? What had the relation between them to do with 'practice'? For example, was the war against Japan 'absolute' in regard to its necessity? Was the present 'movement of class peace' (*chieh-chi ho-p'ing yün-tung*) of relative importance? And what did the 'movement for the liberation of the people' (*min-tzu chieh-fang yün-tung*) have to do with it?[2]

Using a practical example, he attempted to give an answer. The 'progressive youth' believed it was the duty of every Chinese at the present time to defend the homeland and fight against the enemy; however, they often had a false idea of how this struggle should be waged, believing: 'My environment is not good enough, it does not suit me and I do not suit it. I must leave and live in another place!'[3] Whoever thought in this way, wrote Ai, assumed a 'hardened' and 'inflexible' standpoint. Certainly the environment was submerged in 'darkness', but such an attitude did not contribute to breaking through that 'darkness':

The forces of the progressive youth are able to change the environment. Other people around them go through life unconsciously, it is true, but they forget that people who live unconsciously can also be changed. In certain conditions they can be led to consciousness. They, the conscious youth, deepen the darkness and make the people's unconsciousness absolute. They say desperately: 'Let me go to a place where the light has already been lit.'[4]

However, Ai also advises the 'conscious youth' that to flee from their poor environment is wrong because flight is not a method favouring life.

You do not have to be pessimistic, because light will develop out of the darkness. If one does not destroy the darkness, there can be no light. Therefore, you must stay in your environment: only then can there be a possibility that you progressives will carry out your task – of obliterating the darkness. You must not see darkness as absolute!⁵

This 'seeing as absolute' had to be combated. According to Ai the same error occurred in the 'new philosophy' and in the 'new social science': 'absolutism' (*chüeh tui chu-i*). This was revealed in the fact that 'some, who misunderstand the new science, consider the future society as an ideal [*li-hsiang*]'. They wanted to realise it immediately in the world and did not grasp that the starting-point had to be present-day society. This attitude was the 'children's disease of left radicalism' (*tso-ch'ing yu-chih-ping*), which at the same time was a type of 'absolutism' and 'idealism'.⁶

One can initially interpret the biblical-sounding phrases about 'light' and 'darkness' as a naive school-masterly warning to the youth, and leave it at that, but the connection between the 'children's disease of left radicalism' and 'absolutism' given by Ai himself allow for a further interpretation. Moreover, the myth of 'light' and 'darkness' has also been adopted in modern Chinese dictionaries: 'It was the Communist party which led China into the light'⁷ (*Shih kung-ch'an-t'ang pa chung-kuo yin-hsiang kuang-ming*).

What did Ai Ssu-ch'i want to express? He advised the 'progressive' and 'conscious forces' in April 1937 not to enter those areas where 'light' prevailed, or in other words those areas already controlled by the CCP, but rather to stay in the 'kingdom of darkness', i.e. the areas controlled by the Kuomintang, in order to 'destroy' the 'darkness' there and develop 'light from darkness'. Ai used the example of 'light' and 'darkness' in advising the magazine's readers to continue the struggle against the Kuomintang in the areas it controlled and to do so notwithstanding the 'movement of class peace', whose goal was supposedly to unite all classes for the common struggle against Japan. This appeal was, moreover, directly in line with the United Front tactic of the 'dialecticians' that we have described in the preceding chapters. At the same time Ai warned of the sickness of 'left radicalism', which afflicts those who want to have the 'light' all at once, and are thus unwilling to enter tactical compromises with the Kuomintang to obtain long-term strategic goals. These two interpretations contain the word *chüeh-tui chu-i* ('absolutism').

After this, Ai turned to the word *hsiang-tui* – 'relative'. 'Relativism' (*hsiang-tui chu-i*) was for him not a 'children's disease' like 'left radicalism', but – one could almost have guessed as much – a 'sickness of old people',[8] who were not strong enough to 'struggle' against 'evil'. 'Relativism' was a type of 'poison', and those 'infected' with it no longer had a 'fighting spirit for pressing forward'. They were therefore all too ready to compromise with the forces of 'evil' or the 'darkness'. 'Therefore,' he concluded, 'the sickness of right deviationism stems partly from relativism,' and both 'absolutism' and 'relativism' were to be combated.

He then sketched his idea of what were the meanings of 'relative' and 'absolute', and how the relation between them was to be constituted: 'If we recognise the changing character of objects, then we must also recognise its relativity.' But everything that is 'relative' contains an 'absolute', and vice versa: thus the people's struggle against the Japanese was something relative, he said, since imperialism would one day be defeated.

Accordingly, the war against Japan was, in Ai's view, something relative. But what, then, was 'absolute' in this war of resistance?

We recognise that at the present time the common resistance struggle of the entire people is only a demand by the movement for the liberation of the people. Therein lies the 'relative' of the present time. However, we must also say that it is absolutely necessary [*chüeh-tui pi-yao-ti*] in the present period to use the war of resistance of the entire people to realise the movement for the liberation of the entire nation. There is absolutely no other way but this way at the present time . . . A relative object always contains something that is absolute as well. The absolute appears in every essential stage of the relative. That is the relation between relative and absolute.[9]

Accordingly, the struggle against Japan was the relative, and the 'movement for the liberation of the people' the absolute. Furthermore, Ai stressed emphatically – and this passage is underlined in the text – that the struggle against Japan was to serve as a means of obtaining the 'liberation of the people' – which meant, in reality, the United Front and war of resistance were the means whereby the Chinese people were to be liberated from Kuomintang control.

The relation between 'relative' and 'absolute', as Ai had described it and its effect on the role of the Sino-Japanese war in the Chinese revolution, was now valid for the question of 'relative' and 'absolute truth' as well: 'If we now speak of the relative and absolute truth and their relationships to each other, it also behaves in the same way.'[10] The truth develops and consolidates itself continuously, and the truth, as it is seen at a certain time, is of course 'relative'; but it is also 'absolute' in the sense that it is always in progress toward the absolute truth.

Since we have already treated the problem of 'truth' in connection with Ai Ssu-ch'i's 'theory of knowledge' (see above, pp. 84ff.), there is no need to do so again here. Still, with his assertion that 'relative' and 'absolute truth' act in the same way as does the war of resistance in the struggle between the CCP and the Kuomintang, Ai Ssu-ch'i merely provides further proof of our thesis that the purpose of the 'theory of knowledge' of 'dialectical materialism' in China was merely concerned with providing an analogy to the United Front tactic. This is important insofar as we will encounter the problem of 'truth' again, notably in treating Mao Tse-tung's 'On Practice'.

Yeh Ch'ing did not go into great detail on the question of the relationship between 'relative' and 'absolute'. In connection with the relationship between 'materialism' and 'idealism' alone he wrote: 'The contradiction between matter and consciousness is relative, but their unity absolute.' He thus placed unity above contradiction;[11] in other words, the unity of two parties was more important for him in the face of the Japanese threat than the contradictions between them.

We can weigh up Japan's role in relation to China's domestic situation more judiciously by examining Yeh's discussion of 'internal' and 'external causes' (*nei-yin, wai-yin*).

14. ON THE READING OF OLD BOOKS

The relation between 'internal' and 'external causes', 'internal' and 'external contradiction' is an important constituent of materialist dialectic, according to which there is a connection between 'internal' and 'external causes'; and their interrelation has to be considered in any study of the development of an object or a society. The 'internal causes' and contradictions are seen as primary, and the 'external' as being secondary and not decisive. The development of a society is basically determined by the inter-social laws, whereby external affairs can have either a beneficent or a retarding effect on internal ones and thus can only be converted into system-immanent processes.

The Chinese theoreticians treated the problem of causation only briefly, yet it was of vital importance for the CCP in discussing strategy, because its future relations with the Kuomintang were partly to be determined by their estimation of the 'external cause', namely the Japanese threat. The discussion of 'internal' and 'external causes' had already begun by September 1935, a few months after the Seventh World Congress of the Comintern, and was influenced by its decisions. It had already become clear at the Second World Congress of the Comintern in 1921 that the 'internal contradictions' in the colonial powers were to be set aside in favour of cooperation between Communist and bourgeois-national-revolutionary forces, with the aim of strengthening the national struggle in the colonies and thus reducing their profitability for the imperialist states. In this way it was hoped to intensify the endogenous contradictions in these states and consequently help to precipitate the now overdue revolutions in the metropolitan areas. This strategy implied the subordination of 'internal contradictions' in the colonies to the revolutionary aims in the metropolitan areas. Their development was thus no longer determined by themselves but by external factors. The Seventh World Congress of the Comintern drafted a similar strategy in the summer of 1935, albeit under different political conditions. Faced with the threat to the Soviet Union presented by Japan and Germany, the Communist movements were once again to cooperate with bourgeois forces and subordinate 'internal contradictions' in their respective countries to the goal of defending the Soviet Union (see also chapter II). The development of the 'internal contradictions' in the respective states was thus determined by this external strategy.

131

With respect to China, it seemed as if the Comintern's attempt to influence the development of the contradictions between the CCP and the Kuomintang was such a priority that 'internal contradictions' became of secondary importance and the 'external contradiction' – the relationship with Japan – threatened to predominate. It is not surprising, therefore, that only a few months after the Seventh World Congress of the Comintern in September 1935, discussion began on the relationship between 'internal' and 'external causes' and between 'internal' and 'external contradictions'. The discussion was structured in the same way as all those described above: it was 'philosophical-historical', and opened with an argument concerning the necessity of reading the Chinese classics. In his article, Yeh Ch'ing pursued the question of whether the study of the classics was indeed necessary in order to create a new culture.[1] The concept that a new culture develops from an old one according to a set of laws was not fundamentally false, Yeh wrote, but it was not correct for China. Chinese history had not developed in that way: 'it did not develop from a feudalist into a modern culture . . . China's present science, philosophy and literature have all come from abroad.'[2]

For Yeh all the changes that had occurred in China had been the result of foreign influence. China's history since the Opium War had been determined by the United States of America and by Europe. However, the general rule of dialectical materialism, whereby the developmental process of an object or of a society is primarily the consequence of its inherent contradictions, had not been suspended, it remained valid:

All states which are not subjected to external influences develop necessarily from their previous level into modern culture – that is the development of the contradictions of feudalist culture. There are some states in the world which have developed into modern cultures this way [. . .] and there are still feudal states, which still lie far behind them and then come under the influence of the advanced states as a result of commercial relationships and start to modernise. Therefore, history does indeed run according to the laws [of dialectical materialism], if one is talking about world history. However, the history of each state does not follow according to laws.[3]

The course of European history, in Yeh's view, had been in accordance with the rule whereby all development is based on internal contradictions. In this historical epoch, Europe had represented the entire world. On the other hand, since the Opium War, the Yang-Wu movement, the Hsin-hai revolution and the May 4th movement, China's development had been determined by 'external causes', which were merely the result of the 'internal contradictions' of European societies.

The dialectic tells us that in general there is always an exception . . . i.e. some states must necessarily develop on the basis of internal causes. If one fails to understand this point and mechanically applies the development of internal causes [e.g. to China], then one negates reality and advocates a subjective standpoint.[4]

As 'proof' Yeh cited a passage from the *Communist Manifesto* which describes how the bourgeoisie compels all nations to adopt its own mode of production and to import its own civilisation. Those nations had to become 'bourgeois' if they did not want to perish.[5] On the subject of Asian revolutions and their peculiarities, Yeh Ch'ing could have found support from Marx on another point. In connection with the Anglo-Chinese war of 1856–60, Marx wrote that revolutions in Europe were based on endogenous factors, whereas those in Asia were determined from without. For Marx, Asian revolutions were more a reaction to the challenge of Western imperialism, but the causal factors did not lie within the specific society but were imported into it from elsewhere.[6] Now, the 'external causes' which, in Yeh's view, had determined the development of China had already become for him 'internal causes'. In the course of their 'introduction at gunpoint' into China, Western science, philosophy and literature had been transformed into 'internal causes' for the further development of the country. According to Yeh, this, among other things, was revealed by the fact that those 'new philosophers' – the dialectical materialists Ai Ssu-ch'i, Ch'en Po-ta and their friends – would have to depend exclusively on Soviet literature. The 'new philosophy' in China had thus in no way originated from the particular culture of China but was merely a product of 'external causes'.[7]

From Yeh's statements one can infer he considered 'external causes' to be of far greater importance than 'internal' ones. He regarded the changes in China as being solely in reaction to the influences the country had been subjected to as a result of the endogenous contradictions in the industrial states. The consequence of such a point of view could only be that all 'internal contradictions' or 'causes' had to subordinate themselves to 'external' ones. At the beginning of his article Yeh argued that the study of the classics was not necessary for the creation of a new culture, since all developments in the country – including cultural ones – had been, and would continue to be caused by foreign influences. This point of view was related not so much to literature as to the question: which contradiction is more important, that between Japan and China or the one between the CCP and the Kuomintang? The discussion as to whether one should read the Chinese classics or foreign books had the same function as the debate on 'philosophy' and 'science', 'perceptual' and 'theoretical knowledge', and 'formal' and 'dialectical logic'. With his assertion that the cultural development of China was a result of foreign influences, Yeh had provided the answer: the contradiction between the two parties was to be subordinated to the contradiction in relation to Japan. This, of course, had left unanswered the question as to the causes of China's development, but those interested in this question who believe the Chinese theoreticians themselves were seriously concerned with it would be mistaken. This interpretation is by no means an exaggeration, as the articles by Ai Ssu-ch'i reveal:

In 'Should one read the Classics or Foreign Books?', published in September 1935,[8] Ai sharply criticised Yeh's advocacy of the reading of non-Chinese literature. Two further articles followed in January and March 1937, i.e. during the acute phase of the discussion over the United Front.[9] Ai attacked Yeh's assertion that the development of Chinese society was attributable to external causes and that the generally accepted rule of the primacy of 'internal causes' did not apply to China. Instead, he argued that one cannot make an exception in the case of China, and admitted that Chinese history had been strongly affected by foreign influences since the Opium War, but that this was only a part of the wider picture:

External forces have played a large role in modern Chinese history, and one cannot deny this fact. However, one cannot therefore say that the development of China is not based on any internal laws . . . To explain the problem of the development of Chinese society, one must take the internal contradiction of Chinese society as a basis, and investigate in which way the external forces have passed through the internal contradictions and obtained influence, and how the specific contradictions and their movements in China have originated under the influence of external forces. Of course, one must also consider the reality of the external forces, but one must not consider the internal forces as unimportant either. One must always take them as a basis and apply the dialectical theory of the unity of internal and external causes, in which the internal causes always form the basis. One cannot simply reject theories and rules based on the social sciences and fall back into the mechanical materialism of the seventeenth and eighteenth centuries.[10]

This passage, from the March 1937 article, corresponds in large part to the two preceding articles, but contains an important addition. Ai now criticised Yeh Ch'ing's thesis regarding the 'internal' and 'external causes' as a 'compromise' (*che-chung*), and accused him of assuming the same attitude to this as to the relationship between 'formal' and 'dialectical logic'.[11]

It is clear from the above that the discussion of the 'internal' and 'external causes' was merely a variation on the theme of the United Front, and that our interpretation of Yeh's statements on the reading of 'old books' is correct. Here the 'external causes' could refer only to Japanese imperialism. While Yeh Ch'ing advocated the view that Japanese imperialism, as an 'external cause', was to be rated more importantly than 'internal causes' (which could only have meant the contradictions between the two big parties), Ai insisted the 'internal causes' were the determining factor: Japanese imperialism was to be seen only as a function with regard to the 'internal causes'.

To this end Ai discussed the 'mechanical' and the 'dialectical, reciprocal function' (*hu-hsiang tso-yung*) of the two 'causes'. The 'mechanical, reciprocal function' was thus an 'equal-opposed' (*tui-teng*) cause, whereby neither of the two sides was to be placed above or below (*kao-hsia*) the other, since 'this type of reciprocal function represents the compromise theory of Yeh Ch'ing'.[12] Ai was thus firmly convinced that one should not play down the 'internal causes' because of Japanese aggression, according to the principle 'everything through the United Front'. Japanese imperialism was rather to have only one function in relation to the contradiction between the CCP and the Kuomintang: 'Only under this aspect,' he wrote, 'may one apply the theory of the unity of the internal and external causes.'[13]

15. QUANTITY AND QUALITY

Whichever area of the Chinese theoreticians' dialectical materialism one selects, the representation of the relationship between a pair of opposites within the 'unity' always has the purpose of elucidating political and military positions.

We turn now to the relationship between quantity and quality as the next example of this direct correspondence between the 'new philosophy' and the United Front tactic. In *Philosophy for the Masses* Ai had given an illustration of the law of the transformation of quantity to quality (*chih-liang hu-pien-lü*) that could easily be understood, and had characterised it – following the law of the unity of contradictions (*mao-tun t'ung-i lü*) – as the second law of the materialist dialectic. Here too he oriented himself by the Soviet discussions.

The Soviet dialectical materialists saw the essential content of the laws in the transformation of quantitative into qualitative changes, as had already been mentioned by Hegel. Subsequently, all developments moved along the line of a quantitative transformation. If they reached a certain point and then continued beyond it, the result would be a transformation or 'leap' into a new quality. In the view of the dialecticians, this process would hold true for matter and society as well as for consciousness. Examples of such 'leaps' as understood by this law are the transition from inorganic to organic matter, from perceptual knowledge to rational knowledge, and from capitalism to socialism.

In the Soviet Union, the 'philosophical condemnation' of 'left and right deviationists' was explained, among other things, by the fact that they had falsely applied the law of transformation from quantity to quality. They were biased in their consideration of problems in that they saw quantity and quality separately, in absolute terms, without seeing either the connection between the two, or indeed their unity. The error of the 'right deviationists' lay in their emphasis on the continuity of every development in a quantitative sense. Thus they denied 'qualitative leaps', whereas the 'left deviationists' envisioned all developments as taking place only in 'leaps'. The 'dialectical materialists', above all Mitin and Aizenberg, stressed the 'unity of quantity and quality'. This contained the quantitative development as well as the qualitative leap, which always had to have the character of violent revolution where social change was concerned.[1]

The background to the criticism of the 'right deviationists' was the struggle over Stalin's plans for the socialisation of agriculture and, concomitantly to that, the liquidation of the kulaks. The 'right deviationists' advocated the peaceful integration of the large farmers into socialism (which was tantamount to 'quantitative change'), being fearful that enforced collectivisation – the 'qualitative leap' – would harm agriculture. The transition from the period of Lenin's New Economic Policy (NEP) to the construction of socialism was, on the other hand, legitimised theoretically by the 'dialecticians' with the argument that during the NEP period 'quantitative development' had reached a level at which it assumed a revolutionary character and was now transformed by a 'qualitative leap' into socialism.

No extensive discussion of the law of the transformation of quantity to quality had taken place among the Chinese theoreticians, whereas in the Soviet Union the theoreticians had made efforts to 'prove' their respective positions on the basis of examples from the natural sciences. Here the discussion proceeded at a relatively high level, even if it eventually became totally drawn into day-to-day politics.

Ai Ssu-ch'i took the formulation of the law essentially from this discussion.[2] Then, in his work *Methodology of Thought* (October 1936), he linked it to the debate over the United Front. Here he first described the example, mentioned by Engels in his *Dialektik der Natur*, of water, when heated to 100°C, being transformed into a new 'quality' – steam. Through this he explained the various positions within the CCP on the United Front question:

Some people [a formulation used if there is a strong faction holding a different opinion]ido not understand the law of transformation from quantity to quality. They often only see the quantitative changes and overlook the qualitative ones, or they only see the quantitative changes and overlook the qualitative changes.[3] [This formulation is strongly reminiscent of Ai's statement on the relationship between 'syntheses' and 'analysis', cf. p. 92f. above].

The advocates of the first alternative consider every change only as a quantitative increase or decrease. They are 'reformists' because, applied to society, this argument implies it is not necessary to change the quality of society, but merely to carry out gradual changes within the framework of the old society. According to Ai, the 'reformists' were now faced with those who heeded only 'quality'. They insisted on the fact that water should turn into steam and does so before it has reached 100°C. Such people suffered from the by then well-known 'children's disease of left radicalism' (*tso-ch'ing yu-chih-ping*).[4]

'Quantity' and 'quality' are to each other as are 'analysis' and 'synthesis', 'subjective' and 'objective', or 'relative' and 'absolute'. Anyone who stresses the first and overlooks the second is always a 'right deviationist', and anyone who stresses the second and overlooks the first is a 'left deviationist'. Thus one can also replace 'quantity' with 'analysis' or 'subjective' and 'quality' with 'synthesis' and 'objective'. The terms are thus interchangeable and possess no value as evidence in themselves. In other words, it does not matter what 'quantity', 'analysis' or 'subjective' actually mean; all that matters is the mutual relationship in which two opposing terms are placed.

What does the correct application of the law of transition from 'quantity' or 'quality' now mean? If the preceding commentary is accepted, there can only be one answer. The advocates of 'quantitative change' were to be classed with the 'compromise faction', as has been described above, whereas the advocates of 'qualitative change' were opposed to the United Front and were not prepared to distance themselves from their radical ideas. Ai Ssu-ch'i, on the other hand, advocated that the United Front should serve as a device to begin the slow 'cooking' of social conditions – to stick to the metaphor of heating the water – until they were eventually tender enough for the transition into a 'new quality', namely the 'negation' of the Kuomintang.

16. THE 'LAW OF CONTRADICTION'

In the preceding chapters we have already become familiar with a number of contradictions, for example between 'philosophy' and 'science', 'materialism' and 'idealism', 'empiricism' and 'rationalism', 'formal' and 'dialectical logic'. The core of the materialistic dialectic is the 'law of contradiction' or the 'law of the unity of opposites', which supposedly infiltrates all areas of matter, society and thought, and is valid always and without exception. Because it is possible to apply this law analogously, this encourages the tendency to reduce the explanation of a process, like that of an object, to the demonstration of supposed or real inherent contradictions within that process, thereby obviating the need for an empirical examination, because the law is infallible from the beginning. Since it can be applied to any random object, its exemplification by an author through example X also allows conclusions to be formed about his attitudes towards object Y as well; and since the relations between the two sides of a contradiction must always be the same, it does not matter what object is under scrutiny. Hence the objects, concepts and processes under scrutiny become interchangeable, and allow the possibility of using the 'law of contradiction' as a means of discussing explosive political questions without, in regard to the specific point at issue, calling a spade a spade. Consequently Ch'en Po-ta's example of the table which fell apart in the strange contradiction between the table top and the table legs was interpreted by T'an Fu-chih as an analogous statement regarding the United Front (a false one, in his view); for the 'law of contradiction' is valid for the table as for politics.

One can therefore explain everything by the principle of contradiction, without having to know anything about an object; one understands the world, without having grasped it. Analogous thinking permits as many variations as there are objects or processes in the universe, of which there is no shortage. Thus Ch'en Po-ta could just as well have written about a table or a fountain-pen, a pencil or the relations between men and women; the contradiction is concealed in everything, it is the 'driving force' of every development – whatever this 'force' may be –, and the question is merely how the relations between the two sides of a contradiction develop within a certain period, whether they are harmonious, with the stress on unity, or whether in the form of a (marital) quarrel.

Since this type of thought has been the basis of all the texts we have studied, it is no exaggeration to maintain that their authors were concerned not with maximising objective knowledge but rather with the propagation of their subjective and political interests. This runs contrary to European philosophy and science and makes it impossible for us to regard dialectical materialism in China as a philosophy or even as a science.

The 'law of contradiction' contains no ontological or epistemological evidence; instead, the structure of internal party struggles is carried over – projected – into all areas of being. It makes, according to Topitsch, a more or less 'sociomorphic' world picture emerge, from which the course of history is determined without consideration of formal-logical, discursive thought. The legitimative aspect of the 'law of contradiction' is just as obvious here as the belief in the general validity of this 'law': belief and legitimation flow together. For outsiders they form a unity, difficult to grasp, which determines political activity.

Ai Ssu-ch'i had already considered briefly the 'law of contradiction' in *Philosophy for the Masses*,[1] stressing especially the 'absolute' character of contradiction in all things from the beginning to the end. In two further works, the *Ssu-hsiang fang-fa lun* (Methodology of Thought) and the *Che-hsüeh hsüan-chi* (Selected Philosophical Works), he expressed himself more fully and explained the 'law' within the framework of the 'four basic aspects of the materialistic dialectic'.

1. All things pass through the phases of origin, development and decay.

2. The movement of objects is 'absolute' (*chüeh-tui*), but repose is 'relative' (*hsaing-tui*).

In connection with the latter, Ai argued as follows:

When we see things which seemingly have no movement and do not change, but rather are at rest, how do we explain it? This *compromising point of view* [*che-chung k'an-fa* – Ai's own emphasis] is not the real truth . . . We do not want to deny that there is also a relative repose. Every development of an object is also a periodic development. Thus a human being passes through the periods of childhood, adulthood, old age and so on. In each period there is relative rest, but one must pay attention to the fact that it is relative and not absolute. We must see through the external appearance of relative rest, that it is basically in movement.[2]

No one questions Ai's assertion that human beings experience childhood in the course of their lives, become adults and, in most cases, grow old; but what has the 'compromising point of view' to do with the periods of human life? This term suggests instead that Ai, with his statement on the general validity of the principle of movement as exemplified in human development, had his eye on a particular period: namely that of the United Front. This, he wanted to say, has the appearance of a period of rest but is in fact the truce between the two parties and thus only 'relative', while the movement, and consequently the struggle, on the other hand, are 'absolute'. 'Absolute' rest means 'compromise' with the enemy.

What, in Ai's view, was the cause of the movement which pervades all processes and objects in the universe? The cause, he wrote, lies within the objects themselves: 'It is the contradiction within the interior of the objects. If there were no contradiction, then there would be no movement.'[3] Of course, external factors must not be omitted. For example, imperialism influenced the internal development of China, but it could never be the determining factor. All changes are due to internal conditions, not to external influences, with the result that internal contradictions are the driving force behind every change and development in the universe. If one recognises only mechanical movement, and influence through external forces, then one negates the independent movement of objects.

Relations between the CCP and the Kuomintang – and that is what Ai wanted to express – should in no way be allowed to put a stop to the contradictions, bringing about an 'absolute calm'; rather, in the United Front period, 'relative calm' should predominate; the movement, and thus the struggle between the two parties, must continue, since movement was 'absolute'. Ai insisted the war against Japan should never lead to a situation whereby the contradictions between the parties would be suspended and subordinated to it, as the Comintern had wished. This was the political essence of the statement, which he subsequently formulated as follows: 'The unity of contradictions [*mao-tun t'ung-i*] is the most fundamental law of the dialectic. This law reads: the law of the unity of contradiction.'[4] Without anticipating our discussion of Mao's 'On Contradiction', one can establish that the 'law of contradiction', supposedly formulated by Mao at the beginning of the work in 1937, appeared for the first time in October 1936 in Ai Ssu-ch'i's *Methodology of Thought* as an analogy to a certain strategy towards the United Front.

Ai now explained precisely the way in which he wanted the law to be understood: 'Some people misunderstand the law of the unity of contradictions. They see the two sides as equal [*t'ung-teng k'an-tai* – the same characters will later on used by Mao] or lay too much stress on the aspect of negation.' Instead, both sides must be considered differently (*fen-pieh k'an-tai*). The elements of affirmation (*k'en-ting*) and negation (*fou-ting*) must not be seen as equal, nor must the negation be exaggerated. 'This is the greatest misunderstanding of dialectical logic.'[5] It was clear, as we have seen above, that 'some people' had already completely misunderstood the relation between 'perceptual' and 'theoretical knowledge', 'subjective' and 'objective', 'analysis' and 'synthesis', 'absolute' and 'relative'. It was a matter of misunderstanding the 'dialectic' of the correct tactic for the United Front. 'Some people' referred to nobody except the advocates of the 'Wang Ming Line' and the 'left deviationists'.

Thus the 'four basic aspects of the materialistic dialectic', and especially the 'law of contradiction', were Ai Ssu-ch'i's representation of his idea of the United Front, in which he criticised the Comintern's strategy. As he had elaborated at the beginning of his work *Methodology of Thought*, the representation of dialectical materialism was to help in the correction of 'false thought' within the party regarding 'opinions about the United Front' (see above, p. 87). He had thereby described the true function of dialectical materialism; it was not a philosophy, but an instrument of inner-party struggle.

Ai's *Methodology of Thought* appeared in October 1936; so if one assumes he needed several months to formulate his arguments, one can conclude that the struggle within the party must have begun before its publication. The earliest possible date for it to have begun was January 1936, when *Philosophy for the Masses* appeared, in which Ai had continued to advocate that, for example, the solution of the 'contradiction' between 'formal' and 'dialectical logic' had to lie in the absolute rejection of the former (a statement which corresponded to the relationship between the CCP and the Kuomintang at the time). The question of renewed cooperation with the Kuomintang, and the emerging problem of which organisation was to have the leading role within the United Front, had possibly already led to discussions in the early summer of 1936, probably in connection with Wang Ming's argument, officially advocated from May 1936, that the Kuomintang must be drawn into the United Front. And there is no doubt that Ai spoke for a faction within the party which wanted to make clear to the Comintern that it was ready to cooperate with the Kuomintang only with the expectation of the latter's eventual destruction, and not with the goal of a reciprocal and long-term reconciliation.

The second book in which Ai Ssu-ch'i dealt at length with the 'law of contradiction' appeared in 1939, namely his *Che-hsüeh hsüan-chi* (Selected Philosophical Works).[6] These *Works* were important for two reasons. First, they contained Russian writings on dialectical materialism, including Chinese translations of excerpts from Mitin, Sirokov and Aizenberg.[7] On the basis of this translation it is easy to detect how heavily the Chinese theoreticians relied on Russian models, to the extent that one can hardly speak of independence either of thought or formulation. Secondly, Ai Ssu-ch'i had included his own 'Research Theses' (*yen-chiu t'i-kang*) on 'dialectical materialism' as an appendix to the translations.[8] These he regarded as being a total systematic representation of the 'new philosophy'.[9]

It is not necessary to quote extensively from the 'Research Theses' here, since most of them are to be found in Ai's works, already analysed above. So we will cite only those passages which either contain a new argument or allow one that has already been considered to emerge even more clearly.

The 'Research Theses' are divided into six sections: philosophy and politics; materialism and idealism; dialectical materialism; the theory of knowledge of dialectical materialism; the basic laws of materialistic dialectic, and all categories of materialistic dialectic. As in *Methodology of Thought*, in Ai Ssu-ch'i's 'Research Theses' he made a direct equation between the political struggle and the struggle against false thought. Here it was not so much the Kuomintang on which Ai focussed – even Yeh Ch'ing was mentioned only once – but rather 'left radicalism', 'right opportunism' and those 'philosophical' currents within the party related to them – 'subjectivism' and 'Mechanism'. In general, the ideas, embodied in short, numbered 'theses', repeated what was already known. But in the second chapter, 'Materialism and Idealism', Ai enumerated the 'aberrations' of human thought, obviously with the intention of giving the reader a framework for judging exactly where the friends and foes of the Chinese people stood, both inside and outside the party.

'Mechanistic materialism' was once again pre-eminent, with its well-known penchant for 'right opportunism', followed by 'subjective idealism' (*chu-kuan wei-hsin lun*), that form of an 'acute illness' (*chi-hsing ping*) of the consciousness, the symptom of which was an inability to wait for the right moment to make the 'qualitative leap' into the next level of social development – having previously overestimated one's own strength and so been impatient to reach that next level immediately.[10]

There were 'right opportunists' and 'Mechanists' opposed to each other not only within the party, but also inside the enemy's camp. Among the latter were the anarchist, Wu Chih-hui and the future collaborator Wang Ching-wei, whom Ai Ssu-ch'i assigned to the pro-Japanese wing of the Kuomintang. They were considered 'Mechanists' because they acted on the principle that every development was only determined by 'external forces' (i.e. Japan), one's own forces being of no importance.[11] The meaning of the terms 'right opportunism' and 'Mechanism' respectively was thus extended to designate those in the CCP who, because of the war against Japan, were ready to compromise with the Kuomintang, as well as those in the Kuomintang who, because of the war against the CCP, tended towards compromise with Japan. The assertion by 'Mechanism' that an external force was the cause of every movement, and that the cause therefore did not lie within the objects themselves, characterised an attitude of subservience towards an enemy, regardless of whatever enemy it happened to be.

The same was true of 'subjective idealism'. The philosophical concepts of the denial of the possibility of objective knowledge and the overemphasis of subjective perception had its political equivalent in 'subjective, blind activism', which had to be combated. The term 'subjective idealism' embraced, among other things, the empiriomonism of Mach and the philosophy of Hu Shih and Ting Wen-chiang. This strange concoction reveals itself in the extent of Ai's ignorance of Western philosophy and of the philosophy of Hu Shih and Ting Wen-chiang, who had made an effort to spread the pragmatism of Dewey and the empiricism of Pearson as forms of scientific thought in China.[12] Along with 'subjective idealism', which was to be found in the party as well as in society, there was also 'objective idealism', which could not be found in the party. Ai named Chang Tung-sun as its propounder, but the teachings of Sun Yat-sen also come under this heading.[13]

Ai ascribed a special meaning to the term 'dualism'. Previously there had been only two philosophical directions, 'materialism' and 'idealism', but recently a third type of philosophy, 'dualism' (*erh-yüan lun*), had emerged: 'Dualism is the compromise faction, which swings back and forth between materialism and idealism. The solution of dualism for basic philosophical problems is: spirit and matter are objects of the same type, which co-exist in a parallel (or peaceful) manner [*p'ing-hsing ping-ts'un*]. Together, the two form the real origin of the world.[14] According to Ai, the tendency of dualism to compromise was manifested in seeing everything as 'equal' (*p'ing-teng k'an tai*) when one was seeking to find out which of two objects is heavier and which is lighter.[15] Ai saw the cause of this first in the dual character of the 'reactionary classes', but 'dualistic thoughts' would also develop within the revolutionary forces![16] A materialism that was not sufficiently radical could end up following the path of idealism, and it would then assume a standpoint of compromise (*t'uo-hsieh li-ch'ang*). Ai embedded his criticism of the tendency of the compromise fraction towards peaceful co-existence with the Kuomintang in a long philosophical-historical description. As has already been seen with regard to Yeh Ch'ing, European philosophy once more had to serve as justification for certain tactics towards the political and military enemy, and yet again Ai repeated the summary of the history of Western philosophy as perceived by Mitin and other Soviet theoreticians: thus the greatest 'dualist' was still Kant because of his theory of knowledge. From him the path led to neo-Kantianism, in the second half of the nineteenth century, and then to revisionism, to Kautsky and Plekhanov, whose philosophy contained elements of Kant.[17]

Just as unambiguous as the statements about 'dualism' were Ai's comments on the question of how was one to study Marxism in China: 'If one wants to study Marxism and its philosophy in China, one must take the practical tasks of the proletariat as a basis . . . One must combat the disregard of the concrete conditions in China, which makes the mistake of applying Marxism as an empty formula.' The foreign influence on the development of Chinese Marxism was very great, but 'Chinese Marxism must in no case rely upon what has been imported from abroad! . . . It is not enough, when one is studying and resolving problems, to bring in and apply foreign results.'[18] This was a sharp denunciation of the 'internationalists' in the CCP, of the Wang Ming faction. Ai's comment, that one must not rely on Marxism imported from abroad – by which he doubtless meant the Soviet Union – was not without a certain irony, given the extent to which he had patterned himself on Soviet works and used them as an 'empty formula'. The rejection of foreign influence thus referred less to Marxism as a theory than to the Comintern's United Front tactics.

In part III, chapter 5, of his 'Research Theses' Ai discusses the 'law of unity of opposites' (*tui-li t'ung-i fa-tse*). After several statements on the relation between 'quantity' and 'quality' and the principle of movement in matter, he then went on to 'identity and the struggle of opposites'. The opposites within an object or a process existed in fundamental unity with each other, and were identical in three respects:

1. Reciprocal dependence, i.e. the existence of one thing depends upon the simultaneous existence of its opposing aspect, otherwise it must also perish, as, for example, the capitalists and the workers, and the strategy of protracted war [*ch'ih-chiu chan-lüeh*] being dependent on many battles of quick decisions [*su-k'uai ti tou-cheng*]. However, the necessity of reciprocal dependence is based on 2. The relationships of reciprocal penetration, i.e. an object contains or brings forth the effect opposed to itself. If, for example, the capitalist develops, there arises simultaneously the effect that the proletariat develops. The battles of quick decisions cause, as an effect, the protracted war. The Japanese aggression against China resulted in the awakening of China . . . Consequently opposed objects can, under certain conditions, . . . 3. pass into one another or change into each other reciprocally. In other words, the same object, which plays one role under certain conditions, becomes a completely different object, playing a completely opposite role. The effect of the long protracted war through battles of quick decisions was only possible under the conditions of a universal war of resistance. If it should only be a partly and independently led war of resistance, then it could not last long. Defence and retreat did not mean attack. However, under the conditions of mobile warfare and a clever strategy, a defensive retreat could become an attack on the enemy. That is the so-called 'retreat in order to go forward' [*i-t'ui wei chin*].[19]

Ai Ssu-ch'i's example, taken from military strategy, makes clear the great extent to which the theory of contradiction, supposedly valid for all areas of matter, society and thought, was an exact application of the basic strategical principles of Chinese Communist guerilla strategy laid down by Mao in his military writings, especially in chapter V ('The Strategic Defence') of his work *Problems of Strategy in China's Revolutionary War* of 1936, which dealt mainly with the errors of the Comintern line regarding conventional warfare in the civil war. Ai used the same characters for 'protracted war' (*ch'ih-chiu chan-lüeh*), 'battle of quick decisions' (*su-k'uai chan*) and so on as Mao. His statements were a clear defence of the guerilla strategy *vis-à-vis* conventional strategy, with the help of the 'dialectic'. The struggles over these different strategies within the CCP have been dealt with above.

Just how much the representation of the principle 'identity and struggle' had to do with intra-party infighting and with the relationship to the Kuomintang, emerges from the description of the principle of 'struggle', which Ai treated in connection with identity. Struggle expresses itself in reciprocal suppression: an object must suppress its opposite in order to preserve its own existence; consequently every type of unity was a form of struggle. Struggle and identity means the unity of opposites. Struggle caused the division of unified objects, but unity has the effect that struggle assumes a certain form within the unity.

On the one hand, we must pay attention to how the struggle of opposites causes division in an object, and, on the other, to how, under certain conditions, opposing objects become a unified object . . . Without a certain struggle there is no identity; one might say 'He who does not fight does not know himself.' If there is no definite identity, there is also no struggle.[20]

For Ai, therefore, the struggle is 'absolute', whereas identity is 'relative', 'conditional' and 'temporary'. Proceeding from this thought, he went on to criticise 'right opportunism':

Identity or unity do not mean equilibrium [chün-heng] as well. Equilibrium means a condition in which two opposing forces balance themselves reciprocally. In this connection there is no reciprocal dependence of opposites, no reciprocal penetration and no transformation of one into the other . . . The supporters of dialectical materialism must therefore place a special value on the development of one side and not pay attention to how small the one side is. If one believes in the theory of equilibrium, then self-confidence in regard to the aspect of development will not develop; rather right opportunism will do so.[21]

Mention of Bukharin's 'theory of equilibrium', which was described in the first part of the study, could hardly have been included for philosophical reasons, but in view of all that Ai Ssu-ch'i had already written, it could only have referred to the relations between the two parties in the United Front and especially to the faction which propagated peaceful conciliation with the Kuomintang.

What, according to Ai, did the generality of contradiction consist of? All objects, he wrote, existed as a unity of opposites, and that was the generality of contradiction. Elsewhere we find: 'The generality of contradiction not only expresses itself in all objects, but also in the existence of contradiction in the developmental process of one and the same object from the beginning to the end.'[22] In the same paragraph Ai also considered the relation between difference and contradiction: 'Seen from the outside, there are different objects. However, a profound understanding reveals that all differences are contradictions . . . For example, if, during the war of resistance, the opinions of each group are different, they are still in reality the reflection of deep social contradictions.[27] One could not – and this was what Ai wanted to express – reduce the relationship between the CCP and the Kuomintang to a single issue on which they differed and thus remove every point of contention, but they were in contradiction, and would so remain, within the United Front. That this is not a misinterpretation is revealed by Mao, who took the following position regarding the question of difference: 'Proceeding from this standpoint, in the analysis of concrete problems Deborin's school came to the conclusion that under Soviet conditions there were no contradictions, but only differences between the kulaks and the mass of the farmers and thus agreed with the viewpoint of Bukharin.'[24] Deborin's school 'did not grasp that in every difference which exists in the world, a contradiction is contained already, and that difference is simply contradiction'.[25]

In the struggles between Bukharin and Stalin the treatment of the kulaks was the crucial issue on which they differed. Whether or not one understood the relationship between two opposing aspects of an object, and no matter which one, as a difference or a contradiction, could be of great importance for social development, the example of the kulaks and Bukharin showed just how explosive an issue could be concealed behind such a seemingly unimportant statement: all differences are contradictions. Stalin had decided in favour of 'contradiction' instead of 'difference' between the two opposing aspects of an object, a decision to which the kulaks and Bukharin were to fall victim.

Part IV. 'ON PRACTICE' AND 'ON CONTRADICTION'

17. CRITICAL QUESTIONS ON SOURCES

At the beginning of this book we pointed out that a large part of the existing literature on the theoretical basis of Mao Tse-tung's ideology was confined, in its subject-matter, almost exclusively to his works. We hope at this point to have made it clear that most of what one finds in Mao's philosophical works had already been thought out in advance by others, among whom Ai Ssu-ch'i was the most important in regard to the 'new philosophy'. Others such as Ch'en Po-ta, Hu Sheng and Ch'en Chih-yüan had also written on aspects of dialectical materialism, but had not attempted to present a systematic representation.[1] Yeh Ch'ing, who was understandably more interested in a conciliation of contradictions than in the contradiction itself, had not devoted a special chapter or even an article to it but merely demonstrated a systematic unification of all contradictions. An exception is Mao, to whom two basic lectures on dialectical materialism, from 1937, are attributed by official Chinese sources: 'On Practice' and 'On Contradiction'.

Because original versions of these lectures have hitherto been unavailable, it has to be questioned whether they can be used at all to analyse the development of dialectical materialism in the period treated here, and especially for 1937. But because it is clearly ascertainable that the two works referred to the United Front, and because of the importance attached to them in Chinese Communist and Western sources, it therefore seems necessary to deal with them here. Since the analysis has to be based on considerably altered versions of the original works, our conclusions must be treated with great caution, at least until the day the original versions from 1937 are published.

Before analysing Mao's texts, it seems appropriate to present a short summary of the present state of research concerning their origins, and to add some of our own findings. However, our primary concern is not to list once again all the known details of the origin of Mao Tse-tung's 'On Practice' and 'On Contradiction', for this has been comprehensively done by Wittfogel, Takeuchi Minoru, Schram, Lippert and, in recent studies, by Knight and Fogel.[2] Moreover, the subject is worthy of detailed study, since an increasing number of new Chinese sources have provided new openings for research.

There are several versions of the two works by Mao Tse-tung: the official one, from 1950/1952, which was included in the *Selected Works*, and the others, from 1946, which were discovered by Takeuchi Minoru. 'On Practice' appeared as a sub-section of the second chapter of *Dialectical Materialism (Lecture Outlines)*, published in 1938 and 1937 respectively, of which Mao is supposed to have been the author. 'On Contradiction' appeared in the first part of the third chapter of these *Lecture Outlines*.[3] It is possible, though by no means certain, that the versions dating from 1946 and thereabouts are largely identical to the probable original which appeared in 1937, or differ from it only slightly. A linguistic analysis of these two sections and a comparison with the versions in the *Selected Works* has been made by Knight. On the basis of his analysis it has been established that the 1946 version of 'On Practice' was incorporated in the *Selected Works* in a more or less unchanged form, whereas 'On Contradiction' was considerably altered.[4]

No less a figure than the Deputy Director of the Research Centre on Party Literature under the CC, Kung Yü-chih, seems to confirm this point. In an article he mentions a mimeographed edition of *Dialectical Materialism (Lecture Outlines)* from September 1937, which, he claims, contains 'On Practice' and 'On Contradiction' and is the source of all the following reprints.[5] Furthermore, Kung says, the 1937 edition of 'On Praxis' has been included in the *Selected Works* with only minimal changes, whereas 'On Contradiction' was much altered, thus supporting Knight's analysis. Besides some conjunctions such as '*yü*' and '*ho*', and several proverbs, Kung presents three passages from 'On Practice' where the texts differ in content. They are of no importance with regard to political questions, but Kung admits that several sentences have been omitted because they were not clear enough.[6]

Thus for the first time we have semi-official confirmation of what Takeuchi Minoru, Schram, Wittfogel and others have always maintained: namely that Mao was not only the author of 'On Practice' and 'On Contradiction' but also of all the lectures that were included in the course *Dialectical Materialism*. However, this confirmation has not yet completely solved the question of authenticity, since on the one hand the edition mentioned by Kung has no author at all, and on the other, when asked by Edgar Snow in 1965 about his authorship of *Dialectical Materialism*, Mao denied being the author. Moreover, when the interview was reprinted, this denial was reinforced, probably, as Snow supposes, at the request of the Chinese authorities or Mao himself.[7]

We now turn to the question of Mao's authorship of *Dialectical Materialism (Lecture Outlines)*, to which 'On Practice' and 'On Contradiction' belong. According to Kung, there exists a mimeographed edition entitled *Pien-cheng fa wei-wu lun (Chiang-shou t'i-kang)*, printed in September 1937, which does not mention Mao's name. This edition supposedly contains a sub-section to chapter 2 that Kung calls 'On Practice', and a further sub-section to chapter 3 that he calls 'On Contradiction'. It is not clear from Kung's text whether the sections are entitled 'On Practice' and 'On Contradiction', or whether they correspond only to the later versions, or whether they have no other titles. All that he tells us is that 'On Practice' is the last section of chapter 2, and 'On Contradiction' the first section of the third chapter.[8]

The next edition Kung mentions is a serial published by the War of Resistance University (*K'ang-chan ta-hsüeh*) from April to June 1938, probably the same edition which Schram was given by Bernadette Li. Here we find the first reference to Mao as a 'principal lecturer' (*Mao Tse-tung chu-chiang*) but still not as author. From several Chinese sources we learn that 'principal lecturer' and 'author' are not one and the same. The first implies that during a course several lecturers teach a subject, though one of them delivers the majority of the lectures. Furthermore, the term 'principal lecturer' does not necessarily imply that that person himself writes the lectures – they can also be drawn up by somebody else, the lecturer's task being to deliver the texts to the audience.

Therefore we can establish that it seems certain that the publisher of the *K'ang-chan ta-hsüeh* reprint in 1938 did not consider Mao Tse-tung to be the author of the whole of *Dialectical Materialism* course, but only a 'principal lecturer'. If we assume that Mao gave his lectures in 1937, it is possible, but cannot be proved, that he himself had written them, since he was only 'principal lecturer' and this is confirmed only for 1938.

We do not know how many lectures Mao gave as '*chu-chiang*', and who else besides him delivered other lectures, which were then collected in the September 1937 edition of *Dialectical Materialism*. Perhaps the other lectures were compiled by Mao alone. On this point we have to defend him, since his denial of his authorship has simply been brushed aside.[9]

It seems likely that Mao was speaking the truth, since as a 'principal lecturer' (*chu-chiang*) he could not declare that he was the *author* of all the lectures. Furthermore, Snow asked him about the 1940 edition, published in Shanghai, which contained only the first chapter of *Dialectical Materialism*. Schram suggests that Mao perhaps did not want to admit his authorship because in the first chapter of *Dialectical Materialism* he had largely plagiarised Soviet sources. It is true that large parts of this chapter were lifted from Soviet sources sentence by sentence, as Wittfogel has shown, and it is also true that the plagiarism in the second chapter of *Dialectical Materialism* was even more evident, as Schram maintains, but this does not necessarily imply that this was all done by Mao, although several Chinese authors now ascribe all the lectures to Mao as well.[10]

It is most probable that Mao was lecturing in July and August 1937 on 'On Practice' and 'On Contradiction', the two important sections of *Dialectical Materialism*. With regard to 'On Practice', as we know, this is confirmed by Chang Ju-hsin in his articles in the *Liberation Daily* of February 18 and 19, 1942; and regarding 'On Contradiction', we have a hint by Wittfogel that the head of Japanese military intelligence in Shanghai in September 1937 knew of a speech by Mao on contradiction made shortly before in Yenan.[11] As matters stand we can proceed from the assumption that *Dialectical Materialism* was either entirely or only partly drawn up by Mao. I personally subscribe to the latter possibility.

In March 1940 the Shanghai magazine *Min-chu* (Democracy) published the first chapter of *Dialectical Materialism*, wherein Mao is credited as author for the first time. The other two chapters were apparently not published. The next reference occurs in a book published by the Eighth Route Army in Yenan in 1940. It is also entitled *Dialectical Materialism* and, according to Kung, is a reprint of the mimeographed version of the 'Lecture Outlines' from 1937, but, surprisingly, Mao is not mentioned as author. If Mao was the author, it is hard to believe that his name was omitted by the publishing department of the Eighth Route Army. Then in 1942 Chang Ju-hsin referred to this edition when he pointed out the importance of 'On Practice' in studying the political theories of Mao. Moreover, in 1941 and 1942 two further reprints seem to have been produced, one by the National Defence Publishing House of the Political Department of the Hopei Fourth Army, the other by the Hsin-hua publishing house branch in the Chin-Ch'a-Chi region, both of which name Mao as the author. It seemed as if those who supported Mao's authorship were gaining the upper hand, but for the post-war period Kung lists the following reprints: March 1946 by Chung-kuo ch'u-pan she in Shanghai, based on a so-called *mou-pao-she* edition from September 1944; and, furthermore, the reprints by Chang-yüan yin-shua chü and

Ta-lien ta-chung ch'u-pan she. They too bear no date, but also seem to have been printed shortly after the war. In the Ta-lien edition Mao is not listed as author, but he is in the Chang-yüan edition. The same holds true to the *'ch'iu-yin she-pan'* reprints by Chung-kuo ch'u-pan she in Shanghai: according to Kung, some of them include Mao's name on the front and some do not.[12]

However, to bring the pieces of the puzzle together again, from Kung's article we know there exists a mimeographed edition from September 1937 in which there is no evidence of Mao's authorship. Then in the 1938 edition Mao is listed as 'principal lecturer' (*chu-chiang*). Till 1940 he was already credited as author in some reprints, but in relatively important editions, such as the one by the Eighth Route Army, he was not even made '*chu-chiang*'. And what is really puzzling is the fact that after the war, in several identical reprints by the same publisher, Mao's name sometimes appeared on the cover and sometimes did not. Above all, his 'Lecture Outlines' did not appear in the rectification documents and were never mentioned in other sources before 1950 (with the exception of Chang Ju-hsin's article). Neither can they be found in a list compiled by Ai Ssu-ch'i in 1939 containing important books and articles for the study of dialectical materialism.[13] Then, in 1950, 1951 and 1952 Mao's authorship is suddenly officially established in the *Selected Works*, but only for the two revised lectures 'On Practice' and 'On Contradiction', while the whole edition, in which these two lectures were included, was not even mentioned. Finally, the question of Mao's authorship of *Dialectical Materialism* culminates in the suspected author's denial of his presumable authorship.

Because of this eventful publication history, which is undeniably full of contradictions, it is perhaps admissible to include *Dialectical Materialism* in the works of Mao, though not without certain reservations. In this context Schram has argued that the whole text of the work was reprinted in a collected edition by the Philosophy Department of the Peita (Peking University).[14] But even this edition, as official as it may appear to be, together with the statements by several Chinese authors since 1979 (why not earlier?) regarding Mao's authorship, do not outweigh the principal statement by Mao that he was not the sole author of *Dialectical Materialism*. Moreover, it is possible that the editors – as well as Kung and Kuo Hua-jo – did not know of Mao's interview with Snow.

Another interpretation, subscribed to by Takeuchi Minorul as well as by Fogel, is that perhaps Mao had simply collected together some writings which had been presented to him by others, and then signed the 1938 edition 'Mao Tse-tung chu-chiang'. This could be one possible explanation since Kuo Hua-jo, quoting from Mao, describes how Mao had only 'three days and four nights' to prepare for his lectures, a very short time to work on such a long treatise.[15] Perhaps we have to define anew the term 'author': '*chu-chiang* (principal lecturer) seems to be more suitable. To reach a final decision on this question we will have to wait for the day when Mao's handwritten drafts of his lectures are published.

Since the philological approach with regard to the question of authenticity has proved unsatisfactory, we need to introduce further evidence for consideration: first, the materials on philosophy and dialectical materialism that Mao had at his disposal in 1936–7, and second, his relations with Ai Ssu-ch'i. If we examine all three aspects together we may perhaps gain an impression as to the significance of Mao's contribution to the emergence of dialectical materialism in the 1930s.

In terms of the works Mao was reading in Yenan, we now have a detailed list prepared by Hsin Chung, which reveals that Mao studied more than ten books on Marxism. The most important one, from which he took many notes, was *Pien-cheng wei-wu lun chiao-ch'eng* (Course of Instruction in Dialectical Materialism) by Hsi-lo-k'e-fu and Ai-sen-pao (Sirokov and Aizenberg), translated by Li Ta. According to Hsin Chung as well as Kung, Mao had the third and fourth editions (June 1935, and December 1936,) published by *pi-k-eng-t'ang*. In both editions Mao made a lot of notes, writing with his brush in red, black and blue ink around 13,000 characters in the margin and filling up every blank, drawing many circles and lines all over the book. He started reading it in November 1936 and finished the book in April 1937. The longest remark he added was to the third chapter of the work ('Basic Rules of Dialectical Materialism'-'*pien-cheng fa ti ken-pen fa-tse*'), about a thousand characters long. In these comments Mao summarised the essential points of the original texts in a 'pithy style', and the characters were reportedly all written in very pretty calligraphy containing remarks like 'this example is very good', 'sounds very correct', 'that's true', 'most reasonable idea', 'this example is not clear', 'this argument is wrong' and so on.[16]

According to Hsin Chung, the remarks contained many of Mao's ideas on contemporary political problems and the strategic questions of the war of resistance, together with discussions on dialectical materialism. Although Hsin Chung maintains that Mao had read several works by the classical Greek philosophers, by Spinoza, Kant, Goethe,

Hegel and others (of which we have no confirmation), he emphasises that the most important books – besides Sirokov's – were the following: Li Ta's *'She-hui hsüeh ta-kang'* (Outline of the Social Sciences), which appeared in May 1937 in Shanghai, and was sent by Li Ta to Mao, who recommended it as a textbook to the K'ang-Ta – though not before annotating it heavily; Mitin's *Dialectical and Historical Materialism* (which, according to Hsin Chung, was translated by Shen Chih-yüan, although the present author believes this to be incorrect and that it was translated by Ai Ssu'ch'i and Ch'eng I-li), published in Chinese in December 1936, again with many remarks added by Mao; and *Che-hsüeh hsüan-chi* (Selected Philosophical Writings) by Ai Ssu-ch'i, which appeared in 1939. The next book Hsin Chung mentions which profoundly influenced Mao was *Ssu-hsiang fang-fa lun* (Methodology of Thought), also by Ai Ssu-ch'i, published in October 1936. Mao probably read the January 1937 edition, from which he extracted passages (*chai-ch'u*) about 3,000 characters long. Furthermore, Hsin Chung mentions several books which were of less importance.[17] From other sources we learn that Mao had read Ai's *Talks on Philosophy*[18] and Engels' *Anti-Dühring (Fan Tu-lin lun)*.[19]

From Hsin Chung's list one soon learns that Mao's study materials were mainly translations from Soviet texts and manuals by Ai Ssu-ch'i, Li Ta and others, and that he was adopting the philosophical ideas they contained in regard to political and strategical questions related to the war of resistance. Therefore, we can conclude that Mao, who had to prepare his lectures in only four days, had a very limited number of books at his disposal, which, above all, were of little philosophical value.

We now turn to the relationship between Ai Ssu-ch'i and Mao, a question to which Ignatius Ts'ao and Fogel, in particular, have contributed.[20] As we mentioned above, 'On Dialectical Materialism', as well as 'On Practice' and 'On Contradiction', relies extensively on the works of Ai Ssu-ch'i. Wittfogel, Takeuchi Minoru, Schram and Lippert have comprehensively analysed, on the basis of extensive extracts, the correspondence between Mao's 'Lecture Outlines' and the 'Research Theses' and other of Ai's texts in regard to both content and, to some extent, language. In particular, Takeuchi Minoru has compared Mao's 'On Contradiction' with Ai's 'Research Theses', thus showing that some passages by Mao are more or less identical to those by Ai. There would be little point in repeating all these instances of plagiarism in detail, so we will give only one example.

The sub-headings of the chapters in Ai's 'Research Theses' regarding

the 'law of unity of contradiction' correspond closely to those in Mao
Tse-tung's 1952 edition of 'On Contradiction' and the 1937 edition to
that of 1946. In Ai, the sub-headings of the individual sections read as
follows: 'The Universality of Contradictions' (*mao-tun ti p'u-pien hsing*),
'The Particularity of Contradiction' (*mao-tung ti t'e-shu hsing*), 'The Basic
Contradiction and the Leading Contradiction' (*chi-pen mao-tun he chu-tao
ti mao-tun*), and 'The Basic Aspect and the Leading Aspect of
Contradiction' (*mao-tun ti chi-pen fang-mien he chu-tao ti fang-mien*). As
regards construction, there is a great similarity between the two works.
The corresponding chapter headings in Mao Tse-tung follow almost the
same sequence as in Ai and, except for a few characters, are identical.
Thus chapters 2 and 3 in Mao are 'The Generality of Contradiction'
(*mao-tun ti p'u-pien hsing*) and 'The Peculiarity of Contradiction' (*mao-
tung ti t'e-shu hsing*). Chapter 4 in 'On Contradiction' is entitled 'The
Principal Contradiction and the Principal Aspect of Contradiction',
while in Ai Ssu-ch'i one finds two headings which are very similar,
namely 'The Basic Contradiction and the Leading Contradiction' and
'The Basic Aspect and the Leading Aspect of Contradiction'. Instead of
the characters '*chi-pen*' (basic) and '*chu-tao*' (leading), one finds in Mao
the character '*chu-yao*' (principal). In the respective texts as well, there
are no substantial differences. There is only one disparity in the sequence
of headings, in the section 'Identity and the Struggle of Opposites'.
While this appears in Mao as chapter 5, in Ai Ssu-ch'i it occurs at the
beginning. In 'On Contradiction', the heading is 'The Identity and
Struggle of the Aspect of a Contradiction' and in Ai 'The Meaning of
Identity and Struggle' (*t'ung-i hsing he tou-cheng hsing ti i-i*). Of course the
similarity between the two headings says nothing about the resemblance
of the contents; a glance at the texts reveals clear similarities in both style
and content as well.[21]

Further confirmation of the links between Mao's and Ai's writing has
been provided by the Chinese themselves. However, they refer to it
discreetly, making a virtue of necessity, when they write: 'Learn from
Chairman Mao's spirit how to study seriously without feeling ashamed
to ask and learn from one's subordinates.'[22] Ai Ssu-ch'i's 'Philosophy
and Life' was a work which Mao was deeply impressed by, as he
confessed in a letter to Ai in which he sent him the extracts he had taken
from the work.[23] What is interesting in the context of this study is that a
perusal of Mao's remarks and the extracts he took from Ai's book show
clearly that he followed Ai's line regarding Yeh Ch'ing's statements on
'formal and dialectical logic', 'relative and absolute', 'internal and

external cause', 'analysis and synthesis', and so on. All these dialectical concepts, which we have analysed above (Part III, especially chapters 12–15) as symbolic correspondences or analogies, were condemmned by Mao in line with Ai as a 'theory of compromise' (*che-chung chu-i*).[24]

The dating of Mao's extracts – September 1937 – provides further evidence that the political content of Ai's philosophical writings formed the basis of Mao's 'Lectures'; but most interesting is the philosophical poverty of these extracts. They confirm that in September 1937 – i.e. one month after his two lectures 'On Practice' and 'On Contradiction'! – Mao was still familiarising himself with the basic terms and ideas of dialectical materialism and remained unsure about using them. Probably for that reason, in his letter to Ai, which is dated 1938 (no month is given), he asked him to correct the extracts he had drawn from 'Philosophy and Life' in case they were wrong.[25]

While the official versions in the *Selected Works* reveal Mao's dependence upon Ai Ssu-ch'i, as Takeuchi Minoru has shown,[26] his plagiarism becomes even more noticeable in the 1946 version of 'On Contradiction', which does not bear that title but rather 'The Law of Unity of Contradictions' (*mao-tun t'ung-i fa-tse*), a formulation which appears frequently in Ai Ssu-ch'i.

The 1946 version contains a section which was completely omitted from the 1952 revision, for reasons we will deal with below; it bears the title 'The Law of Identity in Formal Logic and the Law of Contradiction in Dialectics'. Reading over these versions it can be established that Mao must have used Ai Ssu-ch'i's texts as models in writing these passages, especially Ai's articles on 'formal' and 'dialectical logic', which we have already analysed. We know that the authors – Kung Yü-chih, Hsin Chung, Wang Jo-shui and Kuo Hua-jo – must have had access to the original works Mao was reading in Yenan, and perhaps to the original manuscripts of 1937. Hsin Chung gives us a vivid and detailed description on Mao's habit of annotating the books he read using red, black and blue ink, circles and lines and so on. Moreover, he even provides us with the number of characters Mao had written in these texts, but despite all these details – by which he indirectly admits that he had the originals in his hand – his quotations are not from the original versions of 'On Practice' and 'On Contradiction' but from the *Selected Works* only.

In view of the foregoing it is undoubtedly possible that two sets of lectures on questions regarding practice and contradiction existed by 1937. There is reason to believe that in 1937 Mao lifted large passages from the aforementioned books, especially from the 'Course of Introduction into Dialectical Materialism' and the works of Ai Ssu-ch'i, put them together with the extracts which, according to Hsin Chung, he had taken from the same books, and added several remarks of his own, thus linking the text with the current political situation. Since large parts of the 'Lecture Outlines' consist of plagiarised passages and extracts, Mao was right to deny that he was the author: he only compiled these writings in order to have teaching materials for his lectures.

Furthermore, on the question of the authenticity of these texts one should not forget that leading politicians always tend to have one or even several ghostwriters, whose work they then paraphrase and, if need be, alter at will. In the struggles against his opponents, mainly those who were schooled in Moscow, Mao had to establish his reputation as a Marxist philosopher, and in doing so he used the writings of Ai. The question as to whether Mao was the author of 'On Practice' and 'On Contradiction', or whether he had only compiled and paraphrased passages from Soviet manuals and texts by Ai Ssu-ch'i (the view which this author subscribes to), is important, of course, but secondary. What really matters is that all the statements attributed to him should be judged according to the same criteria as those applied to the works of the other theoreticians. Apparently, Mao, employing Ai's concepts, spoke about philosophy and epistemology (and it is quite obvious that he believed he was doing so), but in all his philosophical speculations the inner-party struggle over the United Front was his primary concern. Thus if both works were given as lectures or written in 1937, their content should be seen mainly in relation to their political function at that time.

In 1969 Takeuchi Minoru first mentioned that Mao used the term 'contradiction' in 1937 mainly to elaborate his United Front tactic. And several Chinese authors too, now confirm that the adoption of Soviet sources was largely the result of the political struggles with the Kuomintang as well as those within the CCP. To talk about philosophy meant nothing less than keeping politics in mind. Describing Mao's first attempts to master Marxist philosophy, Kung informs us that Mao wrote 'On Practice' and 'On Contradiction' exclusively in order to summarise the revolutionary experiences, and that this was the essential point.[27] Furthermore, in talking about the importance of Mao's two articles, Lin Jen-tung points out that during the first and second revolutionary war the party committed many errors, the most notable offenders being Ch'en Tu-hsiu and Wang Ming. Wang Ming in particular paid no attention to the national conditions of China, he says, and 'lost contact with the concrete praxis of the Chinese revolution'. Because of these errors, according to Lin, Mao wrote his article 'On Practice'.[28]

Yü Lin, in his article 'On Emancipating the Mind, Correcting "Left" Deviation Error and Adhering to Four Basic Principles', emphasises that at the Ts'un-i Conference Mao corrected the false military line; and because of the successful combination of theory and practice in his thought, Mao 'at the beginning of the war of resistance criticised and overcame Wang Ming's right deviation errors "all through the united front", and "everything must be subordinated to the united front" [. . . *tsai k'ang-chan ch'u-ch'i yu p'i-p'an ho k'o-fu-le Wang Ming ti "i-ch'ieh ching-kuo t'ung-i chan-hsien", "i-ch'ieh fu-ts'ung t'ung-i chan-hsien" ti yu ti lu-hsien ts'o-wu*].'[29]

Similar statements are found in an article by Shao Hua-tse, who describes the dialectical materialism of Mao also as a means of overcoming the dogmatism of Wang Ming and his support in the Comintern ('*Che i-ko che-hsüeh ssu-hsiang, shih fan-tui tang-shih kung-ch'an kuo-chi so chih-ch'ih ti Wang Ming ti chiao-t'iao chu-i*') and of developing the synthesis of Marxism-Leninism and the national conditions of China in contradiction to the Comintern, as well as 'the important philosophical foundations: maintain independence and keep the initiative, and regeneration through one's own effort [*tu-li tzu-chu tzu-li keng-sheng ti chung-yao che-hsüeh i-ch'u*].'[30] Here, the basic patterns of Mao's United Front strategy – *tu-li tzu-chu and tzu-li keng-sheng* – are described as 'the important philosophical foundations' of his dialectic. The same argument can also be found in an article by Wang Jo-shui. Dealing with Mao's contribution to the dialectic he stresses the function of 'Mao-tun lun' in the debates about left and right deviation in the 1930s and especially with respect to the United Front. In this context he offers a very important quotation from Mao:

Mao Tse-tung put forward: 'The present politics of the anti-Japanese United Front, neither is it all unity in which struggle is denied [*i-ch'ieh lien-ho fou-jen tou-cheng*], nor is it all struggle in which unity is denied [*i-ch'ieh tou-cheng fou-jen lien-ho*], but it is a politics which synthesises both aspects of unity and struggle [*tsung-ho lien-ho tou-cheng*].'[31]

First, we have here the direct correspondence between the 'law of the unity of opposites' – or 'dialectical law of contradiction' – respectively, and Mao's United Front strategy, but second, according to Wang, this quotation is derived from an article (or whatever it may be) by Mao entitled 'On Politics' ('*Lun cheng-ts'e*), which has never, as far as I know, been published. If such an article exists, then it must have been written in the period before 1942, probably in 1937 or 1938, since in the following sentence Wang says, with respect to the 'law of the unity of opposites', that Mao used this same 'method of rectification applied again in Yenan' ('*Yen-an cheng-feng so-ts'ai-yung ti fang-fa*') in 1942.[32] Here the 'law of the unity of opposites', the supposedly universal law of nature laid down by Mao in 1937 on the basis of Ai's earlier writings, is clearly classified as a 'method of rectifying' false political thought, as an instrument for the inner-party struggle.

If an article or a chapter by Mao entitled 'On Politics' ('*Lun cheng-ts'e*) really does exist, it most probably deals with the United Front tactic. Perhaps it was never published because it contained concrete instructions on how, in the face of Japanese aggression, to deal with the Kuomintang in the United Front.

18. 'ON PRACTICE'

According to the editor of the *Selected Works*, 'On Practice' was to have been delivered as a lecture in July 1937 at the Anti-Japanese Military Political Academy in Yenan, as was 'On Contradiction' (or 'The Law of Unity of Contradictions') in August of that year. The general political frame of reference in which the lectures were given can be inferred from their dates and the fact that it all took place in Yenan.

We should recall that on July 7, 1937, Japanese troops launched a surprise attack close to the Marco Polo Bridge in Peking, and thus initiated the invasion of China proper. Faced with the rapid Japanese advance, there followed intensive negotiations between the CCP and the Kuomintang over the manner of their future cooperation. As early as August 1937, the national government had announced the renaming and integration of the Red Army into the Chinese National Army as the Eighth Route Army. Thus Mao's two lectures were delivered at a decisive phase of the Chinese civil war, characterised by the onset of the Sino-Japanese war and the simultaneous emergence of cooperation between the CCP and Kuomintang. The two lectures are only to be understood in this connection: 'On Practice' and 'On Contradiction' are representations of Mao's United Front tactic, dressed up in the symbolic language of dialectical materialism. The editors of the *Selected Works* pointed this out themselves in an annotation to 'On Practice':

'On Practice' was written in order to expose the subjectivist errors of dogmatism and empiricism in the party, and especially the error of dogmatism, from the standpoint of the Marxist theory of knowledge. It was called 'On Practice' because its emphasis was on exposing the dogmatist kind of subjectivism, which belittles practice.[33]

Accordingly 'On Practice' was to be a work on the Marxist theory of knowledge. But, as we have already seen, Ai Ssu-ch'i had also been concerned with correcting 'false thinking' within the CCP. He had recommended the use of his '*Ssu-hsiang fang-fa-lun*' (Methodology of Thought) as a basis for the evaluation of opinions within the party on the United Front (cf. p. 87 above), and in his works the characters for 'practice' (*shih-chien*) had a concrete military connotation: namely the continuation of the struggle against the Kuomintang within the United Front. The analogous counterpart to this was the 'negation' of 'perceptual' by 'theoretical knowledge'. Furthermore, 'practice' meant the mobilisation of the 'will to resist of the masses' for the military defeat of the enemy, and was thus opposed to the 'Wang Ming line', which advocated peaceful cooperation between the two parties and emphasised conventional warfare in terms of strategy. Moreover, Ai Ssu-ch'i's ideas on the United Front were paralleled in the relationship between 'matter' and 'consciousness'. He equated the 'counter-reaction of the consciousness to matter' in the 'process of knowledge' with the struggle of one's own forces against an enemy with military superiority, whereas in the mechanistic form of the process of knowledge, the pure reflection of the environment without the 'subjective activity' of the person who perceives, was analogous to the strategy of the Comintern – to show restraint towards one's opponent and to compromise. Lastly, the decisive importance of 'practice' in the 'process of knowledge' was analogous to the 'leading role' of the 'proletariat' and its party in the 'present period of social development', that is the United Front.

On the basis of this interpretation of the characters for 'practice' in the works of Ai Ssu-ch'i, and the fact that Mao's lectures are based largely on Ai's texts analysed here, one can conclude that Mao's statements regarding the 'theory of knowledge' were constructed in the same way, with military-strategic goals being projected into the 'theory of knowledge'. The Military Academy was the most suitable place and July–August 1937 the most suitable time: Mao explained to the military cadres the United Front line in opposition to the Comintern, and legitimised it in the form of the 'Marxist theory of knowledge'. That this has nothing to do with epistemology needs no repetition.

Since the structure of the 'process of knowledge' elaborated by Mao corresponds essentially to the relationship between 'perceptual' and 'theoretical knowledge' described by Ai Ssu-ch'i, we will attempt to analyse here only the political references. In one part of his work, Mao stressed two arguments: the importance of the class struggle for human cognition and the dominant role of 'practice' in the 'process of knowledge'. Under the guise of social practice, he said, 'class struggle in particular, in all its various forms, exerts a profound influence on the development of man's knowledge.' The stress on social 'practice' and, especially in this connection, the class struggle appears often in the work.[34] With regard to 'knowledge', class struggle was paramount. If, as Mao maintained, the class struggle was above all 'social practice', and that 'practice' was in turn the basis of 'knowledge', then this could only have meant, in view of the 'movement for class peace' during the United

Front period, that he did not think highly of this movement and favoured instead the continuation of the class struggle within the United Front. Correspondingly, he also expressed his dissatisfaction with all theories that rejected the importance of 'practice', and thus the class struggle, and cut off 'knowledge' from 'practice'. This could only have meant the 'theories of knowledge' in the CCP, which advocated suspension of the class struggle while the United Front existed remained in being.

Like Ai Ssu-ch'i, Mao described the 'process of knowledge' (analogous to his United Front tactic) as a progression from 'perceptual knowledge' (*kan-hsing jen-shih*) to 'theoretical knowledge' (*li-hsing jen-shih*). After the 'period' (*chieh-tuan* – also 'level') of 'perceptual knowledge', there occurred a 'sudden change' (*t'u-pien*) in the human brain regarding the process of 'knowledge', as the result of which 'concepts' emerged. According to Mao, the difference between 'concepts' and 'perceptions' was not only 'quantitative' but also 'qualitative'.[35] With this 'quality leap' the second 'period' (or 'level') of 'theoretical knowledge' was reached. In this connection Mao mentioned an 'observation group', whose members had come from outside Yenan seeking information. This reference gives us a hint of the exact meaning of the 'qualitative leap' in the process of 'knowledge': 'When the members of the observation group have collected various data, and, what is more, have "thought them over", they are able to arrive at the judgement that "the Communist Party's policy of the National United Front against Japan is thorough, sincere and genuine". . . . "The National United Front against Japan can succeed." '[36]

It had to be made clear to every opponent of the United Front that Mao was accusing them of stopping at 'perceptual knowledge' and of having failed to take the 'qualitative leap' to 'theoretical knowledge' regarding the necessity for a United Front and thus of being an 'empiricist'. He then reaffirmed his position. Without bothering to begin a new paragraph, he added his thoughts directly to the last quote by describing the total process of 'knowledge':

The real task of knowing is, through perception, to arrive at thought, to arrive step by step at the comprehension of the internal contradictions of objective things, of their laws and of the internal relations between one process and another – that is, to arrive at logical knowledge.'[37]

Both 'periods' (or stages) of the process of 'knowledge' represented a unity (*t'ung-i*), in which 'theoretical knowledge' would not dispense with 'perceptual knowledge' and vice versa. According to Mao, 'empiricism' in particular made the mistake of stopping at 'perceptual knowledge'. For him the dialectical theory of 'knowledge' consisted rather of the progress from the 'perceptual' to the 'theoretical' stage of 'knowledge'. Whoever did not do this was for Mao a 'vulgar "practical man"', an 'empiricist' and a 'left phrase-monger', of which he wrote that such people:

respect experience but despise theory, and therefore cannot have a comprehensive view of an entire objective process, lack clear direction and long-range perspective, and are complacent over occasional successes and glimpses of the truth. If such persons direct a revolution, they will lead it up a blind alley.[38]

The question we must ask ourselves is: which blind alley? As we ask this, we become aware of the first target of Mao's writings. Apart from their general characteristics, exactly what did this political lapse consist of? According to Mao, the 'process of knowledge', like every process, 'whether in the realm of nature, or of society, progresses and develops by reason of its internal contradiction and struggle, and the movement of human knowledge should also progress and develop along with it.'[39] The only conclusion to be drawn from this is that the Chinese revolution itself cannot be halted as a social process, but, on the basis of internal contradictions, progresses, like 'knowledge', from the 'perceptual' to the 'theoretical' stage (chieh-tuan). Therefore, the error of the 'left deviationists' consisted in not wanting to participate in the step to the next phase of the Chinese revolution, the 'new period' (hsin chieh-tuan), as Mao had described it in another work.[40] They remained immobile in the 'period' (chieh-tuan), of 'perceptual knowledge' instead of progressing to the new 'period' or stage of 'theoretical knowledge'. They did not grasp that cognition always follows the 'objective process' and that the unity between the CCP and the Kuomintang was just as necessary as the unity of 'perceptual' and 'theoretical knowledge'.

But for Mao the most important aspect of this unity, whether concerned with the 'process of knowledge' or the United Front, was 'practice', the 'active function of knowledge', which is expressed particularly 'not only in the active leap from perceptual to rational or theoretical knowledge', but – and this is the essential point – it must manifest itself in the leap from rational knowledge to revolutionary 'practice', namely in the 'revolutionary class struggle', in the 'practice of production' and in 'scientific experiments'.[41]

At this point it is worth reminding ourselves of Ai Ssu-ch'i's views on the matter. For him, 'active knowledge' corresponded to the 'mobilisation of the will of the masses to resist', whereby 'perceptual knowledge' was negated by 'theoretical knowledge' – which corresponded to the negation of the Kuomintang by the CCP in the United Front. Whosoever was not prepared to take the step from 'theoretical' back to 'perceptual knowledge' (that is 'revolutionary practice') acted, according to both Ai as well as Mao, like a (materialistic) 'rationalist', a 'mechanist' and thus like a 'right opportunist'. While this person might advocate the 'unity of the two forms of knowledge' (as well as the necessity of cooperation between the two parties in the United Front), he would still have failed to see that the process of 'knowledge' – and thus the Chinese revolution – could not stop but must continue in this unity through 'practice', through the renewed negation of 'perceptual knowledge' by 'theoretical knowledge' in the form of revolutionary praxis.

This was the distinguishing mark of the second, and by far the most dangerous group in the party: the 'right opportunists' or 'mechanistic materialists'. Theirs was the error of renouncing 'active knowledge' in the 'process of knowledge' and of accepting 'knowledge' as merely a pure reflection of the 'objective environment' in the 'consciousness'. As Ai Ssu-ch'i had stated, this constituted a 'compromising' attitude towards the enemy. The correspondence between the stages of knowledge and of revolution is quite evident in the following passage by Mao from 1937/1946 (interestingly, in the 1952 version the first sentence is omitted): 'The Chinese Ch'en Tu-hsiu-[ism] from 1927 and the Bukharinism in the Soviet Union both belong to that kind of Right opportunism. These people fail to see that the struggle of opposites has already pushed the objective process forward while their knowledge has stopped at the old stage.'[42]

Thus, according to Mao, the thought of the 'left deviationists' as well as that of the 'right opportunists' is detached from 'practice'. The former forgot the 'qualitative leap' to 'theoretical knowledge', and wanted to leap over the period of the United Front, while the latter did not want to make the leap back from 'theoretical knowledge' to 'perceptual knowledge' by 'revolutionary practice', and thus were against the continuation of the struggle within the United Front. 'Practice' in Mao Tse-tung's sense meant, as with Ai Ssu-ch'i, the continuation and not the suspension of the struggle within the United Front – as the 'left deviationists' feared and as the 'right deviationists' demanded.

The following passage from Mao seems to reveal a further, almost cosmological legitimation of and connection between the United Front and the 'theory of knowledge':

Marxists recognise that in the absolute and general process of the development of the universe, the development of each particular process is relative, and that hence in the endless flow of absolute truth, man's knowledge of a particular process at any given stage is only relative truth. The sum total of innumerable relative truths constitutes absolute truth. The development of an objective process is full of contradictions and struggles, and so is the development of the movement of human knowledge.[43]

Here, Mao apparently lost himself in cosmological speculation and thus gave his United Front strategy an almost cosmic consecration. It now appeared as the application of a universal principle, administering the total and absolute developmental process of the universe. It has always been a characteristic of political and military leaders to legitimise their concrete decisions, as well as their general claim to power, by referring to universal principles.

But what did this universal principle have to do with the aforementioned 'right opportunists' and 'left deviationists'? As has been shown above, Ai Ssu-ch'i linked concrete ideas regarding the United Front and the role of Japanese aggression in the Chinese revolution with the characters for 'relative' (*hsiang-tui*) and 'absolute' (*chüeh-tui*): the United Front and the struggle against Japan were 'relative', while the struggle against the Kuomintang was 'absolute'. From the example of this mythical epistemology, Mao's listeners were to grasp the fact that an 'individual, concrete process' like the United Front was merely 'relative' and by no means without contradictions and struggles; rather it was but one of many stages on the path to final victory, just as 'absolute truth' was to be the sum of all 'relative truths'.

Who, in Mao's view, was the bearer of this type of 'knowledge'? 'In the present epoch of the development of society,' he said, 'the responsibility of correctly knowing and changing the world has been placed by history upon the shoulders of the proletariat and its party.'[44] At first sight, this sentence seems to contain nothing that merits serious consideration; but one should read it very carefully: as we know, the 'present epoch of social development' concerns the period of the United Front. In this period 'knowledge' was to be an affair of the proletariat and its party, the CCP, and under no circumstances an affair of the bourgeoisie and its party, the Kuomintang. Since the 'process of knowledge' always followed the 'objective process', the two could thus be placed in an analogous relationship with each other, which can only mean that the CCP and not the Kuomintang was to assume the leadership of the United Front.

19. 'ON CONTRADICTION'

As mentioned above, a comparison of the 1952 version of 'On Contradiction' with texts by Ai Ssu-ch'i, especially the *Research Theses*, reveals great similarities. Now, the study of the 1946 edition confirms once more that Mao must have relied heavily on Ai Ssu-ch'i, especially in those passages that were dropped and not reinstated in the 1952 revision. These include 'The Law of Identity in Formal Logic and the Law of Contradiction in Dialectics' and a section omitted from what is part V of the 1952 edition. They deal with the paraphrasing of passages from Ai Ssu-ch'i's works *Methodology of Thought, Formal Logic and Dialectic* and *Selected Philosophical Works*.[45]

Mao's statements on 'formal' and 'dialectical logic' basically correspond to the descriptions in Ai Ssu-ch'i which we analysed above on pp. 100–11. Ai and all the other theoreticians had used the three laws of 'formal logic' as symbols to distinguish 'right opportunists' and 'left deviationists'. In connection with the law of 'unity of contradictions' (*mao-tun t'ung-i*), Mao now made several statements which confirm unreservedly our comments on his United Front tactics in Part II of this study:

The Chinese proletariat and bourgeoisie have agreed upon an anti-Japanese United Front; this is one aspect of the contradiction. The proletariat must raise its political consciousness and pay close attention to the bourgeoisie's political vacillations, and its corrupting and destructive effect on the Communist Party, in order to guarantee the independence of party and class; this is the other aspect of the contradiction. A United Front of the various political parties with independence for those parties, are the two aspects of the contradiction constituting the present political movement. *There would be no United Front if one of these two aspects, the party's right to determine its own policies, was removed* [author's emphasis].[46]

The correct application of the law of 'unity of contradictions' means, contrary to the three laws of 'formal logic', that the independence of the CCP within the United Front would be guaranteed. This, according to Mao, was only possible if the party retained its independence, and thus had the right to formulate its policy itself and not to let it be determined by either the Kuomintang or by Moscow.

The next point refers to the question of 'leadership' in 'unity', namely which aspect of the contradiction assumes the leading role. Moreover, with regard to this question, there are several paragraphs in the version from the period about 1946, one of which is most surprising:

In China, the antagonistic situation existing internally between the feudal forces and the broad masses of the people is also changing. The people will rely on revolutionary struggle to transform themselves into the leading and dominant force . . . In the relationship in China between the proletariat and the bourgeoisie, because the bourgeoisie has retained the means of production and sovereignty, to the present it still occupies the leading position. However, in terms of leadership of the anti-imperialist, anti-feudal revolution, the proletariat occupies the leading position because of its level of consciousness and revolutionary thoroughness as compared to the vacillation of the bourgeoisie. This point will influence the future of the revolution in China. Only if the proletariat allies itself with the peasantry and the petty bourgeoisie will it be able politically and materially to occupy the leading position. If it can do this, the proletariat will assume the decisive leading function of the revolution.[47]

In this passage the leadership of the CCP in the United Front is stressed repeatedly and with a clarity that leaves no doubt that Mao was unwilling to accept the 'Wang Ming line'. The 'law of contradiction' served here as a 'philosophical' proof of his tactic whereby, in every object in the universe, the two aspects of a contradiction are supposedly transformed into each other and merge, after which a final 'exchange of roles' takes place – that is the 'dominating' become the 'dominated', the 'led' become the 'leaders' and so on. The real surprise, however, is Mao's observation that the situation in China is 'antagonistic': there is no 'considering both aspects as equal' – (t'ung-teng k'an-tai). The contradiction between China and Japan was certainly 'fundamental' (chu-yao), given Japanese aggression, while that between the CCP and the Kuomintang was of secondary importance (tz'u-yao), but only for the present (chan-shih), he added.[48] This obviously did not change anything as far as the 'antagonism' of the contradictions between both parties was concerned.

The Comintern attempt, because of the Japanese threat, to place 'unity' against Japan in the position of the 'contradiction', met with a particularly sharp 'philosophically' legitimised rejection from Mao. After several general statements, obviously taken from Ai Ssu-ch'i's Methodology of Thought, on the contradiction between life and death, which always exist as a unity in every organism and become transformed into one another, whereby the living cells change into dead ones and vice versa, Mao stated: 'from start to finish, the incompatibility of life and death, their mutual rejection, struggle, negation and transformation are unconditional, eternal and absolute.'[49] And analogous to the contradiction in the human body is the contradiction between the proletariat and the bourgeoisie in the United Front, since, 'the United Front between the classes is relative, but the struggle between them is absolute.' . . . Under given conditions the two classes, the proletariat and bourgeoisie, also change from one to another, such that the exploiters change into the exploited and the exploited change into the exploiters, and capitalist society is transformed into a socialist society. The two contradictory entities have an identity under given conditions. This is one problem. The two sides are in a constant struggle. There is struggle within an entity and especially the struggle of revolution. This *unavoidable condition is unconditional, absolute and inevitable*. . . According to this conclusion it is perfectly evident whether or not the so-called theories of class harmony [*chieh-chi t'iao-ho lun*] and the unity of ideology [*ssu-hsiang t'ung-i lun*] still have any standing . . . China too has a so-called theory of class harmony, but this is a tune sung by bourgeoisie reformism. It has no other purpose than specifically to swindle the proletariat so that it will remain forever the slave of the bourgeoisie.'[50]

Like Ai Ssu-ch'i, Mao also mentioned Bukharin's 'theory of equilibrium' (*p'ing-chün lun*), although the passages do not admit of a direct connection with the 'right opportunists' in the CCP. However, viewed from a wider perspective, this connection is certainly admissible when one reads: 'Bukharin has reduced the contradiction to the point of elimination, while Trotskyites have elevated contradiction into antagonism; neither of the two extremes of the right or left wing understand the problem of contradiction.'[51]

If the passages cited here from the 1946 version were indeed part of the lecture given by Mao in August 1937 to military cadres at the Anti-Japanese Military Political Academy, the following conclusions can be drawn.

– Mao characterised as antagonistic the CCP's relationship to a section of the Kuomintang (not the section representing the petty bourgeoisie) at the very moment the United Front was established. Through the example of the 'Law of Contradiction', he condemned harmony between the classes and declared that the struggle against the Kuomintang was 'unavoidable' and 'absolute'.

– The aim of this struggle was to gain the leadership of the United Front and for Kuomintang control to be replaced by CCP control.

– Mao's statements were thus clearly opposed to the Comintern line.

'On Practice' and 'The Law of Unity of Contradictions' were polemics against the China policy of the Comintern and its supporters in China. With the aid of the dialectical materialism adopted from the Soviet Union, Mao Tse-tung, as the first chairman of a Communist Party (the next one was Tito) which was a member of the International, legitimised the CCP's claim to independence from Moscow and its right to 'determine its own policies'. This was the essence of Mao Tse-tung's contribution to dialectical materialism in 1937.

Finally, we now turn to the peculiarities in connection with the editing of 'On Contradiction' in 1952. We will attempt to explain why 'The Law of Identity in Formal Logic and the Law of Contradiction in Dialectics' was dropped from the March 1952 edition and not replaced, or at least indicate where an explanation may be found.

'On Practice' was published in October 1951 in the first volume of the first edition of the *Selected Works of Mao Tse-tung*. Nine months earlier, in December 1950, the work had appeared in the Peking *People's Daily*. According to the chronology, 'On Contradiction' should have followed directly after 'On Practice', but in fact it is at the end of the second volume of the *Selected Works*, which appeared in March 1952. No reprint in book form followed, although it was reprinted in the *People's Daily* in April 1952. The publishers themselves alluded to this point in the second volume and explained that 'On Contradiction' would be placed in the chronologically correct position in the first volume when the second edition of the *Selected Works* came to be published. This curious situation prompts the question: just what could have moved the publishers to abandon an advance printing and not to include the work in the first volume? Their note that the author, Mao Tse-tung, had made several 'additions, abridgments and improvements' for the inclusion of the work in the *Selected Works* can mean one of two things. Either the changes took longer than planned, so that neither an advance printing nor inclusion in the first volume at the proper time was possible, or political developments may have caused the author to cancel the planned publication in the first volume as well as an advance printing, enabling him to revise the work having taken these developments into account. The second alternative is more probable. Regarding the whole outline of 'On Contradiction', it seems incomprehensible that 'The Law of Identity in Formal Logic and the Law of Contradiction in the Dialectic' should have fallen victim to abridgments unless the decision had been politically motivated.

The relationship between 'formal' and 'dialectic logic' had played a central role in the 'philosophical' struggles in 1936–7, and Ai Ssu-ch'i had adopted the contemporary official condemnation of 'formal logic' by the Soviet theoreticians. However, as we have seen (p. 101), the fate of 'formal logic' in the Soviet Union had taken a surprising turn after its official 'rehabilitation' in 1946! The ensuing discussion among Soviet philosophers reached its peak when the magazine *Voprosy Filosofii* intervened in the struggle in February 1950. That discussion lasted till June 1951 when an editorial in the magazine brought it to an end.[52]

In his 1950 'linguistic letters' Stalin began an extensive undermining of the revolutionary components of dialectical materialism in favour of evolutionary ones by renouncing those ideas aiming at violent transformation. As part of the debate *Voprosy Filosofii* made a surprising observation on 'formal logic':

1. Logic is not a part of the superstructure, and therefore it possesses no class character, but belongs to all classes and nations.

2. Formal and dialectical logic both have their own legitimacy.

3. The logical structure of thought and its laws constantly change and develop, but they do so only gradually, like language, and without an 'explosion'.

4. 'Formal logic' is the science of elementary laws and forms of correct thought.[53]

We can hardly assume that the publishers of the *Selected Works of Mao Tse-tung* had no knowledge of the debate in the Soviet Union and of the *Voprosy Filosofii* editorial. If the editorial is compared with statements made by Ai Ssu-ch'i in 1936–7 and by Mao in 1937, one can imagine the difficulties, resulting from contemporary conditions, which the publishers would have experienced over the editing of the first volume and the textual alterations to 'On Contradiction'. It was a fact that only three months separated the editorial in *Voprosy Filosofii* and the publication of the first volume; moreover, a Russian edition was planned for 1952.

True to the ideas of Mitin in the 1930s Ai Ssu-chi'i, and subsequently Mao, had stressed the class character of 'formal logic'. It was by no means the 'science of the elementary laws and forms of correct thought'; rather it was 'bourgeois' and 'metaphysical' and its laws were simply false. It was its fate to be 'sucked up' and finally 'destroyed' by the universally superior 'dialectical logic'.[54] According to the 1946 edition Mao wrote the following: 'We have discussed above the metaphysical and dialectical views of development. The struggle between these two ways of looking at the world constitutes the struggle in methods of thought between formal logic and dialectical logic.'[55] And a few lines later one reads: 'The entirety of formal logic has only one nucleus, and that is the reactionary law of identity.'[56]

In view of these conflicting opinions, expressed respectively in the *Voprosy Filosofii* editorial and the statements of Ai and Mao, the publisher of the *Selected Works* would hardly have considered it opportune to publish Mao's comments on the reactionary character of 'formal logic' at a time when this kind of 'logic' had just been rehabilitated in Moscow, and China found itself heavily dependent upon the Soviet Union. This argument becomes all the clearer as one traces the further history of the relation between 'formal and dialectical logic' in China.

After 1956 the controversy over the two types of logic was renewed, and proceeded in the same way as that of 1936–7. The 'philosophical' struggles reached their climax at the time of the 'Three Red Banners' policy, which brought with it the introduction of the people's communes and at the same time the complete break with the Soviet model of development. The superiority of 'dialectical logic' corresponded here to the policy of the 'Three Red Banners', while 'formal logic' became the symbol for the Soviet model of development, which had been practised in China up till then.[57] To trace the links between this controversy and the CCP's internal party struggles would take far too long; however it is clear that the way the relationship between 'formal' and 'dialectical logic' was represented in 1936–7, as well as in the later 1950s, reflected the struggles over certain political directions, as well as issues in the CCP, that were influenced by the Soviet Union – connected, for example, with Wang Ming in the 1930s and with P'eng Te-huai, the defence minister who was purged in 1958. The pursuit of an independent policy towards the Comintern in 1936–7, in the course of which Wang Ming was named as an advocate of 'formal logic', found its continuation in the break with the Soviet model of development. Here the advocates of 'dialectical logic' at first prevailed, even though the failure of the 'people's commune movement' meant it was little more than a pyrrhic victory over the advocates of 'formal logic'.

Thus the omission of Mao's statements on 'formal logic' in 'On Contradiction' (1952) must have been politically inspired in view of the importance of the struggle between 'formal logicians' and 'dialecticians' in the CCP. The hesitation over the publication of the work, and the fact that this coincided with the period when discussion among Soviet philosophers was at its height, support the view that these two processes were connected.

We should mention, in conclusion, that the long years of the 'Great Proletarian Cultural Revolution' and the fall of the 'Gang of Four' have been followed by signs of a 'rehabilitation' of 'formal logic' in China, too, and that since the 'Four Modernisations' policy the debate on the relation between 'formal' and 'dialectical logic', on 'two combine into one' and 'one divides into two' and the related problems of dialectical contradictions is in full swing again. However, the articles on 'formal logic' and its supposed class character reveal a deeper knowledge of Western literature now than in the 1930s.[58] How long the newly-won recognition of this type of logic will endure is a question which will not be decided by philosophy or by science, but by intra-party struggles over the problems of modernisation.

(This chapter was originally written in 1983 and enlarged in early 1988 for the English edition. The changes in the philosophical debate which followed the T'ien-an-men massacre on June 4, 1989, have not been taken into consideration.)

20. CONCLUSION

In conclusion, we will briefly summarise what we have gleaned up till now and thereby assess Chinese dialectical materialism under ten categories.

In the course of this study it has become clear that dialectical materialism was a self-contained system of analogous thought. All theoreticians used 'philosophical terms' as symbols for the designation of political parties, factions, groups and armies, and the way relations between individual symbols are represented reflects the variety of military and political opinions. Hence, by listing all the pairs of symbols and the relations between individual symbols, we can reproduce the political conflict proceeding at that time.

The following list and classification of the symbols we have examined may serve as a type of glossary for the analysis of future 'philosophical controversies' and the political conflicts they reflect. In this case the classification refers to the United Front, but the system is transferable to other political conflicts, as we have seen in the controversy over 'formal' and 'dialectical logic' in the 1950s. Whereas new 'terms' and pairs of symbols can be introduced, it is in the nature of such a system that the discussion does not increase in intellectual content but merely manifests itself in more varied forms.

The symbols listed are subdivided into four groups: 'Philosophy' and 'Science'; 'Theory of Knowledge'; 'Formal' and 'Dialectical' logic; and 'Basic Rules of Dialectical Materialism'. It is also possible to classify the symbols according to military tactics or the terms 'Mao Tse-tung line' and 'Wang Ming line'. But the 'philosophical framework' remains constant in all the struggles, while the content of the political or military conflicts may change. Moreover, by classifying the symbols according to the philosophical terms, the universal applicability of this 'framework' becomes even more apparent.

'Philosophy' and 'Science'

'New philosophy' (*hsin-che-hsüeh*)	The CCP
'Old philosophy' (*chiu che-hsüeh*)	The Kuomintang and other non-Communist parties.
'Philosophy of opposites' (*tui-li che-hsüeh*)	Open struggle between two parties or armies

174

'Philosophy of alliance' (*lien-he che-hsüeh*)

Coalition between two parties, though without unification

'Abolition of philosophy' (*che-hsüeh hsiao-mieh*)

Surrender of the CCPs independence in the course of unification with the Kuomintang; destruction of the CCP.

'Science[s]' (*k'o-hsüeh*)

Individual parties in the United Front.

Leadership of the 'sciences' by 'philosophy'

The leading role of the CCP in the United Front.

' "Dualism" in "philosophy" ' (Kant's philosophy) (*erh-yüan lun*)

'Right opportunism', 'peaceful existence' and 'separate control', that is areas controlled by the Red Army and the Chinese Nationalist Army cooperating with each other without reciprocal interference.

'Philosophy of identity' (*t'ung-i che-hsüeh*)

Capitulation of the CCP to the Kuomintang; surrender and unification of the CCP and Red Army with the Kuomintang and Chinese Nationalist Army.

'Materialism' (*wu-chih lun, wei-wu lun*)

The CCP

'Idealism' (*kuan-nien lun, wei-hsin lun*)

The Kuomintang and other non-Communist parties

'Matter' (*wu-chih*)

The CCP; but in the relationship of 'consciousness to matter' it means 'hostile environment' or 'hostile armies'.

'Spirit' (*ching-shen*)

The Kuomintang and other non-Communist parties; but in the relationship of 'consciousness to matter' it connotes 'mobilisation of the will to resist of the masses' against the numerically and technically superior hostile armies.

'Unification of matter and spirit' (*wu-hsin tsung-he lun*)

Unification of the CCP and the Kuomintang; unification of the Red Army and the Chinese Nationalist Army.

'Dialectical materialism' (*pien-cheng fa wei-wu lun*)

The CCP, the Mao Tse-tung line'.

'Mechanism' (*chi-hsieh lun*)

Reconciliation instead of struggle between two parties or armies; readiness for compromise with the enemy; setting aside of internal political differences in the face of an external threat; the 'Wang Ming line' ('everything through the United Front'); 'right opportunism'.

'Theory of Knowledge'

'Theory of knowledge' (*jen-shih lun*)

Political and military strategy.

'Process of knowledge' (*jen-shih kuo-ch'eng*)

The developmental process of the Chinese revolution

'Stage of knowledge' (*jen-shih ti chieh-tuan*)

A period (*chieh-tuan*) or level in the development of the Chinese revolution.

'Unity of perceptual and theoretical knowledge' (*kan-hsing jen-shih yü li-hsing jen-shih ti t'ung-i*)

The United Front between the CCP and the Kuomintang

'Unification of perceptual and theoretical knowledge' (*kan-hsing jen-shih yü li-hsing jen-shih ti tsung-he*)

Unification of the CCP and the Kuomintang, and of the Red Army and the Chinese Nationalist Army; 'right opportunism',

'Unification of empiricism and rationalism' (*ching-yen lun yü li-hsing lun ti tsung-he*)

Ibid.

'Mechanistic theory of knowledge' (*chi-hsieh ti jen-shih lun*)

Suspension of the class struggle; renunciation, in the United Front, of the continuation of the struggle against the Kuomintang; readiness to compromise with the enemy; 'right opportunism'.

'Negation of perceptual knowledge' (by the theoretical) (*kan-hsing jen-shih ti fou ting*)

Destruction of the Kuomintang by the CCP.

'Practice' (*shih-chien*)

The leading role of the CCP in the United Front; guerrilla strategy instead of conventional warfare; continuation of the class struggle; continuation of the struggle against the Kuomintang within the United Front; the 'Mao Tse-tung line'.

'Subjective' (*chu-kuan*)

The political and military forces of the CCP.

'Objective' (*k'o-kuan*)	The forces of the political and military enemy.
'Overemphasis of the subjective' (*chu-kuan t'ai-ch'iang*)	Overestimation of one's own strength; no United Front with the Kuomintang; 'left radicalism'.
'Objectivism' (*k'o-kuan chu-i*)	Underestimation of one's own strength; overestimation of the military strength of the enemy; 'right opportunism'.
'Unity of the subjective and objective' (*chu-kuan-yü k'o-kuan ti t'ung-i*)	The United Front together with simultaneous continuation of the struggle against the Kuomintang; the 'Mao Tse-tung line'.
'Exaggeration of "analysis" ' (*fen-hsi*)	'Left radicalism'.
'Exaggeration of "synthesis" ' (*tsung-ho fa*)	'Right opportunism'.
'Unity of analysis and synthesis' (*fen-hsi fa ho tsung-ho fa ti t'ung-i*)	The United Front; 'unity as well as struggle'; the 'Mao Tse-tung line'.
'Relative' (*hsiang-tui*)	The struggle against Japan is the 'relative' element in the developmental process of the Chinese revolution.
'Relative truth' (*hsiang-tui ti chen-li*)	Individual periods of the revolution; the United Front.
'Absolute' (*chüeh-tui*)	The struggle against the Kuomintang is the absolute in the developmental process of the Chinese revolution.
'Absolute truth' (*chüeh-tui ti chen-li*)	Victory of the CCP in the revolution.
The 'epistemological dualism' in Kant, 'thing in itself' and 'phenomenon' (*wu-tzu-t'i. hsien-hsiang*)	'Right opportunism'; 'peaceful co-existence' and 'separate control', i.e. the areas controlled by the Red Army and Chinese Nationalist Army cooperating with each other without reciprocal interference.

'Formal' and 'Dialectical' Logic

'Formal logic' (*hsing-shih lo-chi*)	The Kuomintang.
'Dialectical logic' (*pien-cheng lo-chi*)	The CCP; the 'Mao Tse-tung line'.

'Identity' in 'formal logic' (*t'ung-i*)	Fusion of the Red Army with the Chinese Nationalist Army; the 'Wang Ming line'.
'Law of identity' in 'formal logic' (*t'ung-i lü*)	Rejection of any cooperation with the Kuomintang; 'left radicalism'; regarding unity with the Kuomintang as absolute; 'right opportunism'; 'everything through the United Front', the 'Wang Ming line'.
'Law of contradiction' in 'formal logic' (*mao-tun lü*)	Insistence on one tactic to the exclusion of any other tactic; only 'struggle' or only 'unity'; only 'retreat' or only 'attack'; only 'democracy' or only 'concentration of forces'; 'left radicalism' and at the same time 'right opportunism'.
'Law of the excluded third' in 'formal logic' (*chü-chung lü*)	Any connection between two contradictory political or military tactics is excluded.
'Negation of formal logic' (*hsing-shih lo-chi ti fou-ting*)	Destruction of the Kuomintang by the CCP
'Area of formal logic' (*hsing-shih lo-chih ti ling-yü, ti-p'an*	An area controlled by the Kuomintang.
'Area of dialectical logic' (*pien-cheng lo-chi ti ling-yü, ti-p'an*)	An area controlled by the CCP

'Basic Rules of Dialectical Materialism'

'Materialistic dialectic' (*wei-wu pien-cheng fa*)	The CCP, the 'Mao Tse-tung line'.
'The law of contradiction or the law of unity of opposites' (*mao-tun fa-tse, tui-li t'ung-i ti fa-tse, mao tun t'ung-i lü*)	'Unity as well as struggle'; continuation of the struggle in the United Front.
'Negation' (*fou-ting*)	Destruction of the Kuomintang.
'Reciprocal penetration of the opposites' (*hu-hsiang shen-t'ou*)	Infiltration of the opponent; infiltrate into his territory; infiltrate his organisation; pursue division.
'Sublimation of the positive aspects in the process of negation' (*yang-ch'i*)	Splitting off of the anti-Japanese wing of the Kuomintang and its troops and their incorporation into the CCP camp.

'Negation of the negation'
(*fou-ting ti fou-ting*)

Strengthening of one's own position by dividing the enemy; 'absorbing' (*hsi-shou*) the troops split off and, on the basis of this superiority achieving the final destruction of the enemy.

'Change from quantity into quality' (*liang pien chih*)

Replacing the Kuomintang control with CCP control.

Overemphasis of 'quantity' (*liang*)

Reformism; renunciation of the class struggle and the struggle against the Kuomintang; 'right opportunism'; the 'Wang Ming line'.

'Overemphasis of 'quality' (*chih*)

Rejection of the United Front; struggle exclusively against the Kuomintang; unlimited continuation of the agrarian revolution; 'left radicalism'.

'Developmental process of matter' (*wu-chih ti fa-chan kuo-ch'eng*)

The developmental process of the Chinese revolution.

'External cause' (*wai-yin*)

Japan.

'Internal cause' (*nei-yin*)

The opposition between the CCP and the Kuomintang.

'Subordination of the "internal" to the "external" cause'

Subordination of the struggle against the Kuomintang to the war against Japan; 'everything through the United Front'; the 'Wang Ming line'; 'right opportunism'.

'Unity of internal and external causes' (*nei-yin yü wai-yin ti t'ung-i*)

The link between the struggle against the Kuomintang and that against Japan; 'the internal cause', i.e. the struggle against the Kuomintang remains the determining factor; the war against Japan has only one function for this struggle.

'The theory of equilibrium' (*chün-heng lun*)

Equality of the parties in the United Front; the 'Wang Ming line'. 'To consider two aspects as equal' (*t'ung-teng k'an tai*' or *'p'ing-chün k'an tai*); Bukharinism, Mechanism, Right Opportunism.

1. In all the texts examined it can be established that the content of the terminology as understood in Western philosophy was far from having been taken over by the Chinese dialectical materialists. Although the

theoreticians constantly stressed the objective character of their 'philosophy' and their 'science', we have seen that this merely expressed their subjective and political interests. Philosophy and science were not understood as something separate from the political struggle for power, nor was there any recognition of the idea of objectivity in science. For example, the designations 'subjective' and 'objective' did not stand for truthfulness or falsehood that might or might not exist in regard to a perceivable object, but were used as symbols for the relations between political and military forces. In this way the term 'subjective' referred to one's own forces while 'objective' referred to those of the enemy. Possibly the Chinese characters for 'subjective (*chu-kuan*) and 'objective' (*k'o-kuan*) had encouraged this analogous application. '*Chu-kuan*' means 'view of the host', while *k'o-kuan*' means 'view of the guest' (who also, of course can be an enemy). These characters did not address the question of objectivity in the Western sense, since the 'view of the guest' need not be any more objective than the 'view of the host'.

The understanding of objectivity in the Western sense would have had to be taken from Western science, because no such idea exists in ancient Chinese philosophy. However, this demonstrably did not happen with the dialectical materialists. We will discuss below the extent to which a possible lack of formal-logical reasoning and scientific methodology within Chinese traditional thought had perhaps co-determined the interpretation of Western concepts and their application as analogies.

2. The same observation can be made concerning the 'theory of knowledge' of the 'dialectical materialists'. The relation between 'perceptual' and 'theoretical knowledge', if described according to the pattern of a battle between two armies, indicates – however cautiously one expresses oneself – a far-reaching lack of understanding of the problems connected with epistemology. To have pointed out the social conditions of human thought was a great contribution of Marx. However, the simple equating of the process of 'knowledge' as a whole with the Chinese revolution, and the individual 'stages of knowledge' with the individual periods of this revolution, appear to have been an intellectual short-circuit in which the relation between base and superstructure was simplified into a Chinese shadow-play. Therefore, it is not possible to say that Chinese 'dialectical materialism' possesses a theory of knowledge.

3. The debate on 'formal' and 'dialectical logic' also reflects not the process of contemplating problems of logic, but rather the struggle over the United Front on which all the 'philosophical' statements were based.

The negation of 'formal' by 'dialectical logic' meant nothing more than the negation of the Kuomintang. It became clear, especially in Ai-Ssu-ch'i, that the process of negation, the 'absorbing' of opposites and their subsequent destruction, was merely the 'philosophical' paraphrase for the tactic of 'rolling up' the military opponent, analogous to the negation of 'perceptual' by 'theoretical knowledge'.

The heavy dependence of 'philosophical' thought on military considerations was especially evident in the characters used to represent the dialectical process, which, as we saw in the chapter on 'formal' and 'dialectical logic', originated almost exclusively from the military sphere. 'Formal logic' was to be 'infiltrated', 'fought', 'absorbed', 'overthrown', and 'destroyed'. At the same time the various philosophical schools and concepts were equated with the areas under military control of the respective contenders in the civil war. Here too, as in the 'theory of knowledge', the intellectual world of concepts was only a shadow-play of the struggle for political and military areas of influence and strategies.

4. The 'law of contradiction or the law of unity of opposites' did not contain a general ontological statement, but was rather the military strategy of Mao Tse-tung couched in the language of philosophy. The discussion of the 'law of identity' reflected the strategical principles of the protracted war against conventional warfare, laid down by Mao in his military writings. The principle of 'dialectical negation' was a military strategem that had its origin in the military domain, but it could be applied to any political conflict, whether inner-party, national or international. In this sense, the symbolic language of 'dialectical materialism' had nothing in common with European Marxism, but was more reminiscent of the military theories of the Chan-Kuo period (5th–3rd centuries BC, the era of the warring empires), in which the whole system of military-political strategems was developed. Among them '*ho-tsung*' and '*lien-heng*' were the most important. The '*ho-tsung*' tactic meant the conclusion of an alliance between several weak empires against a strong empire, and the '*lien-heng*' tactic implied subordination to a strong empire and a concerted attack against other empires. The two strategems could be used either simultaneously or consecutively, and in the transition from the first to the second strategem, the other side was 'negated' – to use the language of the Chinese dialectical materialists.

We can therefore describe the controversy over dialectical materialism in China as one about the correct military strategem to be adopted in the struggle against the Kuomintang and the takeover of power in China.

5. The strategem of 'dialectic' ('dialectical logic'), 'unity of opposites', and so on, had another area of application directly connected to the first: in the inner-party struggles, where it served to eliminate the faction that followed the Comintern line.

The history of the origin of 'dialectical materialism' in China thus reveals a characteristic unique throughout the international Communist movement: the language of dialectical materialism was adopted from the Soviet Union, and with it there came a large measure of ideological and political influence. This influence had the opposite effect to that which Moscow had probably hoped for, because 'dialectical materialism' became transformed into a 'theoretical weapon' against the advocates of the Comintern within the CCP. Referring to the 'laws of the dialectic', the faction around Mao Tse-tung legitimised the political emancipation of the party from the Comintern, from which 'dialectical materialism' had only recently been received. There is a certain irony here in that at the very point in time when the inventor of the 'theory of equilibrium', Bukharin, was being led to the firing squad, the Chinese 'dialecticians' were accusing the advocates of the Comintern, and thus indirectly Stalin, of pursuing a 'Bukharinist' policy with regard to the United Front in that they played down the contradictions between the CCP and the Kuomintang in the interests of Soviet security policy, as being 'peaceful opposites'.

6. The Chinese 'dialectical materialism' is not so much an aggregate of 'empty formulae', like its Soviet elder sibling, but an aggregate of symbolic characters. All 'empty formulae' have probably had meaningful content at one time. The process of depletion can be followed in Soviet philosophy. The Chinese theoreticians' reception of the 'empty formulae', and their conversion into Chinese characters, was a prerequisite for their later use as symbols.

Along with its formal reception, the Chinese theoreticians also employed the concept of the function of 'philosophy' in their inner-party struggles. In the process of being legitimised, political power and philosophy were seen as identical to each other and not as being possibly or even fundamentally separate. The idea that thought can and should have another function was not to be found in the Soviet sources. Even today, as recent articles by Chinese authors reveal, philosophy and politics are not regarded as distinct areas of thought, but are linked to political struggles.

7. Because 'dialectical materialism' has been institutionalised in China since 1949 as a generally binding world-view, the precise observation of

'philosophical life' can yield inferences as to the course of political conflicts. The empirical observation of the party, the central committee, the politburo, the military establishment, the ties of loyalty existing within them, local partisanship and so on can be supplemented by a decoding of their 'philosophical representation', thus deepening the analysis of political transformations. This 'philosophical representation' not only reflects existing political conflicts but also is important in that it anticipates them and can point to impending changes that are yet to be established empirically. Thus, in the case of the United Front, the tactic of 'unity as well as struggle' was not empirically provable since there was no pre-existing experience of cooperation with the United Front. Yet this tactic first made an impact upon the controversy in the early summer of 1936, although the United Front did not actually come into being till the autumn of 1937. Hence, by utilising 'philosophical representation' political conflicts can be played out of which one would otherwise become aware only after the political and personal consequences were common knowledge.

Political conflicts found expression not only in the 'new philosophy', but also in the 'new science of history' and the 'new wood-cutting movement' in the 1930s as well as in the 'new literature'. After 1949 this phenomenon was continued in the Hu Hsien 'peasant-paintings', workers' paintings from Shanghai, and in the 'revolutionary romantic' during the Cultural Revolution. Political conflicts pervaded modern Chinese opera as well as the folk dances of the minorities in China, which are permeated with political meaning. The whole cultural milieu, so it seemed, stiffened into a reflex of the political struggle over leadership and direction. Culture and the sphere of political conflict form two parts which refer directly to each other and undergo a reciprocal reaction.

8. In our introductory remarks we suggested several possible answers to the question why did the dialectical materialists use analogy in their political struggle? We will now reexamine this question.

(*a*) First, I do not think that the whole debate was simply a smokescreen for political struggles. This explanation is far too simple. I am convinced that Ai Ssu-ch'i, Mao Tse-tung and other theoreticians regarded dialectical materialism as the most sophisticated and advanced of philosophies, but thinking in analogies was an essential component of traditional Chinese thought. The Chinese characters encourage this, as does a certain lack of formal-logical and analytical thought in Chinese philosophy. However, the thought of the theoreticians in this respect does not follow traditional paths regarding philosophical content, although it does to a certain extent in a formal sense. We return to this problem below.

(*b*) We have seen in this study how the theoreticians used 'terms' consciously for the purposes of analogy and as symbols. Thus it was perhaps not so much that traditional Chinese thought led to the use of analogy, but that the theoreticians possibly saw themselves as obliged to express in encoded language things which they did not dare to say openly. Traditional Chinese thought put into their possession the best prerequisites for this. The press censorship imposed by the Chinese National government forbade free speech, and those who dared to use it were in danger of physical elimination. The CCP, in turn, was organised on the Bolshevik model, and in part was similar to a Chinese secret society – as it had to be in order to survive in the civil war. Free speech was thus hardly a possiblity in the inter-party struggles.

The practice of writing in analogies is thus partially explained by reference to the repressive situation in the 1930s; however, this cannot have been the only reason, since after the CCP's victory 'philosophical' thought followed the same path of analogy, and has continued to do so up till the present day, despite having become more sophisticated in recent years. From this we can infer that even after 1949 the leadership – and individual groups within it – believed themselves to be so gravely threatened that they could not afford to allow the development of open, critical thought and were thus compelled to cloak their political positions in modern myths which, at the same time, served to legitimise their control over the mass of the people. But while this is undoubtedly true, it is by no means the only explanation since it has also been shown that the theoreticians were convinced of the correctness of their world-view, and believed in it.

(*c*) We have already hinted that the thought of the 'dialectical materialists' had mythical attributes. This seems at first to be contradicted by the clear and extremely realistic estimate of the political and military power relationships they had achieved, and by the observation we have just made that, in their thought, they consciously used the terms of Western philosophy as symbols. At the same time, when reading the texts one gains the inescapable impression that they believed firmly in the Western concepts, while possessing only an amorphous idea of their content.

One author, in his personal copy which we were able to copy, had made corrections and revisions by hand, from which it was clear just how strenuously he had grappled with Western philosophy, struggling to find the correct Chinese characters, which he had then, astonishingly, used merely as symbols for the CCP and the Kuomintang. The whole effort, however, was not concerned with itemising the content of Western philosophy, but rather with forming as exact an analogous world picture as possible with regard to the relation between the two parties. This can be explained only by surviving remnants of mythical thought among the Chinese theoreticians, by certain still-functioning traditional thought-patterns. The repressive situation in the 1930s does not seem to offer a sufficient explanation.

The 'dialectical materialism' controversy was therefore not an abstract, theoretical struggle – this has always been foreign to Chinese thought – but rather a 'struggle of the symbols'. In mythical thought, symbols possess a force which is either favourable or ruinous for the object it symbolises. Designations such as 'idealist', 'mechanist', 'Bukharinist', and so on, did not stand for an individual political viewpoint; rather, those who are designated in this way bear these symbols like a tatoo, or like the mark of Cain, or like the white paper hat which political opponents are forced to wear as they are driven through the streets and from which their attachment to a certain faction or social strata can at once be discerned. The Chinese door-signs for the driving away of evil spirits belong to this domain of mythical thought, as does the practice of crossing out the names of political opponents in public wall-newspapers and in books: the belief exists that such a symbolic killing of the opponent anticipates and contributes to his political elimination, and can even banish his power. The symbol is in fact the object or the opponent, and the deletion of his name has an effect on him personally.

For this reason, there is no contradiction between the realistic analysis of the political and military situation and the conscious, and partly even tactical, use of Western 'terms' as symbols which are simultaneously believed in. The content of the belief in the concept of 'materialism' had little to do with what this concept means in Western thought. It is rather to be understood as the force inherent in a myth, which is sometimes able to grip the 'masses', especially in periods of social misery and upheaval. Thus, 'materialism' and 'dialectical logic' were positive myths, possessing 'supernatural power'; they were 'magic weapons' in Ai Ssu-ch'i's formulations, whereas 'Idealism' and 'formal logic' were the negative counterparts that had to be defeated in the eternal struggle between good and evil, light and darkness.

In reading the texts, therefore, one repeatedly encounters the connection between myth and power – the unity of mythical belief, whose intellectual weapon is the symbol – and rational comprehension of political power relationships. This is the true dialectic of Chinese dialectical materialism.

9. We should also address the question whether the tendency towards analogous thought among the Communist theoreticians is valid for other schools of philosophy in China as well. However, to avoid any misunderstanding, we should repeat that this examines only a very small aspect of modern Chinese philosophy and that the statements made about it can be regarded as valid only for that particular area.

Modern Chinese philosophy contains a number of currents, and Chinese Marxism played only a subordinate role in it up till 1949, hence it is not admissible to consider the features of 'dialectical materialism' as characteristic of the whole of modern Chinese thought. The fact that since 1949 only the teachings of Communist theoreticians have been admitted as 'philosophy', with all other schools being forbidden, should not tempt one to assume that these patterns of thought are simply identical to Chinese thought in general, and that 'dialectical materialism' was merely the final political concretisation of the Chinese penchant for dialectic, for which they supposedly cultivated sympathy since the origin of I-Ching, *The Book of Changes*. In the works of Hu Shih, Feng Yu-lan, Chang Tung-sun, Chang Chün-mai, Ting Wen-chiang and other great modern Chinese thinkers, logical-discursive and analytical thought is decisive rather than analogous and dialectical thought.

It is entirely reasonable to ask whether the texts of the dialectical materialists have certain characteristics which are also to be found in the works of their philosophical contemporaries, and whether one can deduce that the dialectical materialists were affected by certain traditional structures of thought to a much greater extent than the theoreticians mentioned above.

Behind this is the question whether the dialectical materialists were influenced by traditional Chinese thought (i.e. of the Ch'un-Ch'iu and Chan-Kuo periods, 770–221 BC), from which they would have derived a predisposition to place a world-view in analogy with party-political issues. Here we will merely suggest the possibility of a further effect of traditional Chinese patterns of thought, or at least not exclude it. We have, of course, to ask the question, how far Chinese dialectical materialism perhaps contains or has incorporated certain elements of traditional Chinese thought – an argument which has been supported by some outstanding Western scholars.

From the profusion of literature on Chinese philosophy,[1] we can identify aspects which are essential in the present context. First, man as a social-historical being, and his ideal, moralistic attitudes have always been at the centre of Chinese philosophy. The goal of this thought was the realisation of the unity of society and the cosmos, in which man followed social principles which had their counterpart in nature and the cosmos. Therefore, the observation of nature was strongly subjective. The concept of nature as a reality independent of man and society, and following its own laws, was foreign to Chinese thought: there was no difference between the ontology, cosmology and the philosophy of life. Cosmology was a part of the philosophy of life, and served as a practical guide for everyday life as well as for social and political affairs; as an independent object of research it did not exist. There were only the beginnings of a systematic contemplation of questions of space, time and matter as independent forms of reality.

This circumstance is related to the fact that modern natural sciences have not developed in China as far as they have in Europe in the last four hundred years. Certainly there was a wealth of inventions, and Chinese inventors often achieved brilliant results, but though their technology was in parts more highly developed than in the West, they lagged behind their Western colleagues where the formation of scientific theories was concerned. Chinese thought was characterised rather by a striking lack of interest in abstract systematisation and logical operations. Natural laws were not important to it, nor did it develop any concept of natural law, but rather one of natural order, which was frequently a projection of the social order.

It is therefore hardly possible to separate political thought in China from other areas of consciousness. Instead one could speak of a politicised cosmology or philosophy, in which the order of the cosmos found its counterpart in the social order, and all thought in that direction was aimed at bringing about harmony between the two orders (*t'ien-jen ho-i*) – the harmony between heaven and man).[2] Correspondingly, the description and explanation of social processes and of the cosmos did not follow by means of logical and systematic analysis and exact definition; it did so with the help of analogies and historical examples of which the works of Chinese thinkers are full.

The logical proof in a line of argument was irrelevant. An opponent's position was not analysed, nor were possible basic contradictions in his logic pointed out, but rather it was rebutted on the basic of historical example, by the use of historical or natural analogies. In this way one 'proved' him to be wrong.

This type of thought is based on a manner of approaching an object which is fundamentally different from Western thought. In the latter the question of 'what' is always decisive; however, in Chinese thought it is the 'how'. The 'how' is also contained in the 'what', but here the main thrust lies in the analysis of the object. The question of the 'how' suggests more an interest in the relation between objects, and the ensuing answer usually takes the form of an analogy instead of a logical conclusion. The following example is just one of many:

Does not life mean nature, just as white means white? Does not the white of a white feather mean the white of white snow, and the white of white snow mean the white of jade? If this is so, then is not the nature of the dog the same as the nature of a cow, and the nature of a cow the same as the nature of a man?[3]

This short example should not give the false impression that all Chinese thought is based on this type of logic alone; but it is, at the very least, an essential element, which becomes of interest in connection with the assessment of Chinese 'dialectical materialism'. We can thus appreciate the difficulties which faced the Chinese theoreticians as they occupied themselves with the formal logic adopted from the West.

There have been many attempts at explaining the different kinds of natural sciences and of formal-logical thought in China, or, as some authors maintain, their non-development. Leibniz had already established that the West, while outshining China in logic, metaphysics, mathematics and military science, was still inferior with regard to the fundamentals of the moral life and of practical philosophy.[4] Herder, Hegel, Schlegel und Humboldt saw in the uniqueness of the Chinese language a serious obstacle to the development of modern natural sciences in China. In later times, Max Weber and Wittfogel devoted their attention to this theme. Weber, on the basis of an examination of the Chinese gentry, concluded that this stratum had been decisively shaped by traditionalistic, particularistic and magical characteristics and was incapable of developing a scientific world-view comparable to that of the West. In contrast to this, Wittfogel saw the basic causes of the non-formation of rational thought in China as lying particularly in the relations of production and the insufficient development of industry.[5]

This theme has also been dealt with in China itself. Chang Tung-sun, a renowned thinker and probably the principal authority on Western philosophy in China, argued in his work *Ssu-hsiang, yen-yü yü wen-hua* (Thought, Language and Culture)[6] that between Western and Chinese thought there were fundamental differences, which on the one hand could be explained sociologically, but which on the other lay in the heterogeneity of the Indo-Aryan languages in relation to the Chinese language. Aristotelean logic was for him unthinkable without the grammatical structure of the Greek language. If this logic were to be transferred to Chinese thought, it would turn out to be unsuitable. For example, according to Chang, the traditional Chinese language lacked both the established form object-subject-predicate-preposition and a character comparable to the word 'be', which is the prerequisite for the ability to envision the concept of 'identity'. In his view, Western thought was largely based on this concept, unlike Chinese thought which, according to Chang, contained neither the concept of 'identity' nor that of 'substance'. Western thought is for him basically dichotomous in form; like 'A and Not-A' it forces thought towards exclusiveness, while Chinese thought does not stress exclusiveness but rather the quality of the relation between opposites. In the sentence 'A is Not-A' or 'A is not A', the negative aspect is easy to determine; however, when one renders this in Chinese as *chia fei i*, it means neither the one nor the other. It does not mean an opposite in the sense of exclusiveness. While Chang designated Western logic, in connection with the grammatical structure of Western languages, as the 'logic of identity', he suggested naming Chinese logic 'logic of correlation' or 'logic of correlation duality',[7] in which the importance of the relations between two opposites would be emphasised.

This is not the place to quote from and comment at length on the writings of Chang Tung-sung. From what has been outlined above we would merely point out the following: the use of Western philosophical concepts as symbols by the 'dialectical materialists' is first of all a result of the adoption of Soviet dialectical materialism; but as it was adopted the 'empty-formula' character of this world-view was combined with some of the distinctive features of traditional Chinese philosophy mentioned above.

However, the 'dialectical materialists' were not alone in being influenced by traditional patterns of thought when adopting Western concepts. The loss of orientation which the traditional Chinese world-view had suffered in face of the challenge of Western science, forced the intellectuals thus affected to seek a new world-view which would enable them to regain their lost certainty regarding the order of the cosmos and society. They believed they had found this new world-view in Western science. The general belief in science which followed won over many intellectuals of all hues and corresponded to the beginnings of scientific research then unfolding at a few institutes. Science and the belief in its 'omnipotence' (*k'o-hsüeh wan-neng*) acquired the character of a myth. From this myth of science many Chinese intellectuals hoped for a new social system as well as a new cosmological one in which the position of man would no longer be determined by Tao, Li or Yin and Yang, but by scientific laws.

The correspondence of the cosmic and the social structures (and vice versa) was revealed also in the personal biographies of the best-known scientists in China. The positivist Ting Wen-chiang, the pragmatist Hu Shih and the philosopher Chang Tung-sun, although scientists, were politicians as well, and saw their scientific concepts as being forever in agreement with their political actions. They never understood the two as separate, but regarded them as a unified whole.

In the 1920s, the belief in the myth of science was characteristic of the advocates of Marxism as well as the advocates of Dewey's pragmatism and English empiricism and sensualism. However, while this myth gradually receded among the advocates of the latter schools because of their intensive occupation with Western thought and independent empirical research, and made way for the concept of science as method for the solution of clearly defined problems, the myth of science now really began to bloom among the dialectical materialists. The lack of knowledge of the content of Western scientific thought resulted in the traditional pattern of thought already mentioned remaining effective and untouched by rational thought. It is one of the curiosities of modern Chinese philosophy that the dialectical materialists, who regarded themselves as the representatives of the supposedly most progressive world-view, remained much more tightly restricted to certain features of traditional Chinese thought than the 'bourgeois' scientists like Hu-Shih and Ting Wen-chiang against whom they struggled and who had made an effort to link the scientific approaches in Chinese thought – especially the beginnings of some kind of empiricism in the Ch'ing era – to Western sciences.

However, this should not be understood as meaning that 'dialectical materialism' represented no more than the continuation of a current within traditional Chinese thought clothed in Western concepts. With regard to content the 'law of the unity of opposites' has very little to do with the teaching of Yin-Yang, not to mention the fact that the latter stresses unity rather than contradiction. There is merely a certain formal similarity in the emblematic and analogical application of Yin and Yang to all areas of society and the cosmos. It is not possible to speak here of a real intellectual continuity. If a continuity has been established, then it was only in the sense that the party ideologists tried to link principles of dialectical materialism to the teachings of Yin-Yang, thus attempting to revive moribund patterns of thought from an extremely advanced culture which had already vanished. Since the patterns of dialectical materialism have been used mainly in a military and power-politics sense, the renaissance seems to be a very questionable one. Furthermore, if one assesses the emergence of dialectical materialism in the 1930s, it is obvious that the attempts to link this kind of philosophy with traditional thought were very shaky. On the contrary, it is not a continuity that emerges from the tradition, but rather one which is forced upon the tradition by selecting and subordinating Chinese philosophy and culture to the goals of the Communist party.

Finally, since Chinese dialectical materialism was composed mainly of paraphrases taken from translations of Soviet manuals in the 1930s, which were of questionable value anyway, we have to ask the following question: namely what will happen if, in the near future, the Stalinistic philosophy, the works of Mitin, Sirokov and others, which provided the basic source materials for Chinese dialectical materialists, are characterised as what they really were – an attempt to legitimise Stalin's persecution of the kulaks and the bloody purges of his adversaries in maybe the darkest period of Russian history – and are finally jettisoned. Will then the Chinese continue to adhere to this ideology adopted from the Soviets as the philosophical foundation of their own political system, or will they have to search for a new one? Free discussion of Stalin's influence on China has only just begun.

10. 'Dialectical materialism' in China is a pre-scientific world-view. It is 'sociomorphic', inasmuch as the struggles between the political camps are magnified as in a distorting mirror. It is in a narrow sense 'factiomorphic – if this expression is permissible – insofar as one finds here the counterpart to the conflicts between the different factions of the CCP over the correct tactics to be employed.

Up till the present, the political representatives of this world-view have found themselves in the unresolved contradiction of having to use Western rationality in the form of science to help them modernise the country, and simultaneously having to restrict it to scientific ghettos while trying to prevent its spreading to other social and political realms. In that process parts of the intelligentsia, educated in rational thought, in recent years have begun increasingly to question the intellectual basis and, correspondingly, – in the view of the party – the basic political structures of the People's Republic of China. The application of

Western sciences seems to be possible only when intellectuals are controlled and, if necessary, repressed. The stormy relationship between the CCP and the country's intellectuals over the past forty years bears this out.

The party's past attempts to make the intellectuals submissive to its aims and bring them into line indicates not so much a lack of loyalty on the intellectuals' part towards the new state but rather a rejection of philosophy and science understood as originating in the analogous structure of dialectical materialism and its function of legitimising the party's politics. The thought-training of cadres and intellectuals in the paths mapped out in this study will not lead to the desperately needed liberation of thought for the development of the country, but rather to its being blocked. Reality will be hidden, not revealed, and rationality will be forced back into that mythical area of classification by 'good' and 'evil', 'materialist' and 'idealist', which has always served to enable rulers, in China and in Europe, to legitimise their power.

NOTES

Introduction

1. Cf. Mao Tse-tung, *Selected Works of Mao Tse-tung*, vol. 1, Peking 1968, pp. 285, 311. The question as to the originality of both these works is treated in part IV of this study.

2. We will mention only the most important of the numerous publications concerning the philosophical contributions of Mao Tse-tung: Stuart R. Schram, *The Political Thought of Mao Tse-tung*, Harmondsworth 1969; 'Mao Tse-tung's Thought to 1949' in John K. Fairbank and Albert Feuerwerken (eds), *The Cambridge History of China*, vol. 13, Pt. 2, *Republican China, 1912–1949*, Cambridge 1986, pp. 789–870; Benjamin Schwartz, 'The Philosopher' in Dick Wilson (ed.), *Mao Tse-tung in the Scales of History*, Cambridge 1977; John Brian Starr, *Continuing the Revolution: The Political Thought of Mao*, Princeton 1979; James Chieh Hsiung (ed.), *The Logic of Maoism*, New York 1974; Frederick Wakeman, Jr., *History and Will: Philosophical Perspectives of Mao Tse-tung's Thought*, Berkeley 1973; Brantley Womack, *The Foundations of Mao Zedong's Political Thought, 1917–1935*, Honolulu 1982; Raymond Wylie, *The Emergence of Maoism*, Stanford 1980; Francis Y.K. Soo, *Mao Tse-tung's Theory of Dialectic*, Dordrecht 1981. Of the literature in German, Ingo Schäfer, *Mao Tse-tung. Eine Einführung in sein Denken*, Munich 1978, is to be recommended.

   For an analysis of the 'Maoism Debates' in the 1960s (involving Wittfogel and Schwartz) and 1970s (involving, among others, Pfeffer, Walder, Meisner, Wakeman and Gurley) from a methodological point of view, see Nick Knight, 'The Marxism of Mao Zedong: Empiricism and Discourse in the Field of Mao Studies', *Australian Journal of Chinese Affairs*, no. 16 (July 1986), pp. 7–22. Regarding the contribution of Marxist, Taoist and Neoconfucianist elements and of traditional Chinese thought in general to Mao's thought, see, for example, Wakeman, op. cit., esp. pp. 238 ff: 'Wang Yang-ming, The Parallel Tradition of Practice'; Schäfer, op. cit., pt. I, chs 1–3; Starr, op. cit., pp. 3–71, but also Francis Y.K. Soo, op. cit., chs 3, 4 and 5.

3. A view propounded, for example, by E. Bauer in his book *Ideologie und Entwicklung in der VR China*, Bochum, 1980, esp. pp. 3 ff., and 77 ff.

4. As to the concept of 'esoteric communication', see Myron Rush, *The Rise of Kruschchev*, Washington, DC, 1958, app. 2, 'The Role of Esoteric Communication in Soviet Politics', pp. 88–94; and William E. Griffith, 'On Esoteric Communications', *Studies in Comparative Communism*, vol. 3, no. (Jan. 1970), pp. 47 ff.

5. See Ernst Cassirer, *Die Begriffsform im mythischen Denken*, Leipzig 1922; L. Lévy-Bruhl, *Die geistige Welt der Primitiven*, Munich 1927; and Emile Durkheim, *Les formes élémentaires de la vie religieuse*, Paris 1912.

6. See Albert Feuerwerker (ed.), *History in Communist China*, Cambridge, Mass., 1968. There exists already an excellent study in German: Mechthild Leutner, *Geschichtsschreibung zwischen Politik und Wissenschaft. Zur Herausbildung der chinesischen marxistischen Geschichtswissenschaften in den 30er und 40er Jahren*,

Wiesbaden 1982. See also Arif Dirlik, *Revolution and History: The Origins of Marxist Historiography in China, 1919–1937*, Berkeley, Calif. 1978.

7. Arthur Cohen, *The Communism of Mao Tse-tung*, Chicago 1968; Dennis J. Doolin and Peter J. Golas, ' "On Contradiction" in the Light of Mao Tse-tung's Essay "Dialectical Materialism" ', *China Quarterly*, no. 19 (July–Sept. 1964), pp. 38–46; Joshua A. Fogel, *Ai Ssu-chi's Contribution to the Development of Chinese Marxism*, Cambridge, Mass. and London 1987; Nick Knight, 'Mao Zedong's "On Contradiction" and "On Practice": Pre-Liberation Texts', *China Quarterly*, no. 84 (1980), pp. 641–88; 'Mao Zedong and the "Sinification of Marxism" ' in C. Mackerras and N. Knight (eds), *Marxism in Asia*, London and Sydney 1985, pp. 62–93; 'The Form of Mao Zedong's "Sinification of Marxism" ', *Australian Journal of Chinese Affairs*, no. 9 (1983), pp. 17–33. Wolfgang Lippert, 'Zur Entstehungsgeschichte von Mao Ze-dongs theoretischen Schriften "Uber die Praxis" und "Uber den Widerspruch" ' in Ch'en-yüeh chi (ed.), *Tileman Grimm zum 60, Geburtstag*, Tübingen 1982, pp. 173–97; Stuart R. Schram, *The Political Thought of Mao Tse-tung*, op. cit.; 'Mao Tse-tung and the Theory of the Permanent Revolution, 1958–1969', *China Quarterly*, no. 46 (1971), pp. 221–44; 'Mao Tse-tung's Thought to 1949', op. cit.; *Mao Zedong: A Preliminary Reassessment*, Hong Kong 1983; Takeuchi Minoru, 'Mō Takutō no "Mujun ron" no genkei ni tsuite" ' (On the Original Form of Mao Tse-tung's 'On Contradiction'), *Shisō (Thought)*, 538, April 1969, pp. 487–526; ' "Mujun ron" no genkei hosetsu' (Additional Theories About the Original Form of 'On Contradiction'), in *Zōho Mō Takutō noto* (Notes on Mao Tse-tung), enlarged edn, Tokyo 1978. Nakajima Mineo, 'Mō Takutō shiso ni okeru ninshiki to jissen: "Jissen ron" o megutte', (Knowledge and Practice in the Thought of Mao Tse-tung: Concerning 'On Practice'), *Koria hyron*, 7, no. 55 (Aug. 1965), pp. 19–23; K.A. Wittfogel and C.S. Chao, 'Some Remarks on Mao's Handling and Problems of Dialectics', *Studies in Soviet Thought*, III, 4 (Dec. 1963), pp. 251–77; Raymond Wylie, op. cit.

8. The three main sources of Chinese dialectical materialism were:

1. *Pien-cheng fa wei-wu lun chiao-ch'eng* (Course of Instruction in Dialectical Materialism), trans. from Russian by Li Ta; the Russian edn. was published in Leningrad in 1931. The members of the Philosophical Institute of the Leningrad branch of the Komakademiia are regarded as having been the authors; among them were Sirokov (Hsi-lo-k'o-fu) and Aizenberg (Ai-sen-pao). The Chinese trans. appeared in Oct. 1932: *Wei-wu pien-cheng fa lun-chan*, edited by Ti-p'ing hsien ch'u-pan she, Chang Tung-sun 1934 (repr. Taipei 1973), p. 26. See also O. Brière, *Fifty Years of Chinese Philosophy*, London 1956, p. 122. Lippert, op. cit., p. 179, and Chen Cheng-ti, '*Shin tetsugaku ronsen to Deborin hihan*' (The Controversy over 'New Philosophy', 1935–1937 – the Criticism of the Deborinites and the Marxist Philosophy in China), *Tōyō bunka* (Oriental Culture), 65 (March 1985), pp. 5–36, esp. p. 14, n. 23. Parts of the *Course in Dialectical Materialism* have also been included as an introduction to Ai Ssu-ch'i (ed.), *Che-hsüeh hsüan-chi* (Selected Philosophical Works), Hong Kong 1939. Cf. the Preface to ibid., p.1, and the introductory chapter '*Hsü-lun, Che-hṣüeh ti tang-hsing*' (Introduction: The Partiality of Philosophy), ibid., pp. 1–37.

2. 'Dialecticheskii materializm' in *Bol'shaia sovetskaia entsiklopediia*, vol. 22 (1935), pp. 45–235. The article was edited and co-authored by Mark B. Mitin and

V.M. Ral'tsevit. Other contributors included G. Adamyan, B. Bychovski, V. Egorsin, M. Konstantinov, S. Lapsin, A. Maksimov, A. Saradzev, E. Sitkovskii, V. Sevkin and A. Sheglov. The Chinese trans. was published in 1936: Ai Ssu-ch'i and Ch'eng I-li (eds), *Hsin che-hsüeh ta-kang* (*Outline of the New Philosophy*), Peking 1936.

3. Mark B. Mitin and I. Razumovskii, *Dialekticheskii i Istoricheskii Materializm* (Dialectical and Historical Materialism), edited by the staff of the Institute of Philosophy, Komakademiia Moscow. Pt. I: Mark B. Mitin (ed.), *Dialekticheskii materializm*, Moscow 1933; Pt. II: *Istoricheskii materializm*, Mark B. Mitin and I. Razumovskii (eds), Moscow 1932. Chs. 1 and 2 of *Che-hsüeh hsüan-chi*, op. cit., form the transl. of Chs. 2 and 3 of *Dialecticheskii i Istoricheskii Materializm*. See the Preface to *Che-hsüeh hsüan-chi*, op. cit., p. I, and Ch. 1: '*Wei-wu-lun he wei-hsin-lun*' (Materialism and Idealism), pp. 39–157; and Ch. 2: '*Bien-cheng-fa wei-wu-lun*' (Dialectical Materialism), pp. 159–220.

9. Loren R. Graham, *Science and Philosophy in the Soviet Union*, New York 1972.

10. N. Knight, 'Mao Tse-tung's "On Contradiction" ', op. cit., pp. 653 ff.

11. Wang Meng-tsou (ed.), *K'o-hsüeh yü jen-sheng-kuan chih lun-chan* (The Controversy over Science and Life Views), Hong Kong 1973 (reprint). An extensive treatment of this controversy is to be found in D.W.Y. Kwok, *Scientism in Chinese Thought, 1900–1950*, New Haven and London 1965, p. 13, and Charlotte Furth, *Ting Wen-chiang. Science and China's New Culture*, Cambridge, Mass. 1970, ch. 5. The controversy over the social history of China is described comprehensively in Arif Dirlik, op. cit.

12. René Ahlberg, *Dialektische Philosophie und Gesellschaft in der Sowjetunion* (Dialectical Philosophy and Society in the Soviet Union), Berlin 1960. This is the most comprehensive description of the controversies over the dialectic between the Mechanists, the Deborinists and Stalin's supporters. On the other hand, I.M. Bochenski, *Der Sowjetische Dialektische Materialismus*, Munich 1950, offers a general perspective. A complete description, which is still indispensable, is Gustav A. Wetter's *Der dialektische Materialismus. Seine Geschichte und sein System in der Sowjetunion*, 5th edn, Freiburg im Breisgau 1960. There is an English trans. of Wetter's book by Peter Heath: *Dialectical Materialism: A Historical and Systematic Survey of Philosophy in the Soviet Union*, New York 1958. A short but excellent analysis of dialectical materialism as a science of legitimation is Oskar Negt's 'Marxismus als Legitimationswissenschaft. Zur Genese der Stalinistischen Philosophie' in Oskar Negt (ed.), *Nikolai Bukharin and Abram Deborin. Kontroversen über dialektischen und mechanizistischen Materialismus*, Frankfurt 1974, pp. 7–50. This edition is a German trans. of works by Deborin, Bukharin and Mitin. David Joravski, *Soviet Marxism and Natural Science, 1917–1932*, New York 1961, also covers the period under review here and gives a detailed report on the change of dialectical materialism from philosophy to what he calls 'caesaropapist dogmatism' (p. 311). A short summary can be found in Richard T. De George, *Patterns of Soviet Thought*, Ann Arbor, Mich. 1966, ch. 10, pp. 179–86. Julius F. Hecker (ed.), *Moscow Dialogues: Discussions on Red Philosophy*, London 1933, consists of interviews with Soviet philosophers on the Mechanistic and Deborinistic trends in Soviet philosophy. A more systematical study is Z.A. Jordan, *The Evolution of Dialectical Materialism, A Philosophical and Sociological Analysis*, New York 1967; see

also Loren R. Graham, op. cit. However the last two studies do not mention the Soviet manuals translated by the Chinese in the 1930s, nor do they analyse the ideological struggles in the 1920s.

13. Lyman P. Van Slyke's *Enemies and Friends: The United Front in Chinese Communist History*, Stanford 1967, offers an overview of the tactics of the United Front since the 1920s. The same is true of his article 'The Chinese Communist Movement during the Sino-Japanese War 1937–1945' in *The Cambridge History of China*, vol. 13, Pt. 2, op. cit. As to the history of Chinese–Soviet relations in this regard, see esp. Charles B. McLane, *Soviet Policy and the Chinese Communists 1931–1946*, New York 1958. There is a short but very detailed description in Jürgen Domes, *Vertagte Revolution. Die Politik der Kuomintang in China, 1923–1937*, Berlin 1969, pp. 647ff. See also Tetsuya Kataoka, *Resistance and Revolution in China: The Communist Party and the Second United Front*, Berkeley, Calif. 1974; James P. Harrison, *The Long March to Power: A History of the Chinese Communist Party*, West Hanover, Mass. 1972; Kuo Heng-yü, *Maos Weg zur Macht und die Komintern*, Paderborn 1975; Gregor Benton, 'The Second Wang Ming Line, 1935–38', *China Quarterly*, no. 16 (March 1975), pp. 61–94. Also important in this context is Raymond Wylie, op. cit. A short summary of the differences between Mao and Wang can be found in Jerome Ch'en, 'The Communist Movement, 1927–1937' in *The Cambridge History of China*, vol. 13, op. cit., pp. 168–229. The most detailed study of this question is Shum Kui-Kwong, *The Chinese Communists' Road to Power: The Anti-Japanese National United Front (1935–1945)*, Hong Kong 1988. New Chinese materials on this period have appeared in two articles by Thomas Kampen: 'The Zunyi Conference and the Rise of Mao Zedong', *Internationales Asienforum*, 3–4 (1986), pp. 347–60, and 'Wang Jiaxiang und der Aufstieg Mao Zedongs', *Asien. Deutsche Zeitschrift für Politik, Wirtschaft und Kultur*, no. 25 (Oct. 1987), pp. 1–19; and, in particular, by John W. Garver, 'The Origin of the Second United Front: The Comintern and the Chinese Communist Party', *China Quarterly*, no. 113 (March 1988), pp. 29–59. A short summary can also be found in Frederick C. Teiwes, 'Mao and His Lieutenants', *Australian Journal of Chinese Affairs*, nos 19 and 20 (Jan. and July 1988), pp. 1–80, esp. pp. 6ff., 35ff.

14. Wang Ming, *Mao's Betrayal*, Moscow 1979 (published in Germany as *50 Jahre KP China und der Verrat Mao Tse-tungs*, Berlin 1981); Chang Kuo-t'ao, *The Rise of the Chinese Communist Party*, vol. II: *1928–1938*, Lawrence, Kansas 1972; Otto Braun, *Chinesische Aufzeichnungen (1932–1939)*, Berlin 1973 (and in an English version as *A Comintern Agent in China, 1932–1939*, trans. Jeanne Moore, London and Stanford 1982); *Wang Ming hsüan-chi* (Selected Works of Wang Ming), vols 1–5, Tokyo 1975. For the Soviet point of view, see K.V. Kukushkin, 'The Comintern and the United National anti-Japanese Front in China' in R.A. Ulyanovski, *The Comintern and the East: The Struggle for the Communist Strategy and Tactics in the National Liberation Movements*, Moscow 1979, pp. 391–5.

15. *Wang Ming hsüan-chi*, Tokyo 1975.

16. Kwok, op. cit.; Brière, op. cit., pp. 34–6, 75–84; and 'L'effort de la philosophie marxiste en Chine', *Bulletin de l'université l'Aurore*, series III, 1947, 8:3, pp. 309–47.

17. Kuo Chan-p'o, *Chin wu-shih-nien Chung-kuo ssu-hsiang shih* (History of Chinese Thought in the last Fifty Years), Peking 1936.

18. Kwok, op. cit., pp. 192ff.

19. Chen Cheng-ti, op. cit., esp. p. 6.

20. Wylie, op. cit., pp. 40–7; Fogel, op. cit., pp. 27–30. Further remarks about Ai and Yeh can be found in two articles by Ignatius Ts'ao, 'Ai Ssu-ch'i: The Apostle of Chinese Marxism. Part One: His Life and Works', *Studies in Soviet Thought*, no. 12 (April 1972), pp. 1–36; and 'Ai Ssu-ch'i's Philosophy. Part Two: Dialectical Materialism', *Studies in Soviet Thought*, no. 12 (Sept. 1972), pp. 231–44.

21. Karl Mannheim, *Ideologie und Utopie*, 3rd edn, 1957; Ernst Topitsch, 'Über Leerformeln, Zur Pragmatik des Sprachgebrauchs in Philosophie und politischer Theorie' in E. Topitsch (ed.), *Probleme der Wissenschaftstheorie*, Vienna 1960; *Gottwerdung und Revolution*, Munich 1973; *Mythos, Philosophie, Politik. Zur Naturgeschichte der Illusion*, Freiburg im Breisgau 1969; Marcel Granet, *La pensée chinoise*, Paris 1934.

Part I (Chapters 2–4)

1. Cf. Wetter, op. cit., p. 149.
2. Ibid., p. 154.
3. Quoted by Ahlberg, op. cit., p. 12. As to Minin and Encmen, cf. Joravski, op. cit., p. 93.
4. Ibid., p. 15.
5. Wetter, op. cit., p. 152; Ahlberg, op. cit., p. 16.
6. Quoted by Wetter, op. cit., p. 164. On the Mechanist faction see also Joravski, op. cit., pp. 119–49; Hecker, op. cit., pp. 157–73; De George, op. cit., pp. 179–83.
7. Ahlberg, op. cit., p. 48.
8. Ivan Petrovitsch Pavlov (1849–1936), the Russian psychologist, became well known for his writings on the effects of internal secretions and 'conditional responses' (*Die höchste Nerventätigkeit von Tieren*, 1926). Cf. Wetter, op. cit., p. 542; Graham, op. cit., pp. 356–62.
9. As to Bukharin cf. S. Heitmann, 'Between Lenin and Stalin: Nicolai Bukharin' in L. Labedz (ed٠), *Revisionism*, London 1962, p. 77; Joravski, op. cit., pp. 49–60.
10. Quoted by Wetter, op. cit., p. 174.
11. Ibid., p. 188.
12. Ahlberg, op. cit., p. 13.
13. Quoted by Ahlberg, op. cit., p. 39
14. Ibid., p. 43.
15. Abram Deborin, 'Materialistische Dialektik und Naturwissenschaft' in Bukharin and Deborin, op. cit., p. 93.
16. Ibid., p. 94.
17. Ibid., p. 108.
18. Ibid., p. 110.
19. Ibid., p. 131.
20. Ibid., p. 104.
21. Ahlberg, op. cit., p. 70.
22. Ibid., p. 79.
23. Wetter, op. cit., p. 155.
24. Ahlberg, op. cit., p. 83.
25. Leonard Schapiro, *The History of the Communist Party of the Soviet Union*, 2nd edn, London 1970, pp. 387–8.

26. J.V. Stalin, 'Die Bucharingruppe und die rechte Abweichung in unserer Partei' in Bukharin and Deborin, op. cit., p. 392.
27. Ibid., p. 394.
28. Cf. his 'Theorie des historischen Materialismus' in Bukharin and Deborin, op. cit., p. 223 and on the theory of permanent revolution, op. cit., p. 260.
29. Ahlberg, op. cit., p. 119.
30. Ibid., p. 104.
31. Ibid., pp. 77, 93. As to the role of Mitin cf. Joravski, op. cit., pp. 251–71; Hecker, op. cit., p. 184.
32. Quoted by Wetter, op. cit., p. 196. See also M.B. Mitin, Judin, I. Raltsevik, '*O Novych zadacach marxistko-leninskoi filosofii*' (On the New Task of Marxist-Leninist Philosophy), *Pravda*, June 7, 1930.
33. Ibid.
34. Cf. Deborin, 'Lenin über Dialektik' in Bukharin and Deborin, op. cit., p. 135.
35. Wetter, op. cit., p. 196, n46.

Part II (Chapters 5–9)

1. Extensive descriptions of China in the 1930s can be found in McLane, Kataoka, Harrison, Domes, Van Slyke, Kuo, Benton, Wylie, Ch'en and Shum—the latter being the most recent study of the United Front. For an excellent survey of newly-available Chinese materials on the origins of the United Front, see John W. Garver, op. cit. G.K. Kindermann, *Der Ferne Osten, dtv-Weltgeschichte des 20 Jahrhunderts*, vol. 6, Munich 1970, offers a short analysis of the international relations of China in the 1930s; for further sources see note 13 of the Introduction.
2. Cf. Günther Nollau, *Die Internationale*, Cologne and Berlin 1959, p. 138.
3. A complete version of the 'manifesto' is to be found in *Kommunistische Internationale*, special issue, Jan. 1936, pp. 101–6. It is published in English as 'An Appeal to the Whole People of China to Resist Japan and Save the Country', *Inprecor*, vol. 15, pp. 1595–7, and in Chinese in Hu Hua, *Chung-kuo hsin min-chu chu-i ko-ming shih ts'an-k'ao tzu-liao* (Reference Materials on the History of the Chinese New Democratic Revolution), Peking 1951, pp. 263–9. According to recently published Chinese sources, there is no doubt that the manifesto was initiated by Wang Ming, thus confirming Kataoka's and Benton's thesis. A detailed account of the origin of the manifesto can be found in Garver, op. cit., pp. 31 ff., and in Hsiang Ch'ing, '*Pa-i hsüan-yen hsing-ch'eng li-shih kuo-ch'eng*' (The Historical Development of the August 1st Manifesto), *Tang-shih tzu-liao ts'ung-k'an* (Collection of Materials on Party History), no. 3 (1983), as well as in Shum, op. cit., pp. 17ff. and 29ff.
4. Domes, op. cit., p. 654.
5. For a copy of the telegram see *Selected Works of Mao Tse-tung*, vol. 1, p. 279, n. 4.
6. Wang Ming, 'The Struggle of the Anti-Japanese People's Front in China', *Communist International*, vol. 13, no. 6, p. 750; cf. also Shum, op. cit., p. 65.
7. G. Dimitroff, 'Zum 15. Jahrestag der Kommunistischen Partei Chinas', *Kommunistische Internationale*, no. 9 (Sept. 1936), pp. 880–3; cf. p. 891; English trans.: 'The Fifteenth Anniversary of the Communist Party of China', *Inprecor*, vol. 14, no. 44 (Sept. 1936), pp. 1207–8.
8. Domes, op. cit., p. 655.
9. *Selected Works of Mao Tse-tung*, vol. I, p. 259 (excerpts), complete text in *Mao Tse-*

tung hsüan-chi, vol. 5, p. 68: '*Chung-kuo kung-ch'an-tang chih Chung-kuo kuo-min-tang shu*'.

10. Cf. *Kommunistische Internationale*, no. 1 (Jan. 1937), pp. 68–76.
11. *Selected Works of Mao Tse-tung*, vol. I, p. 281.
12. Domes, op. cit., p. 656.
13. Ibid., p. 658.
14. Cf. Kuo, op. cit., p. 79; Domes, op. cit., p. 664; McLane, op. cit., pp. 82–8; Kataoka, op. cit., p. 43; Chang Kuo-t'ao, *Wo-ti hui-i*, vol. 3, op. cit., pp. 1239–40.
15. Shum, op. cit., p. 87; Domes, op. cit., pp. 664ff; Kuo, op. cit., pp. 80ff. The Soviet press reacted in a similar fashion: Chiang had been imprisoned because of his pro-Japanese activities, an assertion (later proved to have been baseless) which revealed Moscow's goals: namely to avoid the execution of Chiang, which would have been likely had he refused to meet the demands. This in turn would have brought about a further disintegration of China's military potential rather than a concentration of forces against Japan. Cf. McLane, op. cit., pp. 82ff.; Kuo, op. cit., p. 80.
16. There is a detailed description of the negotiations which led to the release of Chiang Kai-shek in Domes, op. cit., pp. 659.
17. See *Selected Works of Mao Tse-tung*, vol. I, pp. 281–2, n. 7.
18. '*Ken-chüeh ch'ih huo-an*' (Resolution on the Eradication of the Red Danger), *Tung-fang tsa-chih*, vol. 34, no. 6 (March 16, 1937), p. 102. Cf. Domes, op. cit., pp. 677ff.
19. Van Slyke, op. cit., pp. 92ff.
20. Chang Kuo-t'ao, *Wo-ti hui-i*, vol. 3, op. cit., pp. 1295–1300; Otto Braun, *A Comintern Agent in China*, op. cit., pp. 211–13; Kuo, op. cit., p. 94; Shum, op. cit., pp. 94, 106ff.
21. *Selected Works of Mao Tse-tung*, vol. II, p. 67. The Chinese characters '*tu-li tzu-chu*' are translated here as 'independence' and 'initiative'. 'Maintain the independence and keep the initiative' seems more suitable.
22. Ibid., p. 68.
23. Ibid., p. 65.
24. Ibid.
25. Benton, op. cit., p. 65.
26. '*Chung-kuo kung-ch'an-tang tui shih-chü hsüan-yen*' ('Declaration of the CCP on the current political situation', Dec. 25, 1937) in *K'ang-jih min-tsu t'ung-i chan-hsien chih-nan* (Guide to the Documents of the Anti-Japanese People's United Front), edited by Chung-kuo kung-ch'an-tang, Chung-yang wei-yüan-hui, n.p., n.d. vol. 3, pp. 1–5. For an English version see Warren Kuo, *Analytical History of the Chinese Communist Party* (in 4 vols), Taipei 1966–78, vol. 3, pp. 368–71.
27. 'Ch'en Shao-yü, *Mu'ch'ien, k'ang-chan hsing-shih chi jen-wu*' (The Current Situation and Tasks in the War of Resistance) in Kuo Hua-lun, *Chung-kung shih-lun* (History of the Communist Party of China), Taipei 1968, vol. 2, p. 280. For an English trans. see Kuo, *Analytical History*, op. cit., vol. 3, pp. 360–4.
28. Ch'en Shao-yü, '*San-yüeh cheng-chih chü hui-i tsung-chieh*' (Summary of the political situation in the last three months) (March 2, 1938) in *Wang Ming hsüan-chi*, op. cit., vol. 5, pp. 95–116, esp. pp. 106ff.
29. Ibid., p. 105.
30. Ibid., p. 107.

31. Mao Tse-tung, '*Lun hsin chieh-tuan*' (On the New Period) in *Selected Works of Mao Tse-tung*, vol. 5, p. 200. A complete trans. of the report can be found in Kuo, op.cit., p. 139.
32. *Selected Works of Mao Tse-tung*, vol. II, pp. 195–211.
33. Ibid., pp. 195–6.
34. Ibid., p. 213; cf. Shum on Mao's statement at the 6th plenum, op. cit., pp. 138ff.
35. *Selected Works of Mao Tse-tung*, vol. II, p. 219.
36. Further confirmation is provided by Shih Feng, *Fan-tui Wang Ming t'ou-hsiang chu-yi lu-hsien tou-cheng* (The Struggle to Oppose Wang Ming's Capitulationist Line), Shanghai 1976, p. 34. This note is taken from Shum, op. cit., p. 271, n. 47. Ma Ch'i-pin, '*K'ang-chan ch'u-ch'i ti Wang Ming t'ou-hsiang chu-i lu-hsien ts'o-wu*' (The Mistakes of the Capitulationist Wang Ming Line during the Early Stage of the War of Resistance) in *Tang-shih tzu-liao ts'ung-k'an* (Collection of Party History Materials), vol. 1, 1981, pp. 130–2; see also below, pt. IV, notes 28, 29, and 30, for further articles.
37. Ibid., pp. 289–90.
38. Ibid.
39. Cf. Domes, op. cit., pp. 686 ff. Harrison, *The Long March to Power*, op. cit., *pp. 294.ff.*

Part III (Chapter 10)

1. See above, Pt. I, Ch. 2. Ahlberg, op. cit., p. 42.
2. Ibid.
3. After the outbreak of the Sino-Japanese war, Yeh returned to Szechuan and taught at the Central Military Academy; he joined the Kuomintang in 1939 and became the leading theoretician and propagandist of the 'Three People's Principles', the Kuomintang's ideology. In 1949 he became chairman of the propaganda department of the Kuomintang and one year later went to Taiwan (see also *Biographical Dictionary of Republican China*, op. cit., vol. II, pp. 216ff.).
4. Yeh Ch'ing, *Che-hsüeh tao he-chu chü* (Whither Philosophy?), Shanghai 1935.
5. See above, pt. I, Ch. 1, n. 3.
6. Ibid., n. 4.
7. Yeh Ch'ing, op. cit., pp. 1–12.
8. Ibid., p. 17.
9. Ibid., p. 19.
10. Ibid.
11. Ibid., p. 23.
12. Jen Hung-chün (1868–1961), mathematician and close friend of Hu Shih (Kwok, op. cit., p. 111), was one of the most important promoters of Western science in China; he was President of the 'Science Society' in 1914–23, 1934–6 and 1947–50. Luo Chia-lun (1896–) was one of the leaders of the 'May Fourth Movement'; he was also President of the Ch'ing-hua University. Kuo Jen-yüan (1898–) was a noted psychologist and behaviourist. Ting Wen-chiang (1887–1935) was a well-known geologist and advocate of English empiricism in China. See also note 38 below.
13. Yeh Ch'ing, op. cit., p. 50.

14. Ibid., p. 35.
15. Ibid., p. 55.
16. Ibid., p. 51.
17. Ibid., p. 92.
18. Yeh Ch'ing (Tsing Yeh), *Chang Tung-sun che-hsüeh p'i-p'an* (Critique of Chang Tun-sun's Philosophy), 2 vols, Shanghai 1934; and *Che-hsüeh wen-t'i* (Problems of Philosophy), Shanghai 1936.
19. Yeh Ch'ing, *Che-hsüeh wen-t'i*, op. cit.
20. Ibid., pp. 1–20.
21. Ibid., p. 17.
22. Ibid., p. 29.
23. Ibid.
24. Ibid., p. 33.
25. Ibid., pp. 19 and 32.
26. Ibid., p. 34.
27. '*Wu-chih yü ching-shen*' (Matter and Spirit), ibid., pp. 35–51; '*Chi-hsieh-lun yü mu-ti-lun*' (Mechanism and Teleologism), ibid., pp. 52–68; '*Yu-ting yü wu-ting*' (Determinism and Indeterminism), ibid., pp. 69–87; '*Tzu-jan yü jen-lei*' (Nature and Humanity), ibid., pp. 89–106; '*Pi-jan yü tzu-yu*' (Necessity and Freedom), ibid., pp. 197–235; '*T'a-lü yü tzu-lü*' (Heteronomy and Autonomy), ibid., pp. 136–55. '*Ching-yen yü li-hsing*' (Experience and Reason), ibid., pp. 173–93; '*Kan-chüeh yü ssu-wei*' (Perception and Thought), ibid., pp. 193–207; '*Shih-tsai yü kuan-nien*' (Reality and Idea), ibid., pp. 209–21; '*Ming-mu-lun yü shih-tsai-lun*' (Nominalism and Realism), ibid., p. 222–35.
28. Ibid., p. 28.
29. Ibid., p. 37.
30. Ibid., p. 39.
31. Ibid., p. 42.
32. Ibid., p. 44.
33. Ibid., p. 46.
34. Ibid., p. 50.
35. Ibid., p. 271.
36. Yeh Ch'ing, '*Wu-chih yü ching-shen*' (Matter and Spirit), *Yen-chiu yü p'i-p'an* (Study and Critique), vol. 1, no, 4, August 7 1935. This has been reprinted in Yeh Ching (ed.), *Hsin-che-hsüeh lun-chan-chi* (Controversies over the New Philosophy), Shanghai, Oct. 1936, pp. 217–20.
37. Cf. Kwok's description of Yeh Ch'ing's 'philosophy' in Kwok, op. cit., p. 170. Brière, *Fifty Years*, op. cit., pp. 81–4.
38. In regard to Ting Wen-chiang's understanding of science, see the extensive biography by Charlotte Furth, *Ting Wen-chiang*, op cit., esp. pp. 94 and 226. Regarding Hu Shih, Wu Chih-hui, Ch'en Tu-shiu and their understanding of science, see Kwok, op. cit., pp. 33, 59, 85.
39. The works quoted most frequently by Yeh include E. Baudin, *Introduction generale à la philosophie*, Paris 1927; E. Durand, *Histoire de la philosophie*, Paris 1930; E. Brehier, *Histoire de la philosophie*, Paris 1932; Abel Rey, *La philosophie moderne*, Paris 1927; Edmont Globot, *Le système des sciences*, Paris 1930.
40. Yeh Ch'ing, *Che-hsüeh wen-t'i*, op, cit., p. 253.
41. Ai Ssu-ch'i, *Ta-chung che-hsüeh* (Philosophy for the Masses), Shanghai 1936. Cf.

Ts'ao, op. cit., pt. 1, p. 9ff., and Wang Hui-te and Chia Ch'un-feng, '*Chi-nien "Ta-chung che-hsüeh" ch'u-pan wu-shih chou-nien*' (Commemorating the 50th Anniversary of Publication of the 'Philosophy for the Masses'), *Jen-min jih-pao*, March 21, 1986, p. 5.

42. Wang Hui-te and Chia Ch'un-feng, op. cit. For further details of Ai's career see Fogel, op. cit. (on the question of the popularisation of Marxist philosophy in China, see, in particular, Ch. 5 of his book); also Ignatius J.H. Ts'ao, 'Ai Ssu-ch'i: The Apostle of Chinese Communism', parts I and II, op. cit.; and the *Biographical Dictionary of Republican China*, op. cit., vol. I, p. 1ff.

43. Cf. Chs. 11 and 16 of this study.

44. See Chs. 6 and 7 of this study.

45. Ai Ssu-ch'i, *Hsin che-hsüeh lun-chi* (Essays on the New Philosophy), Shanghai 1938, p. 88; this was a collection of essays by Ai written in 1933–5. Ch'en Li-fu (1900–), a full member of the CEC of the Kuomintang, was Director for Political Education of the Chinese National Army in 1929–31, and later became Minister of Education in the National Government (1938–44). His works on 'vitalism' (*wei-sheng-lun*) are connected with the 'New Life Movement' (*hsin sheng-huo yün-tung*), a moralistic revival movement established by Chiang Kai-shek in February 1934 which on the one hand was aimed at stopping the penetration of Marxist thought into China, and on the other hand was to counteract ideologically the increasing moral decay and social disintegration in the country. The designation 'mortal enemy' of 'materialism' can be understood in regard to the situation from which the 'New Life Movement' originated. It began in the seat of the headquarters for the campaign against the Red Army, Nanch'ang, in Kiangsi province. Ch'en Li-fu, *Wei-sheng-lun* (Vitalism), 1934 (no place of publication). As to the 'New Life Movement', see O. Brière, op. cit., p. 60; Domes, op. cit., p. 550.

46. Ai Ssu-ch'i, *Ta-chung che-hsüeh*, op. cit., p. 100. The term 'pragmatism' meant especially the philosophy of Hu Shih; as to the latter see note 38 above.

47. Ai Ssu-ch'i, ibid., p. 14. Cf. *Tu-shu sheng-huo*, vol. 1, no. 3, p. 10, does not contain this passage.

48. Li Ch'ung-chi (alias Ai Ssu-ch'i), '*Niu-chiao-chien lü-hsing chi*' (Report on a Journey to the Tip of a Cow's Horn), *Tu-shu sheng-huo*, vol. 1, no. 9 (March 1935), pp. 18–21.

49. Ibid., pp. 52–9.

50. Ibid., p. 59.

51. Wu Ch'eng-en, *The Adventures of Monkey* (*Hsi-yu-chi*), trans. Arthur Waley, Taipei 1967 (reprint).

52. P'u Sung-ling, *Liao-chai chih-i* (German trans. by E. Schmitt), *Seltsame Geschichten aus dem Liao Chai*, Berlin n.d.

53. In 1697 Swift wrote a pamphlet entitled *The Battle of the Books* in which he mocked, in the manner of the Homeric frog-mice war, the struggle of the old against the new.

54. Ai Ssu-ch'i, '*Yeh Ch'ing hsien-sheng ti che-hsüeh hsiao-mien lun*' (Mr Yeh Ch'ing's Theory of the Annihilation of Philosophy) in 'Yeh Ch'ing (ed.), *Hsin che-hsüeh lun-chan chi* (Controversies over the New Philosophy), Shanghai 1936, p. 145. It also appears as an article in *Tu-shu sheng-huo*, op. cit., vol. 2, no. 12 (Oct. 1935). Ai Ssu-ch'i '*Che-hsüeh chiang-hua p'i-p'ing ti fan p'i-p'ing*' (Critique of the Critique of the 'Talks on Philosophy') in *Hsin che-hsüeh lun-chan chi*, op. cit., p. 8, and *Tu-shu sheng-huo*, op. cit., vol. 4, no. 12 (Aug. 1936).

55. 'Mr Yeh Ch'ing's Theory', op. cit., p. 147.

56. Ibid.

57. Ibid., p. 14.

58. Ai Ssu-ch'i, '*Chung-kuo mu-ch'ien ti wen-hua yün-tung*' (The Present Chinese Culture Movement), *Sheng-huo hsing-ch'i k'an*, vol. 1, no. 19, quoted by T'an Fu-chih in *Che-hsüeh p'i-p'an chi* (Philosophical Critiques), Shanghai 1937, p. 61; and in '*Shih-chieh kuan ti ch'üeh-li*' (The Construction of World-Views), *Hsin shih-chien*, vol. 2, no. 1, quoted by T'an, op. cit., p. 63.

59. Ibid., p. 61.

60. Ibid., p. 63.

61. See Ch. 6 of this study.

62. As to the 'New Enlightenment Movement' (*Hsin ch'i-meng yün-tung*) cf. Wylie, *The Emergence of Maoism*, op. cit., 28–37, 47; Mechthild Leutner, 'Ch'en Po-ta und Ai Ssu-ch'i in der Neuen Aufklärungsbewegung von 1936/7. Zur Anfangsphase der nationalen Neurorientierung der marxistischen Wissenschaft am Vorabend des Antijapanischen Widerstandkrieges' in *Bochumer Jahrbuch zur Ostasienforschung*, 1979, p. 67.

63. Ch'en Po-ta, '*Yeh Ch'ing che-hsüeh p'i-p'an*' (Critique of Yeh Ch'ing's Philosophy), *Hsin shih-chieh*, vol. 1, no. 1. This has been reprinted in *Hsin che-hsüeh lun-chan chi*, op. cit., pp. 22–100.

64. Ibid., p. 89–90.

65. Ibid., p. 85.

66. Ibid., p. 35.

67. Ibid., p. 36.

68. Ch'en Po-ta, '*Wen-hua shang ti ta lien-he yü hsin ch'i-meng yü-tung ti li-shih t'e-tien*' (The Great Cultural Unity and the Historical Peculiarities of the New Enlightenment Movement) in Hsia Cheng-nung, *Hsien chieh-tuan ti Chung-kuo ssu-hsiang yün-tung*, Shanghai 1937, pp. 128–37.

69. Lu Lung-chi, '*Kuan-yü ching-shen yü wu-chih*' (On Spirit and Matter), *Min-hsin yüeh-k'an*, vol. 1 (Sept. 15, 1936). This has been reprinted in *Hsin che-hsüeh lun-chan chi*, op. cit., p. 233.

70. Ibid., p. 234.

71. Ibid., p. 246.

72. Ibid., p. 240.

73. Ai Sheng, *Yeh Ch'ing che-hsüeh p'i-p'an* (A Critique of Yeh Ch'ing's Philosophy), Shanghai 1937.

74. Ibid., p. 67.

75. Ibid., p. 68.

76. Ibid., p. 29.

77. Ibid., p. 34.

78. Ibid., p. 40.

79. Ibid., p. 43.

80. Ibid., p. 93.

81. Ibid.

82. Ibid., p. 93.

83. Ibid., p. 19.

84. Ibid., p. 98.

85. T'an Fu-chih, *Che-hsüeh p'i-p'an chi* (Philosophical Critiques), Shanghai 1937. According to Chen Cheng-ti, op. cit., T'an Fu-chih seems to have been a follower

of Yeh Ch'ing, but afterwards joined the camp of his former critics (p. 12). Lo
Lung-chi and Ai Sheng were both pseudonyms used by T'an Fu-chih (p. 12). This
seems probable, particularly because their arguments are sometimes similar, but we
have no other confirmation of this.

86. Ibid., p. 61.
87. Ibid., p. 65ff.
88. Ibid., p. 96.
89. Ibid., p. 99.
90. Ch'en Po-ta, '*Hsin che-hsüeh che ti tzu-chi p'i-p'an he kuan-yü hsin ch'i-meng yün-tung ti
    chien-i*' (Self-criticism of a New Philosopher and Suggestions for a New
    Enlightenment Movement), *Tu-shu sheng-huo*, vol. 4, no. 9 (Sept. 10, 1936),
    pp. 453–5.
91. T'an, op. cit., p. 126.
92. Ibid., p. 83.
93. Ibid., p. 103.

Chapter 11

1. Ai Ssu-ch'i, *Ta-chung che-hsüeh*, op. cit., p. 60.
2. Ibid., p. 70.
3. Ibid., p. 71.
4. Ibid., p. 73.
5. Ibid., p. 81.
6. Wetter, op. cit., pp. 156, 561, 580.
7. Ai Ssu-ch'i, *Ssu-hsiang fang-fa lun* (Methodology of Thought), Chungking,
   Hongkong, Sian and elsewhere, 1st edn Oct. 1936, 4th edn April 1939. The
   following notes relate to the 4th edn.
8. Ibid., p. 7.
9. Ibid., p. 38.
10. Ibid., p. 22.
11. Ibid., pp. 23–6.
12. Ibid., p. 27.
13. Ibid., p. 28.
14. Ibid., p. 30.
15. Ibid., p. 31.
16. Ibid.
17. Ibid., p. 27.
18. Ibid., p. 35.
19. Ibid., p. 40.
20. Ibid., p. 49.
21. Ibid., p. 79.
22. Ibid., p. 82.
23. Ibid., p. 86.
24. Ibid., p. 87.
25. Ibid., p. 88.
26. Yeh Ch'ing, *Che-hsüeh wen-t'i*, op. cit., p. 173.
27. Ibid., p. 174.

28. Ibid., p. 178.
29. Ibid., p. 176.
30. Ibid., p. 177.
31. Ibid., p. 178.
32. Ibid., p. 181.
33. Ibid., pp. 192, 197.
34. Ibid., p. 193.
35. Ibid., p. 204.

Chapter 12

1. Wetter, op. cit., p. 598. 'Formal logic' has obviously not been adopted in the Soviet Union. The controversy surrounding it is concerned merely with the three basic elements in their simple forms; there is no discussion of either the Aristotelean syllogistic or the development of logic since Frege and Husserl. This would probably have been too complicated for the political struggle, which was tied to the discussion over logic. This applied to the Chinese theoreticians to an even greater degree. As to the history of logic, cf. Günther Patzig, 'Logik' in *Philosophie. Das Fischer-Lexikon*, vol. 2, Frankfurt 1963, pp. 147–60, as well as the literature he refers to.
2. See also Yeh Ch'ing, *Lun-li-hsüeh wen-t'i* (Problems of Logic), Shanghai 1937, pp. 149, 154. Wetter, op. cit, p. 598.
3. Quoted by Wetter, op. cit., p. 599.
4. Ibid.
5. Yeh Ch'ing, *Lun-li hsüeh wen-t'i*, op. cit., p. 149.
6. Ibid., p. 155; Ai Ssu-chi and Cheng I-li (eds), *Hsin che-hsüeh ta-kang*, op. cit., p. 412.
7. Cf. Pt. I of this work.
8. Wetter, op. cit., p. 600; Bochenski, op. cit., p. 88.
9. As to the reception of logic in China, cf. the works by Chin Yüeh-lin, *Lo-chi* (Logic), Peking 1935; Lin Chung-ta, *Tsung-he lo-chi* (Synthetic Logic), Chung-hua shu-tien 1936; Wang Chang-huan, *Lun-li hsüeh ta-kang* (Survey of Logic), Shanghai 1930; Yen Fu, *Mu-Le lo-chi* (Mill's Logic), Shanghai 1902; Hu Shih, *The Development of the Logical Method in Ancient China*, Yatung shu-chü 1922. Cf. also O. Brière, p. 84.
10. Ai Ssu-ch'i, *Ta-chung che-hsüeh*, op. cit., p. 140; cf. *Tu-Shu sheng-huo*, vol. 2 (July 1935), p. 252.
11. Ibid., p. 253.
12. Cf. Pt. II of this work.
13. Ai Ssu-ch'i, '*Kuan-yü 'hsing-shih lo-chi yü pien-cheng lo-chi*' (On Formal and Dialectical Logic) in *Che-hsüeh yü sheng-huo* (Philosophy and Life), Shanghai, April 1937, p. 17. The article, however, dates from the autumn of 1936, since it was reprinted in Dec. 1936 in *Hsin che-hsüeh lun-chan chi*, op. cit. Chen Cheng-ti, op. cit., also mentions that Ai changed his opinion of the relevance of 'formal logic' at that time (p. 21).
14. Ai Ssu-ch'i, *Che-hsüeh yü sheng-huo*, op. cit., p. 27.
15. Ai Ssu-ch'i, *Ssu-hsiang fang-fa lun*, op. cit., p. 109.

16. Ibid., p. 111.
17. *The Pinyin Chinese-English Dictionary*, Hong Kong 1979, p. 148.
18. *A New Practical Chinese-English Dictionary*, Taipei 1971, p. 174.
19. Ai Ssu-ch'i, '*Hsing-shih lun-li hsüeh he pien-cheng fa*' (Formal Logic and Dialectic) in Ai Ssu-ch'i, *Lun Chung-kuo t'e-shu hsing chi ch'i-t'a* (On the Peculiarity of China, *inter alia*), Hong Kong 1941, pp. 147–74.
20. Ibid., p. 149.
21. Ibid.
22. Ibid., p. 150.
23. As to the question of the defence of Wuhan, see Benton, op. cit., p. 86. Mao Tse-tung, 'Uber die neue Periode' in Kuo Heng-yü, op. cit., p. 162.
24. Ai Ssu-ch'i, '*Hsing-shih lun-li hsüeh he pien-cheng fa*', op. cit., p. 147.
25. Cf. Pt. II of this work; see also Mao Tse-tung, 'Policies, Measures and Perspectives for Resisting the Japanese Invasion, July 23, 1937' in *Selected Works*, vol. II, pp. 13, 17. As to the position of Wang Ming, see Benton, op. cit., p. 78.
26. Ai Ssu-ch'i, '*Hsing-shih lun-li hsüeh he pien-cheng fa*', op. cit., p. 153.
27. Ibid., pp. 157–8.
28. Yeh Ch'ing, *Lun-li hsüeh wen-t'i*, op. cit.
29. Ibid., p. 16.
30. Ibid.
31. Ibid., p. 26.
32. Ibid., p. 35.
33. Ibid., p. 38.
34. Ibid.
35. Ibid.
36. Ibid., p. 40.
37. Ibid., p. 41.
38. Ibid., p. 43.
39. Ibid.
40. Ibid., p. 50.
41. The connection between 'dualism' and 'eclecticism' can even be found in Lenin, though without concrete political implications: 'The materialist elimination of the "dualism of spirit and body" [i.e. materialist monism] consists of the fact that the spirit, the secondary, is a function of the brain, the reflection of the external world. The idealistic elimination of the "dualism of spirit and body" [i.e., idealistic monism] consists of the fact that the spirit is not a function of the body, that the spirit is consequently primary . . . there can be no other type beyond these two diametrically opposed types of elimination of the "dualism of spirit and body", apart from eclecticism, i.e. the absurd mixing of materialism and idealism.' Trans. from V.I. Lenin, *Gesammelte Werke*, vol. 14, 1961, p. 83.
42. Yeh Ch'ing, '*Kuan-yü cheng-chih tang-p'ai*' (On Political Parties) in Mao Tse-tung et. al, *T'ung-i chan-hsien hsia tang-p'ai wen-t'i* (The question of parties under the United Front), Yenan 1938, p. 66. Cf. Van Slyke, op. cit., p. 102.
43. Yeh Ch'ing, *Lun-li hsüeh wen-t'i*, op. cit., p. 33.
44. Ibid., pp. 154, 159.
45. Ibid., p. 185.
46. Ch'en Po-ta, '*Yeh Ch'ing che-hsüeh p'i-p'an*' (Yeh Ch'ing's Critique of Philosophy) in *Hsin che-hsüeh lun-chan chi*, op. cit., p. 61. The senselessness of 'formal logic' was

also maintained by Miao Nan: '*Yeh Ch'ing "Hsing-shih lo-chi yü pien-cheng lo-chi" p'i-p'an*' (Critique of Yeh Ch'ing's 'Formal Logic and Dialectical Logic') in *Shi-tai lun-t'an*, vol. 1, no. 7 (July 1936), pp. 336–9, quoted in Chen Cheng-ti, op. cit., p. 20.

47. Ibid., p. 60.
48. Ibid., p. 69.
49. Ibid., p. 75.
50. Ibid., p. 68.
51. Ibid.
52. Ibid., p. 75.
53. Ibid., p. 78. Yeh's comment is found in Ch'en's article, which Yeh had criticised systematically.
54. Cf. Pt. II of this work.
55. Ch'en Po-ta, '*Hsin che-hsüeh che ti tzu-chi p'i-p'an ho kuan-yü hsin ch'i-meng yün-tung ti chien-i*', op. cit., p. 127.
56. Quoted by T'an, op. cit., p. 127.
57. T'an, op. cit., p. 114.
58. Ibid., p. 124.
59. Ibid., p. 43.
60. Ibid., p. 49.
61. Ibid., p. 50.
62. Ibid., p. 51.
63. Wolfgang Lippert, *Entstehung und Funktion einiger chinesischer marxistischer Termini*, Wiesbaden 1979, p. 258.
64. Ai Sheng, op. cit., p. 43.

Chapter 13

1. Ai Ssu-ch'i, '*Hsiang-tui yü chüeh-tui*' (Relative and Absolute) in Ai Ssu-ch'i, *Che-hsüeh yü sheng-huo*, op. cit., pp. 1–10.
2. Ibid., p. 2.
3. Ibid., p. 3.
4. Ibid.
5. Ibid.
6. Ibid., p. 5.
7. *The Pinyin Chinese-English Dictionary*, Shanghai 1979, p. 252.
8. Ai Ssu-ch'i, op. cit., p. 7.
9. Ibid., p. 9.
10. Ibid., p. 10.
11. Cf. Yeh Ch'ing, *Che-hsüeh wen-t'i*, op. cit., p. 253.

Chapter 14

1. Yeh Ch'ing, '*Fan tu-ching lun chung ti wen-t'i*' (Problems which Result from the Rejection of the Theory of Reading the Classics) in *Yen-chiu yü p'i-p'an*, vol. 1, no. 8, Dec. 20, 1935, repr. in Yeh Ch'ing (ed.), *Hsin che-hsüeh lun-chan chi*, op. cit., pp. 277–87.

2. Ibid., p. 278.
3. Ibid.
4. Ibid., p. 279.
5. K. Marx and F. Engels, *Communist Manifesto*, Frans. S. Moore, Moscow, p. 55.
6. Karl Marx, *Die Revolution in China und Europa, MEW*, vol. 9, Berlin 1960, pp. 95–102.
7. Yeh, op. cit., p. 278
8. Ai Ssu-ch'i, '*Tu-ching ma? Tu wai-kuo-shu ma?*' (Should one read the Classics? Should one read Foreign Books?) in *Tu-shu sheng-huo*, vol. 2, no. 10 (Sept. 25, 1935), p. 427.
9. Ai Ssu-ch'i, '*Lüeh-shuo wai-yin lun yü nei-yin lun*' (Comments on the Theory of Internal and External Causes) in *Hsin-che-hsüeh lun-chan chi*, op. cit., p. 269. It can be found in *Tu-shu sheng-huo*, vol. 4, no. 2 and '*Kuan-yü nei-yin lun he wai-yin lun*' (On Internal and External Causes) in ibid. Ai Ssu-ch'i, *Che-hsüeh yü sheng-huo*, op. cit., p. 33; and *Tu-shu sheng-huo*, vol. 4, no. 4, repr. in *Hsin che-hsüeh lun-chan chi*, op. cit., pp. 297–307.
10. Ai Ssu-ch'i, *Kuan-yü nei-yin lun yü wai-lin lun*, op. cit., p. 44.
11. Ai Ssu-ch'i, *Che-hsüeh yü sheng-huo*, op. cit., p. 32.
12. Ibid.
13. Ibid.

Chapter 15

1. Wetter, op. cit., pp. 154, 166; Ahlberg, op. cit., pp. 74, 127.
2. Ai Ssu-ch'i, *Ta-chung che-hsüeh*, op. cit., p. 124.
3. Ai, Ssu-ch'i, *Ssu-hsiang fang-fa lun*, op. cit., p. 139.
4. Ibid., p. 141.

Chapter 16

1. Ai Ssu-ch'i, *Ta-chung che-hsüeh*, op. cit., p. 116.
2. Ai Ssu-ch'i, *Ssu-hsiang fang-fa lun*, op. cit., p. 118.
3. Ibid., p. 123.
4. Ibid., p. 125.
5. Ibid., p. 132.
6. Ai Ssu-ch'i (ed.), *Che-hsüeh hsüan-chi* (Selected Philosophical Works), Shanghai 1940.
7. Cf. the titles of the works trans. from Russian given by Ai in the preface of *Che-hsüeh hsüan-chi*, ibid., p. 1.
8. Ibid., pp. 431–543.
9. Ibid., p. 2.
10. Ibid., pp. 450, 454.
11. Ibid., p. 452.
12. Ibid., p. 458.
13. Ibid., p. 463.
14. Ibid., p. 442.
15. Ibid., p. 459.

16. Ibid., p. 460.
17. Ibid., p. 460.
18. Ibid., p. 437.
19. Ibid., p. 497.
20. Ibid., p. 498. Cf. Mao, op. cit., p. 330.
21. Ai Ssu-ch'i, *Che-hsüeh hsüan-chi*, op. cit., p. 498.
22. Ibid., p. 500.
23. Ibid.
24. Mao, op. cit., p. 318.
25. Ibid.

Part IV (Chapters 17–19)

1. Cf., for example, Ch'en Chih-yüan's work: *Hsien-tai che-hsüeh ti chi-pen wen-t'i* (Fundamental Problems of Philosophy), Shanghai 1936; '*Yeh Ch'ing che-hsüeh wang he-ch'u ch'ü*' (Where is Yeh Ch'ing's Philosophy Heading for?), *Tu-shu sheng-huo*, vol. 4, nos. 4 and 5 (Jan. 1936), repr. in *Hsin che-hsüeh lun-chan chi*, op. cit., pp. 106–24. The nature of Ch'en's works calls for his inclusion in the Ai Ssu-ch'i and Ch'en Po-ta line, as does that of Hu Sheng with his work *Pien-cheng fa wei-wu lun ju-men* (Introduction to Dialectical Materialism), n.p. 1938. The only systematic description is found in Ch'en Wei-shih, *Hsin che-hsüeh t'i-hsi chiang-hua* (Conversations on the System of New Philosophy), Shanghai, April 1937. This 400-page work differs from those of Ai Ssu-ch'i solely in the order of the chapters and thus needs no special analysis. Nevertheless, it is, apart from the works of Ai, the only systematic introduction to the philosophy of dialectical materialism. In particular, Ch. 5: 'Basic rules of dialectical materialism' (*pien-cheng fa ken-pen fa-tse*) contains a description of all the essential elements of the 'law of the unity of opposites' (*mao-tun t'ung-i lü, tui-li t'ung-i fa-tse*), op. cit., pp. 296–305.
2. An account of the question of authenticity is given by Fogel, op. cit., pp. 61–71, and by Schram: *Mao Tse-tung's Thought to 1949*, op. cit., pp. 837–44. Cf. also the literature on this theme in note 7 of the Introduction; esp. Takeuchi Minoru, '*Mō Takutō no "Mujun ron"* ', op. cit., and 'Mujun ron no genkei hosetsu', op. cit.; Lippert, 'Zur Entstehungsgeschichte', op. cit.; Knight, 'Mao Zedong's "On Contradiction" and "On Practice" ', op. cit.; Schram, 'Mao Tse-tung and the Theory of the Permanent Revolution', op. cit., pp. 223–4.
3. '*Mō Takutō shu hokan*' (*Mao Tse-tung chi pu-chüan*), op. cit., vol. 5, pp. 187–280, 220–34, pp. 240–78 (*Mao-tun t'ung-i fa-tse*, respectively *Mao-tun lun*).
4. Knight, 'Mao Zedong's "On Contradiction" and "On Practice" ', op. cit., p. 643. There also exists a complete translation of the text by Nick Knight: *Mao Zedong's 'On Contradiction': An annotated translation of the pre-liberation text*, Nathan, Queensland 1981.
5. Kung Yü-chih, '*Shih-chien lun' san-t'i*' (Three Points regarding 'On Practice') in *Lun Mao Tse-tung che-hsüeh ssu-hsiang*, op. cit., pp. 66–87, esp. pp. 66–72.
6. Ibid., p. 67.
7. Edgar Snow, *The Long Revolution*, London 1973, pp. 194–5; see also Schram, *Mao Tse-tung's Thought*, op. cit., p. 838, n. 109.
8. Kung, op. cit., p. 67.

9. Schram says that confirmation of Mao's authorship of 'Dialectical Materialism', and of the fact that the Ta-lien edition of 1946 was a reprint of the 1937 edition, 'has been provided recently from an extremely authoritative source', and he mentions the article by Kung, op. cit. (Schram, *Mao Tse-tung's Thought*, op. cit., p. 840, n. 112). In my view, the only authoritative confirmation would be the publication of Mao Tse-tung's handwritten manuscripts and of the 1937 edition. The characterisation of Mao as '*chu-chiang*' seems to make it clear that in 1938 the publisher responsible for the War of Resistance University series did not regard Mao as the author. For Knight's opinion see his article in *China Quarterly*, op. cit., and for Fogel's position cf. Fogel, op. cit., pp. 66ff.

10. Schram, *Mao Tse-tung's Thought*, op. cit., p. 838; Wittfogel, op. cit., p. 264. Besides Kung, op. cit., Kuo Hua-jo maintains that Mao wrote the 'Lecture Outlines'. See Kuo Hua-jo, '*Mao chu-hsi k'ang-chan ch'u-ch'i kuang-hui ti che-hsüeh huo-tung*' (Chairman Mao's Brilliant Philosophical Activities at the Beginning of the War of Resistance), *Chung-kuo che-hsüeh*, no. 1, 1979, pp. 34ff., 31–7. See also Wen Chi-tse, *Mao chu-hsi tsai Yen-an tsen-yang chiao-tao wo-men hsüeh che-hsüeh* (How Chairman Mao taught us to study Philosophy in Yenan), *She-hui k'o-hsüeh chan-hsien* (Social Science Front), vol. 5, no. 3(19), 1982, pp. 1–8.

11. Wittfogel, op. cit., p. 252.

12. Kung, op. cit., p. 68.

13. See Takeuchi Minoru, '*Mō Takutō no "Mujun ron"* ', op. cit, pp. 490–2; Doolin and Golas, op. cit., pp. 38ff., and Ai Ssu-ch'i, '*Tsen-yang yen-chiu pien-cheng fa wei-wu lun*' in *Ai Ssu-ch'i wen-chi*, vol. 1, pp. 449—59.

14. *Mao Tse-tung che-hsüeh ssu-hsiang (chai-lu)*, ed. by the Pei-ching ta-hsüeh che-hsüeh hsi; cf. Schram, *Mao Tse-tung's Thought*, op. cit., p. 838, n. 108.

15. Takeuchi Minoru, ' *"Mujun ron" no genkei hosetsu*', op. cit., pp. 261–3, and Fogel, p. 68. Kuo Hua-jo, op. cit, p. 34.

16. Hsin Chung, '*Mao chu-hsi tu-shu sheng-huo chi-shih*' (Some Records of Mao Tse-tung's life in reading), *She-hui k'o-hsüeh chan-hsien* (Social Sciences Front), vol. 4, no. 4/16 (1981), pp. 1–15, esp. pp. 7ff.

17. The other books were *Niao-li-ya-jo-fu, Wei-wu lun yü ching-yen p'i-p'ing lun*, (Materialism and Empiriocriticism), trans. from the Russian by Po Tse-tung, Shen-chou, and Kuo-kuang-she, 1935; V.I. Lenin, *Wei-wu lun yü ching-yen p'i-p'ing lun* (Materialism and Empiriocriticism), Shanghai 1930, trans. Ti Ch'iu and Chu T'ieh-sheng; Chang Ju-hsin, *Che-hsüeh kai-lun* (Outline of Philosophy), 1935; Hsueh-ko-lo-fu (ed.), *Hsi-yang che-hsüeh shih chien-pien* (Short Course in the History of Western Philosophy), trans. Wang Tsu-yeh, 1943; *Hei-ko-erh che-hsüeh p'i-p'an* (Critique of Hegel's Philosophy), by Fei-erh-pa-ho (Feuerbach) *et al.*, trans. Yang Jo-shui, Shanghai 1935; *Hei-ko-erh che-hsüeh ju-men* (Introduction to the Philosophy of Hegel), trans. Shen Ying-ming, Shanghai 1936; Mi-ting (Mitin) (ed.), *Pien-cheng fa wei-wu lun tz'u-tien* (Dictionary of Dialectical Materialism), P'ing Sheng *et al.*, 1939; *P'u-lieh-ha-no-fu* (Plekhanov), *Lun i-yüan lun li-shih kuan chih fa-chan* (On the Development of Monistic Historicism), trans. Po Ku, Chieh-fang she, 1945; *Pu-ha-lin*, (Bukharin), *Li-shih ti wei-wu lun* (Historical Materialism), trans. Liu Po-ying, Shanghai 1930; *Lang-ko wei-wu lun shih* (Lange's History of Dialectical Materialism), trans. Li Shih-ts'en and Kuo Ta-li, Chung-hua shu-chü, 1936; *Shih-t'o-li-ya-no-fu, Chi-hsieh lun p'i-p'an* (Critique of Mechanism), trans. Jen Pai-ko, Shanghai 1932; Yen Ch'un, *Ya-li-shih-to-te-chih lun-li ssu-hsiang* (The Logical

Thought of Aristotle), rev. by Chang Chün-mai, Shang-wu yin-shu kuan 1933. Cf. Hsin Chung, op. cit., p. 9.

18. Wang Tan-i, '*Kuan-yü Mao chu-hsi kei Ai Ssu-ch'i t'ung-chih hsin ti chi-tien hui-i*' (Reminiscences of Certain Points in Chairman Mao's Letter to Comrade Ai Ssu-ch'i), *Chung-kuo che-hsüeh* (Chinese Philosophy), vol. 1, 1979, pp. 41–3.

19. Wu Li-p'ing, '*Mao chu-hsi kuan-hsin "Fan-tu-lin lun" ti fan-i*' (How Chairman Mao was interested in the translation of *Anti-Dühring*), *Chung-kuo che-hsüeh*, vol. 1, 1979, p. 44. Wu Li-p'ing talks about how Mao was interested in his translation of *Anti-Dühring* in Yenan, and complains especially of Wang Ming's 'treacherous' behaviour after he returned to Yenan in the winter of 1937: Wu, ibid.

20. T'sao, op. cit., pt. I, pp. 15ff; Fogel, op. cit., pp. 61–71.

21. See *Che-hsüeh hsüan-chi*, op. cit., pp. 502, 497; *Selected Works of Mao Tse-tung*, vol. 1., pp. 311–47; '*Mō Takutō shu hokan*', vol. 5, p. 240. Cf. also Takeuchi, '*Mō Takutō no "Mujun ron"* ', op. cit., pp. 63–72 (495–505); see also Schram, 'Mao Tse-tung and the Theory', op. cit., pp. 223–4, n. 5.

Mao Tse-tung writes in his work 'On Practice': 'Logical knowledge differs from perceptual knowledge in that perceptual knowledge pertains to the separate aspects, the phenomena and the external relations of things, whereas logical knowledge takes a big stride forward to reach the totality, the essence and the internal relations of things and discloses the inner contradictions in the surrounding world. Therefore, logical knowledge is capable of grasping the development of the surrounding world in its totality, in the internal relations of all its aspects' (*Selected Works of Mao Tse-tung*, vol. I, p. 298).

Obviously a passage from 'Course of Instruction in Dialectical Materialism' (*pien-chang fa wei-wu lun chiao-ch'eng*) served here as a copy, for one finds the same train of thought, only formulated more concisely: 'Logical knowledge differs from perceptual knowledge in that it makes it possible, through the revelation of internal contradictions, to comprehend reality in its totality, in connection with all of its aspects.' Cited in German in Lippert, *Zur Entstehungsgeschichte*, op. cit., p. 180. Cf. also the other passages, in which Lippert contrasts various extracts by Mao and by Ai Ssu-ch'i, ibid., p. 180.

22. See Wang Tzu-yeh, '*Hsüeh-hsi Mao chu-hsi jen-chen tu-shu pu-ch'ih hsia-wen ti ching-shen*' (Learn from Chairman Mao's spirit how to study seriously without feeling ashamed to ask and learn from one's subordinates), *Chung-kuo che-hsüeh*, vol. 1, 1979, pp. 38–40, as well as Kuo Hua-jo, op. cit., p. 31.

23. See Mao Tse-tung, '*Kei Ai Ssu-ch'i t'ung-chih ti i-feng hsin*' (A letter to Comrade Ai Ssu-ch'i), *Chung-kuo che-hsüeh*, vol. 1, op. cit., pp. 3 and 4; also in '*Mō Takutō shu hokan*', op. cit., vol. 5, p. 165.

24. Cf. Mao Tse-tung, '*Ai chu Che-hsüeh yü sheng-huo chai-lu*' (Extracts from Ai's Philosophy and Life), *Chung-kuo che-hsüeh*, op. cit., pp. 25–30.

25. Mao Tse-tung, '*Kei Ai Ssu'ch'i t'ung-chih*', op. cit.

26. Takeuchi Minoru, '*Mō Takutō no "Mujun ron"* ', op. cit.; see chart on p. 73 (505) below.

27. Ibid., p. 75 (507); Kung, op. cit., pp. 84–5.

28. Lin Jen-tung, '*Kuan-yü "Shih-chien lun" chi-ch'i tui Ma-k'o-ssu chu-i che-hsüeh ti chu-yao kung-hsien*' ('On Practice' and its main contributions to Marxist Philosophy) in *Lun Mao Tse-tung che-hsüeh ssu-hsiang*, n.p., 1983, pp. 87–107, 90.

29. Yü Lin, '*T'an-t'an chieh-fang ssu-hsiang hsiu-cheng "tso"-ch'ing ts'o-wu yü chien-ch'ih ssu-hsiang chi-pen yüan-tse wen-t'i*' (On emancipating the mind, correcting 'left' deviationist error and adhering to your basic principles), *She-hui k'o-hsüeh chan-hsien* (Social Science Front), vol. 4, no. 2/14 (1981), pp. 1–8, p. 3. The same arguments can be found in Wen Chi-tse's article '*Mao chu-hsi tsai Yen-an tsen-yang chiao-tao women hsüeh che-hsüeh*' (How did Chairman Mao teach us to learn philosophy?), *She-hui k'o-hsüeh chan-hsien* (Social Science Front), vol. 5, no. 3 (19), 1982, pp. 1–8, p. 1.

30. Shao Hua-tse, '*Lien-hsi "Chüeh-i" hsüeh-hsi ho yün-yung Mao Tse-tung che-hsüeh ssu-hsiang*' (Integrate the 'Resolution' in the Study and Application of Mao Tse-tung's Thought) in *Lun Mao Tse-tung che-hsüeh ssu-hsiang*, op. cit., pp. 1–22, p. 5.

31. Wang Jo-shui '*Pien-cheng-fa ti ming-yün-Ts'ung Lieh-ning tao Ssu-ta-lin tsai tao Mao Tse-tung, ping t'an-tui chung-p'ing "ssu-wei ho ts'un-tsai ti t'ung-i hsing" yü "Ho-erh erh-i" chih wo-chieh*' ' (The Destiny of Dialectics: from Lenin to Stalin to Mao Tse-tung also Talking about my Opinion on Reviewing 'The Unity of Thinking and Being' and 'Two Combine into One'), *She-hui k'o-hsüeh chan-hsien* (Social Science Front), vol. 4, no. 3/15 (1981), pp. 1–19.

32. Ibid.

33. *Selected Works of Mao Tse-tung*, vol. 1, p. 296.

34. Ibid., pp. 296ff.; '*Mō Takutō shu hokan*', vol. 5, pp. 221ff.

35. '*Mō Takutō shu hokan*', ibid., p. 223; *Selected Works of Mao Tse-tung*, ibid., p. 298.

36. Ibid.

37. Ibid.

38. Ibid.; '*Mō Takutō shu hokan*', ibid.; *Selected Works of Mao Tse-tung*, ibid., p. 303.

39. '*Mō Takutō shu hokan*', ibid., p. 231; *Selected Works of Mao Tse-tung*, ibid., p. 308.

40. '*Lun hsin chieh-tuan*' (On the New Period) in *Selected Works of Mao Tse-tung*, vol. 6., pp. 163–340.

41. '*Mō Takutō shu hokan*', ibid., pp. 229–30; *Selected Works of Mao Tse-tung*, ibid., p. 304.

42. '*Mō Takutō shu hokan*', ibid., p. 233; *Selected Works of Mao Tse-tung*, ibid., p. 307.

43. Ibid.

44. '*Mō Takutō shu hokan*', ibid., p. 234; *Selected Works of Mao Tse-tung*, ibid, p. 308.

45. Ai's *Ssu-hsiang fang-fa lun* (Methodology of Thought), which we have analysed above, was published in 1936. Pt. V (Basic Rules of Dialectical Materialism, pp. 123–50) contains the section '*Mao-tun t'ung-i lü*' (The Law of Unity of Contradiction), pp. 123–34, from which Mao seems to have paraphrased several passages. One passage by Mao reads as follows: 'Within an organism, the death of old cells is the precondition for the production of new cells, and is the precondition for the process of life. The two contradictory aspects of life and death are united within an organism, and also change into each other; live cells change into dead cells, and dead cells change into live cells [live cells are regenerated (*tuotai*) from dead cells],' ('*Mō Takutō shu hokan*', ibid, p. 257). Here I have drawn on Knight's translation 'Mao Zedong's "On Contradiction" and "On Practice" ', op. cit., p. 666. The following passage appears in Ai's *Methodology of Thought*: 'Why can humans grow? Because in the human body, there is a continual replacement of the old by the new, i.e. in the human body millions of old cells die constantly, dissolve, while simultaneously millions of new cells are created and grow. On the one hand, old things die, simultaneously new things are born, and in the human

body there exists this constant contradiction between life and death, and only in this way can the human body grow' (section 1, 'The Law of unity of contradiction' ['*mao-tun t'ung-i lü*']), of part V, *Ssu-hsiang fang-fa lun*, op. cit., pp. 123–4.

The section headed 'The Law of Identity in Formal Logic and the Law of Contradiction in Dialectics' is found in Knight, ibid., p. 661, and the second section in ibid., p. 666. A complete trans., also by Knight, is *Mao Zedong's 'On Contradiction': An Annotated Translation*, op. cit. Cf. also Ch. 12 (the first two sections, pp. 100–11) of the present study; there are several translations by Ai Ssu-ch'i's on 'logic'. Comparable passages are also found in Ai Ssu-ch'i's *Methodology of Thought*, op. cit., pp. 94–112, and in *hsing-shih lun-li hsüeh ho pien-cheng fa* (Formal Logic and Dialectic) in *Lun Chung-kuo t'e-shu hsing chi ch'i-t'a*, op. cit., p. 147.

46. Quoted by Knight, ibid., p. 665; it also appears in '*Mō Takutō shu hokan*', ibid., p. 270.

47. '*Mō Takutō shu hokan*', ibid., p. 263; Knight, ibid., p. 664.

48. '*Mō Takutō shu hokan*', ibid., pp. 260ff. Here Mao uses the same formulation as Ai: '*t'ung-teng k'an-tai*' (also '*p'ing-chün k'an-tai*'); cf. Ai, '*Ssu-hsiang fang-fa lun*', p. 132ff., and p. 104 of the present study.

49. '*Mō Takutō shu hokan*', ibid., p. 274; Knight, ibid., p. 667.

50. '*Mō Takutō shu hokan*', ibid., pp. 273, 275; Knight, ibid., p. 667.

51. '*Mō Takutō shu hokan*', ibid., p. 277; Knight, ibid., p. 652.

52. Cf. Wetter, op. cit., p. 598.

53. Quoted by Wetter, op. cit., p. 606.

54. See p. 103 of this study.

55. '*Mō Takutō shu hokan*', ibid., p. 244; Knight, ibid., p. 661.

56. '*Mō Takutō shu hokan*', ibid., p. 247; Knight, ibid., p. 663.

57. Cf. Robert Schumann's 'Die formale Logik und ihr Verhältnis zum dialektischen Materialismus. Eine philosophische Debatte in der Volksrepublik China', Ph. D. diss., University of Bonn 1977. Schumann shows that there was a sudden increase in the number of articles on 'formal' and 'dialectical logic' in 1956, and that the struggle first ebbed in 1959–60 (p. 29). He examined the articles, however, as to their 'philosophical' contents; only in his conclusion did he begin to suspect that perhaps they too could also be seen in a political connection.

58. Cf., for example, the articles in *Che-hsüeh yen-chiu*, 1979 (nos 2, 3, 4, 5, 8, 10, 11, 12); 1980 (no. 2); 1981 (no. 2). The three laws of 'formal logic' are now supplemented by a fourth: the 'law of sufficient reason' (*ch'ung-tsu li-yu lü*), discovered by Leibniz. Cf. *Che-hsüeh yen-chiu*, no. 3 (1979), pp. 63–6, 67–72, and no. 10, pp. 60–5.

Conclusion

1. Cf. the bibliography in Charles Wei-Hsün Fu and Wing-tsit Chan, *Guide to Chinese Philosophy*, Boston 1978; Joseph Needham, *Science and Civilisation in China*, vol. 2: *History of Scientific Thought*, Cambridge 1970; *Wissenschaftlicher Universalismus. Über Bedeutung und Besonderheit der chinesischen Wissenschaft*, translated, edited and introduced by Tilman Spengler, Frankfurt 1977. (As to the non-development of modern natural sciences, see Spengler's introduction, p. 7.) The best description of the

differences between Western and Chinese thought are to be found in Chang Tung-sun, '*Ssu-hsiang yen-yü yü wen-hua*' (Thought, Language, Culture), *She-hui hsüeh-chieh*, no. 10 (June 10, 1938). It appeared in English as 'A Chinese Philosopher's Theory of Knowledge', *Yenching Journal of Social Studies*, vol. 1, no. 2 (Jan. 1939), pp. 155–91. A comparative description is also given by Hans O.H. Stange, 'Chinesische und abendländische Philosophie. Ihr Unterschied und seine geschichtlichen Usachen' in *Saeculum*, vol. 1, 1950, pp. 380–98. As to sources for the comparison between individual Chinese and Western thinkers, see the bibliography in Charles Wei-Hsün and Wing-tsit chan, *Guide to Chinese Philosophy*, Boston 1978, op. cit., p. 233.

2. In view of the benefits as well as the mortal threats posed to mankind by the results of research in the natural sciences, it is invidious to have to judge which of the two approaches to nature is better: the Chinese or the Western. Perhaps a synthesis of the two offers the best way forward.

3. Cf. the explanations of Chang Tung-sun, op. cit., as to the importance of analogy in Chinese thought, esp. p. 180 (in the English trans.).

4. Cf. Otto Franke, 'Leibniz und China', *Zeitschrift der Deutschen Morgenländischen Gesellschaft*, 82 (1928), pp. 155–78.

5. Tilman Spengler gives an overview of the various models for the non-development of the natural sciences in China in his introduction to Needham, *Wissenschaftlicher Universalismus*, op. cit., pp. 7–52.

6. Chang Tung-sun, op. cit.

7. Ibid., p. 171.

BIBLIOGRAPHY

LITERATURE IN CHINESE

Ai Sheng, *Yeh Ch'ing che-hsüeh p'i-p'an* (A Critique of Yeh Ch'ing's Philosophy), Shanghai 1937.

Ai Ssu-ch'i, *'Che-hsüeh chiang-hua p'i-p'ing ti fan p'i-p'ing'* (Critiques of the Critiques of Talks on Philosophy) in Yeh Ch'ing (ed.), *Hsin che-hsüeh lun-chan chi* (Controversies over the New Philosophy), Shanghai 1936.

——, *Che-hsüeh yü sheng-huo* (Philosophy and Life), Shanghai 1937.

——, *'Che-hsüeh cheng-lun ti hui-i'* (Review of the Philosophical Controversies), *Shen-Pei kung-hsüeh k'ai-hsüeh chi-nien t'e-k'an* (Special Number for the Start of Classes at the North Shensi Academy), Nov. 1, 1937, pp. 16–20.

——, *'Chung-kuo mu-ch'ien ti wen-hua yün-tung'* (The Present Chinese Culture Movement), *Sheng-huo hsing-ch'i k'an*, vol. 1, no. 19 (Sept. 1936). •

——, *'Hsiang-tui yü chüeh-tui'* (Relative and Absolute) in Ai Ssu-ch'i, *Che-hsüeh yü sheng-huo* (Philosophy and Life), Shanghai 1937.

——, *Hsin che-hsüeh lun-chi* (Essays on the New Philosophy), Shanghai 1938.

——, *'Hsing-shih lun-li hsüeh he pien-cheng fa'* (Formal Logic and Dialectic) in Ai Ssu-ch'i, *Lun Chung-kuo t'e-shu hsing chi ch'i-t'a* (On the Particularity of China), Hong Kong 1941, pp. 147–74.

——, *'Kuan-yü hsing-shih lo-chi yü pien-cheng lo-chi'* (On 'Formal' and 'Dialectical' Logic) in Ai Ssu-ch'i, *Che-hsüeh yü sheng-huo*.

——, *'Kuan-yü nei-yin lun yü wai-yin lun'* (On Internal and External Causes) in Ai Ssu-ch'i, *Che-hsüeh yü sheng-huo*; also published in *Tu shu sheng-huo*, vol. 4, no. 4.

——, *'Lüe-shuo wai-yin lun yü nei-yin lun'* (Remarks on the Theory of External and Internal Causes) in Yeh Ch'ing (ed.), *Hsin che-hsüeh lun-chan chi* (Controversies over the New Philosophy), Shanghai 1936.

——, *Lun Chung-kuo t'e-shu hsing chi ch'i-t'a* (On the Particularity of China *inter alia*), Hong Kong 1941.

—— [alias Li Ch'ung-chi], *'Niu chiao-chien lü-hsing chi'* (Report on a Journey to the Tip of a Cow's Horn), *Tu-shu sheng-huo*, vol. 1, no. 9 (March 1935), pp. 18–21.

——, *'Shih-chieh kuan ti ch'üeh-li'* (The Establishment of World-Views), *Hsin shih-chieh*, vol. 2, no. 1 (Oct. 1936).

——, *Ssu-hsiang fang-fa lun* (Methodology of Thought), Chungking, Hong Kong, Sian and elsewhere, 1936.

——, *Ta chung che-hsüeh* (Philosophy for the Masses), Shanghai 1936.

——, *'Tu-ching ma? Tù wai-kuo shu ma?'* (Should one read the Classics? Should one read Foreign Books?), *Tu-shu sheng-huo*, vol. 2, no. 10 (Sept. 25, 1935).

——, *'Yeh Ch'ing hsien-sheng ti che-hsüeh, hsiao-mieh lun'* (Mr Yeh Ch'ing's

Theory of the 'Annihilation of Philosophy') in Yeh Ch'ing (ed.), *Hsin che-hsüeh lun-chan chi*, (Essays on the New Philosophy) Shanghai 1936.

——, *'Yen-chiu t'i-kang'* (Research Theses) in *Che-hsüeh hsüan-chi* (Selected Philosophical Writings), Shanghai 1940, pp. 431–543.

—— (ed.), *Che-hsüeh hsüan-chi* (Selected Philosophical Writings), Shanghai 1940.

——, *Ai Ssu-ch'i wen-chi* (Works of Ai Ssu-ch'i), 2 vols, Peking 1981 and 1983.

——, and Ch'eng I-li (eds), *Hsin che-hsueh ta-kang* (Outline of the New Philosophy), Peking 1936.

Chang Kuo-t'ao, *Wo-ti hui-i* (My Recollections), 3 vols, Hong Kong 1971–4.

Chang Tung-sun, *'Ssu-hsiang yen-yü yü wen-hua'* (Thought, Language and Culture), *She-hui hsüeh-chieh*, no. 10 (June 10, 1938).

Ch'en Chih-yüan, *Hsien-tai che-hsüeh ti chi-pen wen-t'i* (Basic Problems of Contemporary Philosophy), Shanghai 1936.

——, *'Yeh Ch'ing che-hsüeh wang he-ch'u-ch'ü'* (Where is the philosophy of Yeh Ch'ing heading for?), *Tu-shu sheng-huo*, vol. 4, nos. 4 and 5, Jan. 1936; reprinted in Yeh Ch'ing (ed.) *Hsin che-hsüeh lun-chan chi*, pp. 100–24.

Ch'en Li-fu, *Wei-sheng lun* (Vitalism), n.p. 1934.

Ch'en Po-ta, *'Hsin che-hsüeh che ti tzu-chi p'i-p'an he kuan-yu hsin ch'i-meng yün-tung ti chien-i'* (Self-criticisms of a New Philosopher and Suggestions for a New Enlightenment Movement), *Tu-shu sheng-huo*, vol. 4, no. 9 (Sept. 10 1936).

——, *'Wen-hua shang ti ta lien-he yu hsin-ch'i meng yün-tung ti li-shih t'e-tien'* (The Great Cultural Unity and the Historical Peculiarities of the New Enlightenment Movement) in Hsia Cheng-nung (ed.), *Hsien chieh-tuan ti Chung-kuo ssu-hsiang yun-tung* (The Thought Movement of the Present Period), Shanghai 1937, pp. 128–37.

——, *'Yeh Ch'ing che-hsüeh p'i-p'an'* (Critique of Yeh Ch'ing's philosophy), *Hsin shih-chieh*, vol. 1, no. 1; reprinted in Yeh Ch'ing (ed.), *Hsin che-hsueh lun-chan chi*, pp. 22–100.

Ch'en Shao-yü [Wang Ming], *'Mu'ch'ien k'ang-chan hsing-shih chih jen-wu'* (The Current Situation and Tasks in the War of Resistance) in Kuo Hua-lun (ed.), *Chung-kung shih-lun* (History of the Communist Party of China), Taipei 1968, vol. 2, p. 280.

——, *'San-yüeh cheng-chih chü hui-i tsung-chieh'* (Summary of the Political Situation in the Last Three Months, March 2, 1938) in *Wang Ming hsüan-chi* (Selected Works of Wang Ming), op. cit., vol. 5, pp. 95–116.

Ch'en Wei-shih, *Hsin che-hsüeh t'i-hsi chiang hua* (Talks on the System of the New Philosophy), Shanghai 1937.

Chin Yüeh-lin, *Lo-chi* (Logic), Peking 1935.

'Chung-kuo kung-ch'an-tang tui shih-chü hsüan-yen' (Declaration of the CCP on the current political situation, Dec. 25, 1937) in Chung-kuo kung-ch'an-tang, Chung-yang wei-yüan hui (eds), *K'ang-jih min-tsu t'ung-i chan-hsien chih-nan*

(Guide to [Documents of the] Anti-Japanese People's United Front), n.p., n.d., vol. 3, pp. 1–5.

Hsiang Ch'ing, '*Pa-i hsüan-yen hsing-cheng li-shih kuo-ch'eng*' (The Historical Development of the Appearance of the August 1st Manifesto), *Tang-shih tzu-liao ts'ung-k'an* (Collection of Materials on Party History), no. 3, 1983.

Hsin Chung, '*Lun Mao Chu-hsi tu-shu sheng-huo chi-shih*' (Some Records of Mao Tse-tungs's Life in Reading), *She-hui k'o-hsüeh chan-hsien* (Social Science Front), vol. 4, no. 4(16), Oct. 1981, pp. 1–15.

Hu Hua, *Chung-kuo hsin min-chu chu-i ko-ming shih ts'an-k'ao tzu-liao* (Reference Materials on the History of the Chinese New Democratic Revolution), Peking 1951.

Hu Sheng, *Pien-cheng-fa wei-wu lun ju-men* (Introduction to Dialectical Materialism), n.p. 1938.

Jen-min ch'u-pan she (ed.), *Lun Mao Tse-tung che-hsüeh ssu-hsiang*, Hu-pei 1982.

'*Ken-chüeh ch'ih huo-an*' (Resolution on the Eradication of the Red Danger), *Tung-fang tsa-chih*, vol. 34, no. 6 (March 16, 1937).

K'o-hsueh yu jen-sheng kuan chih lun-chan (The Controversy over Science and Life Views), Wang Meng-tsou (ed.), repr. in Hong Kong 1973.

Kung Yü-chih, ' "*Shih-chien lun*" *san-t'i*' (Three Points regarding 'On Practice') in *Lun Mao Tse-tung che-hsüeh ssu-hsiang*, Hu-pei 1982, pp. 66–87.

Kuo Ch'an-po, *Chin wu-shih nien Chung-kuo ssu-hsiang shih* (History of Chinese Thought in the Last Fifty Years), Peking 1935.

Kuo Hua-jo, '*Mao Chu-hsi k'ang-chan ch'u-ch'i kuang-hui ti che-hsüeh huo-tung*' (Chairman Mao's Brilliant Philosophical Activities at the Beginning of the War of Resistance), *Chung-kuo che-hsüeh*, no. 1 (1979), pp. 31–7.

Kuo Hua-lun [Warren Kuo], *Chung-kung shih-lun* (History of the Communist Party of China), 4 vols, Taipei 1969.

Lin Chung-ta, *Tsung-he lo-chi* (Synthetic Logic), n.p., 1936.

Lin Jen-tung, '*Kuan-yü "Shih-chien lun" chi-ch'i tui Ma k'o-ssu chu-i che-hsüeh ti chu-yao kung-hsien*' (On 'On Practice' and its main contributions to Marxist philosophy), *Lun Mao Tse-tung che-hsüeh ssu-hsiang*, pp. 87–107.

Lu Kuo-ying and Yeh Tso-ying,'*Ai Ssu-ch'i wen-chi ti-i-chüan pien-chi kung-tso yi-ching wan-ch'eng*' (Editorial work on the First Volume of the *Works of Ai Ssu-ch'i* has been completed), *Che-hsüeh yen-chiu*, no. 12 (1979), pp. 74–7.

Lu Lung-chi, '*Kuan-yü ching-shen yü wu-chih*' (On Spirit and Matter) in Yeh Ch'ing (ed.), *Hsin che-hsüeh lun-chan chi* (Controversies over the New Philosophy), Shanghai 1936.

Ma Ch'i-pin, '*K'ang chan ch'u-ch'i ti Wang Ming t'ou-hsiang chu-i lu-hsien ts'o-wu*' (The Mistakes of the Capitulationist Wang Ming Line During the Early Stage of the War of Resistance), *Tang-shih tzu-liao ts'ung-k'an* (Collected Materials on Party History), no. 1 (1981), pp. 130–2.

Mao Tse-tung, '*Ai chu che-hsüeh yü sheng-huo chai-lu*' (Extracts from Ai's work Philosophy and Life), *Chung-kuo che-hsüeh*, vol. 1 (1979), pp. 25–30.

——, 'Kei Ai Ssu-ch'i t'ung-chih i-feng hsin' (A letter to Ai Ssu-ch'i), *Chung-kuo che-hsüeh* (Chinese Philosophy), no. 1 (1979), pp. 4–24.

Mao Tse-tung chi (Collected Works of Mao Tse-tung), edited by Takeuchi Minoru, vols 1–10, Hong Kong 1976.

Mao Tse-tung hsüan-chi (Selected Works of Mao Tse-tung), 4 vols, Peking 1968.

Miao Nan, 'Yeh Ch'ing "Hsing-shih lo-chi yü pien-cheng lo-chi" p'i-p'an' (Critique of Yeh Ch'ing's 'Formal logic and dialectical logic'), *Shi-tai lun-t'an*, vol. 1, no. 7 (July 1936), pp. 336–9.

Mō Takutō shu (Collected Works of Mao Tse-tung), edited by Takeuchi Minoru, 10 vols, Tokyo 1970–2.

Mō Takutō shu hokan (Supplements to the Collected Works of Mao Tse-tung), 9 vols and 1 supplement, Tokyo 1983–5.

Shao Hua-tse, 'Lien-hsi "Chüeh-i" hsüeh-hsi ho yün-yung Mao Tse-tung che-hsüeh ssu-hsiang' (Integrate the 'Resolution' in the Study and Application of Mao Tse-tung's Thought) in *Lun Mao Tse-tung che-hsüeh ssu-hsiang*, pp. 1–22.

Shih Feng, *Fan-tui Wang Ming t'ou-hsiang chu-i lu-hsien tou-cheng* (The Struggle to Oppose Wang Ming's Capitulationist Line), Shanghai 1976.

T'an Fu-chih, *Che-hsüeh p'i-p'an chi* (Philosophical Critiques), Shanghai 1937.

Wang Chang-huan, *Lun-li hsüeh ta-kang* (Outline of Logic), Shanghai 1930.

Wang Hui-te and Chia Ch'un-feng, 'Chi-nien "ta-chung che-hsüeh" ch'u-pan wu-shih chou-nien' (Commemorating the 50th Anniversary of Publication of the 'Philosophy for the Masses'), *Jen-min jih-pao*, March 21 1986, p. 5.

Wang Jo-shui, 'Pien-cheng-fa ti ming-yün: Ts'ung Lieh-ning tao Ssu-ta-lin tsai tao Mao Tse-tung; ping t'an-tui chung-p'ing "ssu-wei ho ts'un-tsai ti t'ung-i hsing" yü "ho-erh erh-i" chih wo-chien' (Destiny of Dialectics: from Lenin to Stalin to Mao Tse-tung; also Talking about my Opinion on Reviewing 'The Unity of Thinking and Being' and 'Two Combine into One'), *She-hui k'o-hsüeh chan-hsien* (Social Science Front), vol. 4, no. 3 (1981), pp. 1–19.

Wang Ming hsüan-chi (Selected Works of Wang Ming [Ch'en Shao-yü]) 5 vols, Tokyo 1975.

Wang Tan-i, 'Kuan-yü Mao chu-hsi kei Ai t'ung-chih hsin ti chi-tien hui-i' (Reminiscences of Certain Points in Chairman Mao's Letter to Comrade Ai Ssu-ch'i), *Chung-kuo che-hsüeh*, no. 1 (1979), pp. 41–3.

Wang Tzu-yeh, 'Hsüeh-hsi Mao chu-hsi jen-chen tu-shu pu-ch'i hsia-wen ti ching-shen' (Learn from Chairman Mao's Spirit How to Study Seriously Without Feeling Ashamed to Ask and Learn from one's Subordinates), *Chung-kuo che-hsüeh*, vol. 1 (1979), pp. 38–40.

Wei-wu pien-cheng fa chiao-ch'eng (Course of Instruction in Dialectical Materialism), trans. from the Russian by Li Ta, n.p. 1932.

Wei-wu pien-cheng fa lun-chan (Controversies over Dialectical Materialism), Ti-p'ing hsien ch'u-pan she (ed.), repr. Taipei 1973.

Wen Chi-tse, 'Mao chu-hsi tsai Yen-an tsen-yang chiao-tao wo-men hsüeh che-hsüeh' (How Chairman Mao taught us to study Philosophy in Yenan), *She-hui k'o-hsüeh chan-hsien* (Social Science Front), vol. 5, no. 3 (19) (1982), pp. 1–8.

Wu Li-p'ing, 'Mao Chu-hsi kuan-hsin "Fan Tu-lin lun" ti fan-i' (Chairman Mao's

Concern with the Translation of *Anti-Dühring*), *Chung-kuo che-hsüeh*, vol. 1, 1979, p. 44.

Yeh Ch'ing (Tsing Yeh), *Chang Tung-sun che-hsüeh p'i-p'an* (Critiques of the Philosophy of Chang Tung-sun), 2 vols, Shanghai 1934.

——, *Che-hsüeh wen-t'i* (Problems of Philosophy), Shanghai 1936.

——, '*Che-hsüeh tao he ch'u-ch'ü*' (Whither Philosophy?), Shanghai 1935.

——, '*Fan tu-ching lun chung ti wen-t'i*' (Problems which result from the Rejection of the Theory of Reading the Classics), *Yen-chiu yü p'i-p'an*, vol. 1, no. 8 (Dec. 20 1935), repr. in *Hsin che-hsüeh lun-chan chi*, pp. 277–88.

——, *Hu Shih che-hsüeh p'i-p'an* (Critique of Hu Shih's Philosophy), 2 vols, Shanghai 1934.

——, '*Kuan-yü cheng-chih tang-p'ai*' (On Political Parties), in Mao Tse-tung *et al.*, *T'ung-i chan-hsien hsia tang-p'ai wen-t'i* (The Questions of Parties under the United Front), Yenan 1938.

——, *Lun-li hsüeh wen-t'i* (Problems of Logic), Shanghai 1937.

——, '*Wu-chih yü ching-shen*' (Matter and Spirit), *Yen-chiu yü p'i-p'an*, vol. 1, no. 4 (Aug. 7, 1935).

—— (ed.), *Hsin che-hsüeh lun-chan chi* (*Controversies over the New Philosophy*), Shanghai 1936.

—— (ed.), *Wei fa-chan hsin che-hsüeh erh chan* (Struggles to Develop the New Philosophy), Shanghai 1937.

Yeh Tso-ying, '*Ai Ssu-ch'i chu-yao chu-i nien-p'u* (Chronology of Ai Ssu-ch'i's major writings), *Hsüeh-shu yen-chiu*, no. 1 (1983), pp. 48–53; no. 3 (1983), pp. 46–50.

Yen Fu, *Mu Le lo-chi* (Mill's Logic), Shanghai 1902.

Yü Lin, '*T'an-t'an chieh-fang ssu-hsiang chiu-cheng "tso"-ch'ing ts'o-wu yü chien-ch'ih ssu-hsiang chi-pen yüan-tse wen-t'i*' (On Emancipating the Mind, Correcting 'Left' Deviation Error and adhering to Four Basic Principles), *She-hui k'o-hsüeh chan-hsien* (Social Science Front), vol. 4, no. 2 (14) (1981), pp. 1–8.

LITERATURE IN OTHER LANGUAGES

Ahlberg, René, '*Dialektische Philosophie' und Gesellschaft in der Sowjetunion*, Berlin 1960.

'Appeal to the Whole People in China to Resist Japan and Save the Country', *Inprecor*, vol. 15, Nov. 30, pp. 1595–7.

'Aufruf des ZK der Kommunistischen Partei Chinas – Für den aufrichtigen Zusammenschlub der Kuomintang und der Kommunistischen Partei, für die Fortsetzung des bewaffneten Widerstandes gegen Japan, für den endgültigen Sieg', *Kommunistische Internationale*, no. 5 (May 1938), pp. 458–60.

Bauer, Edgar, *Ideologie und Entwicklung in der VR China*, Bochum 1980.

Benton, Gregor, 'The "Second Wang Ming Line" (1935–38)', *China Quarterly* no. 61, (March 1975), pp. 61–94.

Bochenski, I.M., *Der sowietische dialektische Materialismus*, Munich 1950.

Boorman, Howard C. (ed.), *Biographical Dictionary of Republican China*, 4 vols, New York 1967.

Braun, Otto, *Chinesische Aufzeichnungen (1932–1939)*, Berlin 1975; English trans. *A Comintern Agent in China, 1932–1939*, London and Stanford 1982.

Brière, O., *Fifty Years of Chinese Philosophy, 1898–1950*, London 1956.

——, 'L'effort de la philosophie marxiste en Chine', *Bulletin de l'Université l'Aurore*, 3rd series, 8, no. 3 (1947), pp. 309–47.

Cassirer, Ernst, *Die Begriffsform im mythischen Denken*, Leipzig 1922.

Chang Kuo-t'ao, *The Rise of the Chinese Communist Party, 1929–1938*, vol. 2 of the *Autobiography of Chang Kuo-t'ao*, Lawrence, Kansas 1972.

Chang Tung-sun, 'A Chinese Philosopher's Theory of Knowledge', *Yenching Journal of Social Studies*, vol. 1, no. 2 (Jan. 1939), pp. 155–91.

Chen Cheng-ti, 'Shin tetsugaku ronsen to Deborin hihan' (The Controversy over the "New Philosophy", 1935–1937: Criticism of the Deborinites and Marxism in China), *Toyo bunka* (Oriental Culture), no. 65 (March 1985), pp. 5–36.

Ch'en, Jerome, 'The Communist Movement, 1927–1937' in *The Cambridge History of China*, vol. 13/2; John K. Fairbank and Albert Feuerwerker (eds), *Republican China, 1912–1949*, Cambridge 1986, pp. 168–229.

Chen Shao-yü [Wang Ming; Wan Min], 'The Struggle of the Anti-Japanese People's Front in China', *Communist International*, vol. 13, no. 6, p. 750.

——, 'Der Kampf um die antijapanische Volksfront in China', *Kommunistiche Internationale*, no. 5 (May 1936), pp. 402–11.

——, *50 Jahre KP Chinas und der Verrat Mao Tse-tungs*, Berlin, 1981.

Chi, Wen-shun, *Ideological Conflicts in Modern China: Democracy and Authoritarianism*, New Brunswick, NJ, and Oxford 1986.

Chin, Steven S.K., *The Thought of Mao Tse-tung: Form and Content*, Hong Kong 1979.

Cohen, Arthur, *The Communism of Mao Tse-tung*, Chicago 1964.

Conquest, Robert, *The Great Terror: Stalin's Purges of the Thirties*, New York 1975.

De George, Richard T., *Patterns of Soviet Thought: The Origins and Development of Dialectical and Historical Materialism*, Ann Arbor, Mich. 1966.

Dimitroff, G., 'Zum 15. Jahrestag der Kommunistischen Partei Chinas', *Kommunistische Internationale*, no. 9 (Sept. 1936), pp. 880–3; English trans. 'The Fifteenth Anniversary of the Communist Party of China', *Inprecor*, vol. 14, no. 44 (Sept. 1936), pp. 1207–8.

Dirlik, Arif, *The Origins of Marxist Historiography in China, 1919–1937*, Berkeley, Calif. 1978.

Domes, Jürgen, *Vertagte Revolution – Die Politik der Kuomintang in China, 1923–1937*, Berlin 1969.

Doolin, Dennis J. and Peter J. Golas, ' "On Contradiction" in the Light of Mao Tse-tung's Essay "Dialectical Materialism" ', *China Quarterly*, no. 19 (July–Sept. 1964), pp. 38–46.

Durkheim, Emile, *Les formes élementaires de la vie religieuse*, Paris 1912.

Feuerwerker, Albert (ed.), *History in Communist China*, Cambridge, Mass. 1968.

Fogel, Joshua A., *Ai Ssu-chi's Contribution to the Development of Chinese Marxism*, Cambridge, Mass. and London 1987.

Fu, Charles Wei-Hsün and Wing-tsit Chan, *Guide to Chinese Philosophy*, Boston 1978.

Furth, Charlotte, *Ting Wen-chiang: Science and Chinese Culture*, Cambridge, Mass. 1970.

Garver, John W., 'The Origins of the Second United Front: The Comintern and the Chinese Communist Party', *China Quarterly*, no. 113 (March 1988), pp. 29–59.

Graham, Loren R., *Science and Philosophy in the Soviet Union*, New York 1972.

Granet, Marcel, *La pensée chinoise*, Paris 1934; German trans. *Das chinesische Denken*, Munich 1963.

Griffith, William, 'On Esoteric Communications', *Studies in Comparative Communism*, vol. 3, no. 1 (Jan. 1970).

Harrison, James P., *The Long March to Power: A History of the Chinese Communist Party*, West Hanover, Mass. 1972.

Hecker, Julius F. (ed.), *Moscow Dialogues: Discussions on Red Philosophy*, London 1933.

Heitmann, S., 'Between Lenin and Stalin: Nicolai Bukharin' in L. Labedz (ed.), *Revisionism*, London 1962.

Holubnychy, Vsevolod, 'Der dialektische Materialismus Mao Tse-tungs', *Der Ostblock und die Entwicklungsländer*, Sept. 1962, pp. 15–59.

——, 'Mao Tse-tung's Materialistic Dialectics', *China Quarterly*, no. 19 (July–Sept. 1964), pp. 3–37.

Hsiung, James Chieh, *Ideology and Practice: The Evolution of Chinese Communism*, New York 1970.

—— (ed.), *The Logic of Maoism*, New York 1974.

Joravski, David, *Soviet Marxism and Natural Science, 1917–1932*, New York 1961.

Jordan, Z.A., *The Evolution of Dialectical Materialism: A Philosophical and Sociological Analysis*, New York 1967.

Kampen, Thomas, 'The Zunyi Conference and the Rise of Mao Zedong', *Internationales Asienforum*, nos. 3/4, Oct. 1986, pp. 347–60.

——, 'Wang Jiaxiang und der Aufstieg Mao Zedongs', *Asien. Deutsche Zeitschrift für Politik, Wirtschaft und Kultur*, no. 25 (Oct. 1987), pp. 1–19.

Kataoka, Tetsuya, *Resistance and Revolution in China, the Communist Party and the Second United Front*, Berkeley, Calif. 1974.

Kelly, D.A., 'Chinese Controversies on the Guiding Role of Philosophy over China', *Australian Journal of Chinese Affairs*, 14 (1985), pp. 21–35.

Kindermann, G.-K., *Der Ferne Osten (Weltgeschichte des 20. Jahrhunderts*, vol. 8), Munich 1970.

Knight, Nick, 'Mao Zedong's "On Contradiction" and "On Practice"': Pre-Liberation Texts', *China Quarterly*, no. 84 (1980), pp. 641–88.

——, *Mao Zedong's "On Contradiction": An Annotated Translation of the Preliberation Text*, Nathan, Queensland 1981.

——, 'Leninism, Stalinism and the Comintern' in C. Mackerras and N. Knight (eds), *Marxism in Asia*, London and Sydney 1985, pp. 24–61.

'The Form of Mao Zedong's "Sinification of Marxism" ', *Australian Journal of Chinese Affairs*, 9 (1983), pp. 17–33.

——, 'The Marxism of Mao Zedong: Empiricism and Discourse in the Field of Mao Studies', *Australian Journal of Chinese Affairs*, 16 (1986), pp. 7–22.

Kukushkin, K.V., 'The Comintern and the United National Anti-Japanese Front in China' in R.A. Ulyanovski, *The Comintern and the East: The Struggle for the Communist Strategy and Tactics in the National Liberation Movements*, Moscow 1979, pp. 391–5.

Kuo, Heng-yü, *Maos Weg zur Macht und die Komintern*, Paderborn 1975.

Kuo, Warren, *Analytical History of the Chinese Communist Party*, 4 vols, Taipei 1966–78.

Kwok, D.W.Y., *Scientism in Chinese Thought, 1900–1950*, New Haven and London 1965.

Labedz, L. (ed.), *Revisionism*, London 1962.

Leutner, Mechthild, 'Ch'en Po-ta und Ai Ssu-ch'i in der Neuen Aufklärungsbewegung von 1936/37. Zur Anfangsphase der nationalen Neuorientierung der marxistischen Wissenschaft am Vorabend des Antijapanischen Widerstandskrieges' in *Bochumer Jahrbuch zur Ostasienkunde*, Bochum 1979.

——, *Geschichtsschreibung zwischen Politik und Wissenschaft. Zur Herausbildung der chinesischen marxistischen Geschichtswissenschaft in den 30er und 40er Jahren*, Wiesbaden 1982.

Lévy-Bruhl, L., *Die geistige Welt der Primitiven*, Munich 1927.

Lippert, Wolfgang, *Entstehung und Funktion einiger chinesischer marxistischer Termini*, Wiesbaden 1979.

——, 'Zur Entstehungsgeschichte von Mao Zedongs theoretischen Schriften "Über die Praxis" und "Über den Widerspruch" ' in *Ch'en-yüeh chi. Tileman Grimm zum 60. Geburtstag*, Tübingen 1982, pp. 173–97.

Mao Tse-tung, *Selected Works of Mao Tse Tung*, vols. 1–4, Peking 1968.

McLane, Charles B., *Soviet Policy and the Chinese Communists 1931–1946*, New York 1958.

Meissner, Werner, *Philosphie und Politik in China. Die Kontroverse über den dialektischen Materialismus in den dreissiger Jahren*, Munich 1986.

Minoru, Takeuchi, 'Mō Takutō no "Mujun ron" no genkai ni tsuite' (On the Original Form of Mao Tse-tungs's 'On Contradiction'), *Shiso* (Thought), 538 (April 1969), pp. 487–526.

——, 'Mujun ron' no genkei hosetsu (Additional theories about the Original Form of 'On Contradiction') in *Zoho Mo Takuto noto* (Notes on Mao Tse-tung), enlarged edn, Tokyo 1978.

Mitin, Mark B. and I. Razumovskij, *Dialekticeski i istoriceskij materializm* (Dialectical and Historical Materliasm) 2 vols, Moscow 1932, 1933.

Nakajima, Mineo, '*Mō Takutō shisō' ni okeru ninshiki to jissen: "Jissen ron'o megutte"* ' (Knowledge and Practice in the Thought of Mao Tse-tung: Concerning 'On Practice'), *Koria hyoron*, 7, no. 55 (Aug. 1965), pp. 19–23.

Needham, Joseph, *Science and Civilisation in China*, vol. 2: *History of Scientific Thought*, Cambridge 1970.

——, *Wissenschaftlicher Universalismus. Über Bedeutung und Besonderheit der chinesischen Wissenschaft*, trans. and ed., with an introduction, by Tilman Spengler, Frankfurt 1977.

Negt, Oskar (ed.), *Nicolai Bukharin und Abram Deborin. Kontroversen über dialektischen und mechanizistischen Materialismus*, Frankfurt 1974.

——, 'Marxismus als Legitimationswissenschaft. Zur Genese der stalinistischen Philosophie' in *Nikolai Bukharin und Abram Deborin*,. . . . op. cit., pp. 7–50.

Nollau, Günther, *Die Internationale*, Cologne and Berlin 1959.

——, *International Communism and World Revolution: History and Methods*, New York 1961.

Patzig, Günther, 'Logik' in *Philosophie. Das Fischer-Lexikon*, vol. 11, Frankfurt 1963, pp. 147–60.

Rue, John, 'Is Mao Tse-tung's "Dialectical Materialism" a Forgery?', *Journal of Asian Studies*, 26, no. 3 (May 1967), pp. 464–8.

Rush, Myron, *The Rise of Khruschchev*, Washington, DC 1958.

Schapiro, Leonard, *The History of the Communist Party of the Soviet Union*, 2nd edn, London 1970.

Schäfer, Ingo, *Mao Tse-tung. Eine Einführung in sein Denken*, Munich 1978.

Schram, Stuart R., *The Political Thought of Mao Tse-tung*, Harmondsworth 1969.

——, 'Mao Tse-tung as Marxist Dialectician' (review article), *China Quarterly*, no. 29 (Jan.–March 1967), pp. 155–65.

——, *Das politische Denken Mao Tse-tungs*, Munich 1975.

——, 'Mao Tse-tung and the Theory of Permanent Revolution, 1958–69', *China Quarterly*, no. 45 (1971), pp. 221–44.

——, *Mao Zedong: A Preliminary Reassessment*, Hong Kong 1983.

——, 'Mao Studies: Retrospect and Prospect', *China Quarterly*, no. 97 (March 1984), pp. 95–125.

——, 'Mao Tse-tung's Thought to 1949' in *The Cambridge History of China*, vol. 13/2: John K. Fairbank and Albert Feuerwerker (eds), *Republican China, 1912–1949*, Cambridge 1986, pp. 789–870.

Schumann, Robert, 'Die formale Logik und ihr Verhältnis zum dialektischen Materialismus. Eine philosophische Debatte in der Volksrepublik China', unpubl. Ph.D. thesis, University of Bonn 1977.

Schwartz, Benjamin, 'The Philosopher', in Dick Wilson (ed.), *Mao Tse-tung in the Scales of History*, Cambridge 1977.

Shum Kui-Kwong, *The Chinese Communist Road to Power: The Anti-Japanese National United Front (1935–1945)*, Hong Kong 1988.

Soo, Francis Y.K., *Mao Tse-tungs's Theory of Dialectic*, Dordrecht 1981.

Spengler, Tilman, 'Zur Entdeckung der chinesischen Wissenschafts- und Technikgeschichte' in Joseph Needham, *Wissenschaftlicher Universalismus*, trans. and ed. by Tilman Spengler, Frankfurt 1977, pp. 7–52.

Stange, Hans O.H., 'Chinesische und abendländische Philosophie. Ihr Unterschied und seine geschichtlichen Ursachen' in *Saeculum. Jahrbuch für Universalgeschichte*, 1 (1950), pp. 380–96.

Starr, John B., *Continuing the Revolution: The Political Thought of Mao*, Princeton 1979.

Teiwes, Frederick C., 'Mao and His Lieutenants', *Australian Journal of Chinese Studies*, nos 19/20 (Jan./July 1988), pp. 1–80.

Topitsch, Ernst, 'Zur Pragmatik des Sprachgebrauchs in Philosophie und politischer Theorie' in Ernst Topitsch (ed.), *Probleme der Wissenschaftstheorie*, Vienna 1960.

——, *Mythos, Philosophie, Politik. Zur Naturgeschichte der Illusion*, Freiburg im Breisgau 1969.

——, *Gottwerdung und Revolution*, Munich 1973.

Ts'ao, Ignatius J.H., 'Ai Ssu-ch'i: The Apostle of Chinese Communism', part I: 'His Life and Works', *Studies in Soviet Thought*, 12 (1972), pp. 2–36.

——, 'Ai Ssu-ch'i's Philosophy, Pt. II: Dialectical Materialism', *Studies in Soviet Thought*, 12 (1972), pp. 231–44.

Van Slyke, Lyman P., 'The Chinese Communist Movement during the Sino-Japanese War, 1937–1945' in *The Cambridge History of China*, vol. 13/2: John K. Fairbank and Albert Feuerwerker (eds), *Republican China, 1912–1949*, Cambridge 1986, pp. 609–722.

——, *Enemies and Friends: The United Front in Chinese Communist History*, Stanford 1967.

Wakeman, Frederic, *History and Will: Philosophical Perspectives of Mao Tse-tung*, Berkeley, Calif. 1973.

Wetter, Gustav A., *Dialectical Materialism: A Historical and Systematic Survey of Philosophy in the Soviet Union*, New York 1958.

——, *Der dialektische Materialismus. Seine Geschichte und sein System in der Sowjetunion*, 5th edn, Freiburg im Breisgau 1960.

Wittfogel, K.A. and C.S. Chao, 'Some Remarks on Mao's Handling and Problems of Dialectics', *Studies in Soviet Thought*, vol. 3, no. 4 (Dec. 1963), pp. 251–77.

Womack, Brantly, *The Foundations of Mao Zedong's Political Thought, 1917–1935*, Honolulu 1982.

——, 'Politics and Epistemology in China Since Mao', *China Quarterly*, no. 80 (Dec. 1979), pp. 768–92.

Wylie, Raymond, *The Emergence of Maoism*, Stanford 1980.

INDEX

Ai Sheng: 79, 86, 130; attack on Yeh, 81ff., 117
Ai Ssu-ch'i: 1, 8, 12, 15, 50; attack on Yeh, 72ff.; 77, 95, 102, 149, 161f, 165, 169, 171, 183, 186; comparison of Ai's work with Mao's, 154ff.; on absolute, 127ff., on relative, 127ff., on external and internal causes, 129ff.; on dialectical logic, 142; on Comintern, 142; on dualism, 144; on law of identity, 106ff.; on perceptual and theoretical knowledge, 84ff.; on practice, 86f, 92ff.; on objectivism, 87ff.; on subjectivism, 90; on the law of contradiction, 140ff.; on the law of transformation of quantity in quality, 136ff.; on the law of unity of opposites, 145; on United Front, 87; on Yeh Ch'ing, 102, on formal and dialectical logic, 100ff.
Aizenberg, 101–2, 117, 139, 143, 154
analogous counterparts, 9
analysis: in the theory of knowledge, 92ff.; and synthesis, 92ff.; and United Front, 93ff.
Anselm of Canterbury, 55
Antisthenes, 55
Aristippus of Cyrene, 55
Aristotle, 64, 55
Avenarius, 16

Bacon, 55, 64
Berkeley, 55
Bogdanov, 16, 50
bourgeoisie, 46
Braun, O., 14
Brière, O., 60
Bukharin, N.: 19, 70, 102, 148, 182; theory of equilibrium, 147, 169
Bukharinism, 11f, 110
Büchner, 55

capitulationism, 42
Cassirer E., 8
Ch'en Chih-yüan, 149

Ch'en Po-ta: 13, 77, 117, 139, 151; attack on Yeh, 72ff., 118ff.; on contradiction, 118ff., on formal and dialectical logic, 119ff., on United Front strategy, 121
Ch'en Shao-yü, see Wang Ming
Ch'en Tu-hsiu, 161
Ch'ü Shih-ying, 53
Chang Chün-mai, 64, 186
Chang Hsüeh-liang, 34
Chang Ju-hsin, 152
Chang Kuo-t'ao, 14
Chang Tung-sun: 53, 142, 186; on Western philosophy, 189
Chang Wen-t'ien, 41
Chaplin, C., 85
Chiang Kai-shek, 30ff., 37, 71, 103, 116; and Hsi-an Incident, 37ff.
Chinese Communist Party (CCP): 1, 8, 10, 14, 30, 37, 56, 84, 120, 131, 141, 185; and United Front, 35ff., 45ff.; leadership in the United Front, 168; unification with Kuomintang, 59ff., 69ff.; compromise with Kuomintang, 77; and Kuomintang, 147; and intellectuals, 192; and the laws of formal logic, 125ff.; and dialectical logic, 126; and theory of knowledge, 96
Chou Fo hai, 50
Chou Li-po, 65
Chou Yang, 65, 71
Chu Ch'i-hua, 50
Comintern (Communist International): 14, 19, 34ff., 47, 83, 117, 131, 162, 168, VII World Congress, 31; and Wang Ming, 47; and United Front, 91, 100
Communist Academy, 24
Communist Manifesto, 133
Communist Party of the Soviet Union, 49
Comte, Auguste, 51, 64
concepts, philosophical, 4, 5, 6, 12
Condillac, 50, 55
contradiction: 8, 19; law of 124, 139ff.,

DATE DUE

BRODART, INC.   Cat. No. 23-221